Peer-Impact Diagnosis and Therapy

Peer-Impact Diagnosis and Therapy

A Handbook for Successful Practice with Adolescents

Vivian Center Seltzer

NEW YORK UNIVERSITY PRESS

New York and London

NEW YORK UNIVERSITY PRESS
New York and London
www.nyupress.org

© 2009 by New York University
All rights reserved

Library of Congress Cataloging-in-Publication Data

Seltzer, Vivian Center.
Peer-impact diagnosis and therapy : a handbook for
successful practice with adolescents / Vivian Center Seltzer.
p. cm.
Includes bibliographical references and index.
ISBN-13: 978-0-8147-4042-2 (cl : alk. paper)
ISBN-10: 0-8147-4042-1 (cl : alk. paper)
1. Adolescent psychology. 2. Adolescence. I. Title.
BF724.S3988   2009
155.5'182—dc22   2009009079

New York University Press books are printed on acid-free paper, and
their binding materials are chosen for strength and durability. We
strive to use environmentally responsible suppliers and materials to
the greatest extent possible in publishing our books.

Manufactured in the United States of America

10 9 8 7 6 5 4 3 2 1

This book is dedicated to nine adolescents or aspiring adolescents—cousins who make up a unique Peer Arena—who I watch grow and develop, each of whom I love dearly. Brad, Jack, and Ben . . . Hanna, Olivia, and Cassandra . . . Veronica, Kate, and Alexandra.

May you achieve your dreams . . . gm (gem)

Contents

Acknowledgments

Library materials, domestic and cross-cultural research findings, clinical experiences with adolescents and families, teaching graduate and undergraduate students and interacting with talented colleagues from many countries of the world, counsel with statistical consultants, exchange with professionals in my field, and raising three adolescents all in some way contributed to the ideas found in this volume. Although I make no specific designation, I am very appreciative and thank all of you. However, there are colleagues at the University of Pennsylvania from fields other than my own whom I acknowledge for special kinds of support: Louis A. Girifalco, university professor of materials science; Marion Kant, senior lecturer in dance history; Jonathan Steinberg, Annenberg professor of history; and Richard Waterman, a past professor and current adjunct professor of statistics at the Wharton School with whom I collaborated on early cross-national studies; and Robert Cosner, former director of youth protective services of Bucks County Pennsylvania and lecturer at the School of Social Policy and Practice, for his assistance in the third replication of my early study, and to those staff and volunteers at Philadelphia Young Playwrights whose cooperation was invaluable. Ellen DeMarinis, research librarian at the Van Pelt Library was very helpful and gracious in assisting me. I also acknowledge the assistance of two students, Orkun Sak, Ph.D. student at the Wharton School, for statistical work on international findings that supported anecdotal and clinical findings with adolescents, and Sara Flanagan, for work-study assistance in accessing library materials and retyping initial drafts. I am most appreciative for the permission granted me by John Wiley Publishers to cite my work in *The Psychosocial Worlds of the Adolescent: Public and Private* (1989).

I was privileged to have Jennifer Hammer serve as my editor. She was a part of the of the project from initiation to end. Her brilliance in carrying out her role was evident at all periods—first draft through to completed manuscript. In addition, I also thank you, Jennifer, for prompt responses so crucial to keeping the travel energized. I am appreciative of the work of the production staff at New York University Press.

I value the concern and the implicit encouragement from my three adult children, Jonathan, Francesca, and Aeryn, and from my in-law children, Andrew, Bruce, and Liza, their spouses. Of course, there is a last but not least acknowledgment, this time to my partner in life, my husband Bill, whose meaningful and quiet support was ever present despite the demands of this project. For all I am most grateful.

Introduction

This book is meant to aid professionals in understanding their adolescent clients by offering a theory and method of practice with adolescents. It differs from books in current circulation in connecting both normative and troubling behaviors to development and growth dynamics. With perhaps the exception of methods influenced by psychoanalytic theory, most current practice with adolescents has not been anchored in a theoretical road map. Yet without such a road map, it is not possible to determine which behaviors are deviant and which are not or what the therapeutic task is. Thus, this book fills an empty space in the professional literature on adolescents. It offers information with which to construct an imaginary road map of the adolescent's journey from puberty to psychological maturity: attaining psychological identity and arriving into early adulthood.

Kurt Lewin, considered a brilliant social psychologist and the individual who led development of the field of group dynamics, convincingly argued for a seamless relationship between theory and practice—that theory informs practice and practice informs theory (Lewin 1939). This book takes theory about adolescent growth and behavior and translates it into practice principles and methods for you to use. It offers reformulations of customary thought about adolescent dynamics and discussion of deviant family and environmental influences and whether such influences are significant; it also provides instruments to inform your practice more quickly about issues with which adolescents are dealing and provides a group therapy model exclusive to adolescents.[1]

The contents of this book derive from a theoretical model entitled Dynamic Functional Interaction (DFI), a theory of adolescent psychosocial development that blends pertinent adolescent theory and literature together with social psychology theory and experiment. It sets the adolescent task as individuation and the age-mate peer as the most relevant "other" of the stage. In doing so, it veers away from popular notions of adolescent rebellion and parent-child difficulties as the primary explanations of adolescent behavior. Indeed, regardless of the nature of the problem, many professionals immediately ask adolescents about their home life and issues of family. What do they fight about? How often? What are their feelings about the outcome? Unless an adolescent's behavior is extreme or dangerous, a common approach is to interpret rebellious behavior as normative and use appropriate strategies to reduce conflict between adolescents and parents/family. Some strategies succeed, but not enough. By assuming family dynamics to be the root cause of many behavioral problems, and crafting treatment plans accordingly, professionals are likely to miss the central role played by peers in shaping adolescent behavior, thereby failing to address real problems and failing some clients in treatment.

In contrast, the DFI model sets the core of adolescent behavior as flowing from responses to psychological interactions with peers. Comparison dynamics, as adolescents assess and evaluate themselves in relation to their age-mates in order eventually to settle on the self they wish to have, forge the axle of the adolescent wheel. Inevitably, cognitive and emotional aftermaths, as adolescents rank themselves against their peers, affect their changing system benignly or harshly. To be unaware of these processes is to miss the essence of the stage. Professionals must understand the crucial influence peers have on adolescents' development as arbiters of what works and what does not, both in the present and in contemplation of their future life. In so doing, professionals will also understand the pressure that adolescents feel about conforming and about maintaining an acceptable status relative to peers. The goal of this book is to help professionals attain that knowledge so they will possess the keys to successful practice with adolescents.

Not Rebellion but Work

Adolescents are not rebelling when they resist being with family and relatives. They are merely trying to do their jobs. They are trying to grow up. They are trying to individuate. They do so by looking around and comparing with other adolescents to see how they are doing, what they are doing, what they are singing, how they dance, what they read, what they watch on television, what is the latest gadget they are carrying round, what they talk about. This process is adolescents' developmental school. It is their informal instruction. They carry out these comparisons about everything important to them at the moment. As they review the outcomes, they find out that by comparison they are at times quite superior, at other times quite inferior, and sometimes right in between. Of course, it is only logical that when one comes out superior one is happy and when inferior it is bad news. If the latter occurs too often, an adolescent may take flight to *defensive glitches,* which are sometimes visible in problem social behaviors and at other times not readily discernable. These glitches are traced to unbearable feelings of failure in adolescents' perceptions of how they rank relative to their attachment figures—peers.

The purpose of this book is to help readers understand adolescents better and to be better equipped to work with them. Issues of rebellion against parents are not the most important when it comes to adolescents. Behaviors that may be considered rebellion are often more properly regarded as *individuation.* Or an adolescent may be communicating, "I am having some difficult times, and the only folks I can really take it out on are the people with whom I feel the safest." Or it might be something far different. As professionals, it is our job to find out, and not to assume ahead of time. To understand what confronts the adolescent who is seeking help, we must have a good idea of what point an adolescent has reached in his or her development and compare it with the normative growth level at the adolescent's age. By assessing where each adolescent is in relation to these norms we are able to evaluate the suitability or unsuitability of externally observable behaviors. Furthermore, with the knowledge that adolescence has a psychological goal—maturity—professionals can ask adolescents where they are along the road to putting together something of a "self." We need to recognize when the perception of their progress is overblown and exaggerated purposely to make them feel better about themselves and when it is authentic.

This book deals with what adolescents are like just prior to adolescence, what changes in four domains of growth take place, how adolescents manage these changes, and how the changes are reflected on the outside, when important integrations in each of the domains take place, as well as when all the domains catch up to one another and maturity is reached. This road map provides benchmarks as to what can be expected and when, as well as how to identify whether development is behind or ahead for a particular individual. Each pace may be manifested outwardly in observable behavior, which may make an adolescent appear smart or dumb when he or she is neither. Rather, what is happening is that the adolescent is either an early or late developer, a factor that we readily recognize when it is displayed in physical height but that we do not recognize as easily with regard to cognitive and emotional development.

Many books cover children *and* adolescents, thus subtly reinforcing the notion that the two groups are similar except for variations in height, weight, and physical sexual characteristics. But this conflation between children and adolescents may contribute to our so often failing to reach adolescents or to their feeling misunderstood. Until professionals truly grapple with the "why" behind strong adolescent desire *not* to be regarded—and related to—as a child, results of efforts to be helpful will often last only a brief time or keep failing. The essence of adolescence is a quest for maturity. So long as an understanding of adolescents' goals and perceptions continues to elude professionals and parents alike, we will not be able to help adolescents' anomie and social problem behaviors.

Adolescents are a unique group, different from all others in any period of the life span. Since the developmental tasks of children and adolescents *are not the same*, each group needs very different therapeutic planning.

Development Brings a Difference

Puberty brings highly significant changes in four domains of growth: physical/biological, cognitive, emotional, and social. It marks the onset of adolescence. A good example of how distinct adolescence is from childhood is cognitive growth. Prepubertal children must see an object before they can think in the abstract about it—for example, once they see a chair, then they can imagine all different kinds of chairs. But *they must see it to think about it.* But, only several years after puberty, adolescents no longer need to see the object before they can think in the abstract about it. Once they achieve the last stage of cognitive development, formal operations, they are able to hold up to 16 combinations or permutations of thought in their heads at the same time.[2] Adolescents can ponder about abstract principles and unseen concepts such as civilization or altruism, whereas children are restricted to enlarging on what they view. With adolescents, it becomes possible to discuss benefits and consequences of actions in the abstract, whereas children must see them actually occur. This difference is stunning, and it opens broad doors for professional practice.

Unique to adolescence is that choices in relationships and activities look casual but are developmentally deliberate. They are geared to a central goal: growing up. This process involves unearthing "who I am" and connecting that discovery to "who I wish to be" in future life. This aspect of adolescence is what makes it so different from any other period of growth.

Benchmarks of development provide a road map to the adolescent's growth into maturity. Professionals will find their task more certain if their practice road map takes this sequence into account. What happens internally influences external behaviors in the same manner that growing taller makes shooting a basketball into the basket easier.

Psychological outcomes of peer interaction are the bricks and mortar of reaching each benchmark. The benchmarks are not automatic or easy for anyone to recognize, and they need to be examined and assessed, as is covered more thoroughly in the chapters to come. Adolescents are extremely sensitive to similarities and differences between self and other, and they are concerned about the implications not only for their popularity but for their getting ahead. How and why peers play such an important role in their development is central to understanding adolescent psychology and to practicing efficiently.

The well-renowned epistemologist of the twentieth century Jean Piaget introduced the world of cognitive development to the literature.[3] His work is influential to a considerable degree to the basis for this book's insistence that without a real understanding of the course of normal development from childhood to maturity, valid insight cannot follow into why and when maladaptations in development occur or how they morph into real deviations. Investigations should be focused on the point in development at which the problem behavior began to occur, not on chronological age alone. At a certain age, behavior may be troublesome and unpleasant, but it may not necessarily be a maladaptation or deviant. An abbreviated case study serves as an example:

> *A sixth-grade, 12½-year-old female with whose parents I had a general acquaintance was displaying problem behavior in school. Meghan was seen by a school psychologist, who worked hand in hand with a consulting psychiatrist. They agreed on prescriptions of Ritalin to reduce her restlessness and Prozac to ease her "depression." Out of parental need for reassurance, the situation came to my attention as a friend of the family. Meghan was different from the rest of the class, and she was often annoying to them. She laughed at the wrong things and not at what the others considered funny. Her classmates told the teacher that she was weird. Meghan's parents, a puzzled set of professionals who were respectful of other professionals, were planning to proceed with the directives of the psychologist and psychiatrist, but they intuitively felt mystified. The child was*

not unhappy at home, nor was she destructive. And it was not a case of an overly strict household leading to acting out in school.

Using a developmental perspective, some deviations from the norm became clear. This cognitively advanced new adolescent was bored in school. She was making life as interesting for herself as possible in many antisocial ways to garner attention and make friends. The attempt failed, and she was very unhappy at school. Meghan had no friends, saying, "no one likes me." She expressed this feeling to her parents, who had consulted the school administrators. Diagnostically, it was clear that Meghan was developing physically right on time with the general norm, since she reached menarche shortly after her 12th birthday. Yet she was emotionally behind. There was some emotional deprivation, not expressed, due to lack of attention by busy parents and an overabundance of responsibility because she was very capable. Cognitively she was well ahead of the norm, which interfered with appropriate socialization. Her responses were so complicated that she could not find a way to connect with age-mates. To summarize the outcome of Meghan's case, her mother was guided in how to make private time a regular daily occurrence, tasks were reduced or made joint efforts, and conversations about and strategies for making and keeping friends were inaugurated. Within less than six months, Meghan had friends, and the attention-getting behaviors were for the most part dropped. It could be that she was adept enough to take on the new social mannerisms that she had been taught, that she was no longer attention hungry, that counselors had coached teachers to praise rather than ridicule her, or very simply that her classmates caught up. In three years, she was elected president of her class.

This case study, in which a youngster might have been unnecessarily treated with powerful drugs, illustrates the importance of a multidomain developmental lens when diagnosing and treating individuals who are still not full grown. This emphasis might be new, even to experienced professionals. Much primary emphasis in current practice and graduate preparation is still on *emotions*—an artifact of early 20th-century Freudian psychoanalytic theory and the later 20th-century introduction of its variants. Certainly quantity, quality, and direction of emotions is highly important to functioning well. Valid arguments can be made for the effectiveness of treatments that focus on emotions when such treatments are used appropriately. However, because there are four domains of development that are en route to completion, each of the four types of growth must be taken into account, as well as their interrelationships.

Erik Erikson, who amended his psychoanalytic training with an emphasis on the importance of social factors, introduced to the literature just how important the peer is in the adolescent period.[4] From the field of social psychology, followers of Leon Festinger, the father of social comparison theory, studied what people do when they are uncertain.[5] Among these followers of Festinger, social psychologist Stanley Schachter identified what people who are uncertain do to judge the validity of their uncertainty. His findings revealed that they look to others who are uncertain about the same matter—similar others—and engage social comparison behavior to judge the correctness of the extent of their own uncertainty.[6] Who is more similar to adolescents than their age-mate peers?

In early adolescence, immediately after puberty, a condition that I term *frameworklessness* surfaces. It is the result of psychological distancing from parents, which adolescents' new physical, emotional, and cognitive condition stimulates. They wish to think on their own—to individuate. But, having abdicated guideposts of past times, they are left without familiar reference points, which creates a sense of helplessness and lack of a framework in which to exist comfortably.

The British physician John Bowlby, who observed infants closely during the London bombings of World War II and subsequently authored his conclusions about what he saw, posited an instinctual need in infancy: attaching to the mother. This psychological attachment is accomplished through use of all the senses. Bowlby further held that the degree and quality of attachment would be prototypic of the depth of future relationships. Very simply, infant anxiety is relieved by food from the mother's breast, which resolves painful hunger, and by the warmth from her body, which approximates the warmth of the womb. Rooting to the source of nurturance begins and is reinforced by frequent daily repetitions.[7] Bowlby connected with the work of the ethologist Konrad Lorenz, who studied imprinting behavior in ducklings and chicks, observable as instinctually lining up directly behind the first creature they see upon hatching, usually the mother, and following her wherever she goes.[8] Lorenz's work inspired Bowlby's development of his formulation of instinctual attachment behavior in infants to their mother. Infant attachment is reciprocal: a mother offers milk to satisfy an infant's hunger drive; the infant's sucking milk out of the breast in turn reduces the mother's pain of swollen breasts. Each also experiences mutual emotional satisfaction. It is achievement of a solid attachment to mother that gives young children security to venture away for increasingly longer amounts of time, freed to investigate their world and others in it.[9]

Bowlby's work lays the foundations for the importance placed on peer attachment in this book. Peer attachment is a response to the depth of precariousness that frameworklessness sets off in early adolescence. Psychoanalyst and author of respected books and articles Anna Freud and her followers regard adolescents as so unsteady that they caution that adolescence could be likened to near-psychosis.[10] The pubertous adolescent may be seen to experience reactivation of the intense defenselessness of the neonate. This sense of helplessness, combined with increasing social pressure to individuate, to be oneself, leads to a "rooting instinct," similar to that in the Bowlby formulation, to resolve the pain of vulnerability. Adolescents are thus inspired to find a new attachment figure.

In adolescence, the drive is not for actual food to feed the hunger to grow but for others who supply the food of psychological growth: information. This food is supplied by a nurturer who is not the parent but the age-mate, and it does not come from the breast but from developmental "food" to try out: physical appearance, mannerisms, habits and speech, characteristics, talents, opinions, values, and attitudes. Peer attachment works reciprocally: each is actor and audience member simultaneously. It is a back-and-forth relationship, just as in the relationship between infant and mother. These exchanges can both yield information and bring the comfort of relational back and forth.

Adolescent attachment is not decided on consciously but driven internally by urgent motivation from within to be with peers. Once there, comparative acts begin. The more data, the better. To gain information about one's place on the continuum and thus understand the value of an action, there need to be sufficient numbers of others with whom to compare.[11] Comparing with just a few peers is insufficient.

Attachment in infancy and in adolescence thus differ as to numbers necessary. Infants need a solo attachment other—far better for emotional purposes if it is always the same person. Adolescents require many others. Early adolescent months and years are fed by modeling and feedback from peers on almost everything to do with one another. As adolescents advance cognitively to play with ideas, they see that they must function without direction from parents, no matter how deep their love for one another. This parting is one of growth. Peers stand for the present and future. That realization increases pressure to be around age-mate peers and learn from them, and it is outwardly expressed in an all-consuming drive to be with one another.[12] Just as the infant instinctively seeks the breast for nurturance to guarantee survival, so adolescents seek nurturance from one another. There is no leader as there is in the Lorenz model of mother duck and duckling followers. Adolescents *all are followers*.

Indeed, adolescents are motivated by internally driven, attachment-based imperatives to affiliate with their peers in order to be able to watch them, see what they do, listen to them, hear their thoughts, and understand why they make the decisions they do. They watch the outcomes to judge what brings success or failure. It is an all-consuming task. In adolescence, it is peers who nurture development. Adolescents need data on what works in life, and they do not want answers from parents and elders. Age-mates are seen as the only ones who understand enough about the quest to offer *functional information*. Adolescents have little desire to spend precious time in nonfunctional company. They wish to be at home for short periods of time, primarily to refresh. This desire is *not* a rejection of parents. Contrary to Freudian theory, the action is not "*to be away from*" but is positive, "*to be near to*." Parents can be fine, even great, but adolescents want updated contemporary models. Most of what they want from parents is support for their desire to be with peers. There is a goal to reach—getting to adulthood—and time is limited. Or so it seems to them.

Ironically, contemporary parents of very young children concern themselves with making sure that their children get together with other young children to satisfy socialization purposes. Conversely, when offspring reach adolescence, parents often become concerned by the "excessive" time offspring devote to peers and peer issues. They fear a negative impact of too much time with peers. Yet in order to fulfill legitimate developmental needs, all adolescents need to attach to peers.

Straight from Adolescents

A primary reason that practice with adolescents fails is that, commonly, actual adolescent concerns are not addressed. Rather, professionals have been addressing matters they believe are as important to adolescents as they are to mental and public health professionals. Findings from a small study completed several years ago reinforce this position. My colleagues at Philadelphia Young Playwrights and I examined what 354 adolescent high school students living in Philadelphia and its suburbs were worried or concerned about by studying the themes from their original plays. Among other fascinating findings, one was most stunning. The central themes were not about matters clinicians and public health professionals tend to consider important such as adolescent pregnancy, drug abuse, or dropping out of school. The central themes in the plays of a statistically significant number of the adolescents focused on relationships with one another and on their futures. The leading characters were adolescents.[13] This outcome reminded me of the first directive from professors in practice seminars in the early days of my graduate education: "start where the client is." This advice referred to knowing a client's options, plans, conditions of life, past goals, disappointments, parents' positions and reasons, and friends, if any, and the gender and significance of those friends. Clients' beliefs about reasons for their behaviors and problems are always important, as are whether they have supporters, who those supporters are, and why they support them. Finally, one must also assess clients' current status, their dreams and goals, and their plans, if any.

Adolescent Rebellion Examined

For quite some time, "adolescent rebellion" has been firmly engrained in the minds of professionals and laypeople alike. It also is found in academic literature and pop psychology books. Most parents besieged by confusion, hurt, and frustration welcome an explanation: "That's it! Adolescents rebel!" Because this proclamation refers to *all* adolescents, parents can feel relieved that it is not only their own child that is acting out the worrisome behavior and that rebellion is to be anticipated since it is "normal to rebel."

This perspective has become an expectation, so that parents start preparing for problem behavior years in advance, do not worry too much when the behavior occurs, and have confidence that the behavior will pass. In addition, parents are enabled to engage with other parents in socially permissible complaints and to read popular magazines for tips or quick fixes.

Sigmund Freud's theories introduced the notion of adolescent rebellion early in the 20th century. Its popularity has diminished only slightly in spite of new approaches such as behavioral and family therapies.[14] Centuries ago, prevailing preformationist notions of infants coming into the world fully formed except for physical height and weight thus regarded adolescents as small adults, who were expected to meet rigid prescriptions for proper behaviors. In Rousseau's time, at the other extreme, there was a focus on the natural playfulness of youth, combined with a plea to support natural but harmless behavior.[15]

Why has the notion of rebellion persisted for so long? A major reason is that adolescent clients/patients are quite clever. They join the back and forth of this type of emphasis because when they do, they are viewed as cooperative, the therapist feels progress is under way, and most important the real subject is never touched. So, the idea of rebellion is a good deal for adolescents and it rarely hurts. By buying into the idea of rebellion against parents, adolescents can continue to keep their defenses intact and untouched, while the professional feels competent in mastering application of complex theory. Parents hear their adolescents willingly engage in the back and forth. In fact, adolescents exhibit "signs of trust" by revealing painful problems with parents and family members. Professionals continue to be pleased. Therapeutic sessions gain focus. When sessions with parents follow, parents' frustrations are listened to and supported. In the end, all meet together to try to "work it out." It feels good to both parent and professional to appear to be getting to the root of it all, though from the adolescent's perspective his or her true concerns remain hidden and private.

In fact, adolescent life is not confined to—or even primarily located in, in most cases—the home but takes place in interaction with others just like themselves—similar others. These others are found in school and in other group gatherings. Most adolescent group members look very engrossed and appear to be having a good time. They are good actors and only occasionally fail to hold back fears about how all this change and changing is going to end. In the early adolescent years, most insecurity is about chances of "making it" day by day with one another. All this is generally kept verbally hidden but is evident in nonverbal tenuousness and hesitation. Uncertainty and insecurity in our society are not admired. Their existence is certainly a well-kept secret of adolescence.

A Note on Terms: Reformulated Concepts

Almost 50 years have passed since the British educational psychologist John Coleman advised of an "adolescent society," one quite separate from the society of adults.[16] The past 10 years have seen an expansion of communication options that extend Coleman's observation exponentially. Separate mores and values in this adolescent society are implicit, and the rising numbers and varieties of social problem behaviors among adolescents make the sloughing off of outmoded methodologies imperative. The time has come to adopt orientations to practice that are relevant to contemporary adolescence, just as the time arrived in the early '60s and '70s for the introduction of cognitive therapy[17] and family therapy.[18] In order to adopt this new relevant lens, the model for practice espoused in this book includes reversals in thought, exchange of new functions for old, strict adherence to stage-specific developmental theory bases for diagnostic planning and therapeutic management, creation of pertinent protocols for diagnosis and unique adolescent-only group therapy.

Before proceeding, it is important to note that in what follows I have reformulated some important familiar terms and concepts and offered some substitutions. Although elaborations of these revised definitions can be found in the chapters of this book, I briefly describe six of them here: conformity, importance, competition, separation, supports, and rebellion.

Functional Conformity versus Conformity

Conformity is commonly used to describe behavior that observes the norms, habits, and patterns of the general society and in one's favored subgroups. Adolescent conformity is more *functionally* than socially motivated. It is essential to psychological progress in resolving growth tasks associated with development to maturity and the creation of one's identity. The motive is to remain securely a part of the group or groups. Proximity to others perceived as similar is considered paramount, since peers model choices in behavior, language, attitude, and opinion that may be assessed and tried on for fit. Thus, conformity in adolescence is not stimulated by uncertainty alone or for status reasons. It functions to secure membership.

Relevance versus Importance

Importance is usually attributed to a person or a status that is understood to represent a substantial quality, position, access, or influence. In this book, I replace *importance* with *relevance*, which implies significance. For example, parents can be important, but they are not relevant unless they are perceived as having consequential views about a very broad number of situations. Adolescents deal daily with issues of today and an unknown tomorrow, and peers meet the criteria for relevance.

Comparison versus Competition

Competition is generally understood as a contest or rivalry toward achieving or winning a goal of some kind. But the application of the concept to adolescents is an incorrect interpretation of relationships between adolescents and age-mates. The challenge in adolescence is to determine "how I am doing in relation to another or others." Thus, the dynamic is not one of competition but of *comparison*. Comparison implies a far more neutral emotional component.

Frameworklessness versus Separation

Separation is most often seen as a parting of some type; it can be physical, emotional, or even intellectual. In this book, *frameworklessness* replaces *separation*. *Frameworklessness* describes the state of adolescents—how they think and feel—as they distance themselves from parents psychologically.[19] Adolescents are lonely and uncertain, but they do not feel separate from parents; they want parents to be around. Like room and board, parents offer basic support.

Similar Others versus Supports

Supports in common parlance refers to people who aid others to better circumstances, lift their spirits and encourage them, and if necessary, offer them comfort or goods when matters go badly. In this book, *similar* or *similar others* replaces *supports*. Peers are immediately available, in school and afterward, and adolescents' uncertainties are soothed by the physical and emotional experiences they share side by side while they are all in a state of changing.[20]

Attachment and Individuation versus Rebellion

Rebellion is normally understood to mean defiance or resistance to authority or a controlling power. In this book, it is replaced by *attachment*, the ultimate purpose for which is individuation.

Order of the Book

The book starts in chapter 1 with a short tour of historical trends in the adolescent literature up to contemporary times in order to review information about the four domains of adolescent growth. This discussion begins with late-middle childhood and examines growth and change—physical/biological, cognitive, emotional, and social—in order to set the foundation for the methods of practice offered in the rest of the book. The following chapters in part 1 then explain the comparative and evaluative psychological processes activated when adolescents are together and the way these processes affect their development, for good or ill, as well as the cultural background influences that may collide and preferences that deviate from the norm.

Part 1 concludes with a chapter devoted to issues of home base, including an acknowledged conundrum: how to deal with adolescent changes. Professionals will recognize in this revisionist approach to parental confusion and questions of self-regard in the parent-adolescent relationship surprisingly familiar facets of the adolescent experience. The chapter explains the information that parents require to recast what they perceive as their adolescent's rejection of them within a framework of the adolescent's positive growth needs. Concrete recommendations are provided, as are examples to learn from.

The book then moves in part 2 to explain what can happen psychodynamically to adolescents during the course of growth: some adolescents do get off track. Part 2 explains defensive glitches, and part 3 offers original protocols specially designed to guide the therapist during initial interviews with adolescents and with other pertinent persons. The protocols assist in reaching the real adolescent problem, thus avoiding treatment based on only an assumed problem. Thirty protocols are offered, the vast majority for use specifically with adolescents. The protocols are geared to history, relationships, and experiences with people who matter the most to adolescents: their peers.

Part 4 introduces a model for a special type of group therapy called Peer Arena Lens (PAL) group therapy. The structure of this model is built around the basic premises of DFI theory, and it is exclusive to adolescents.

A Personal Note

My interest in adolescents began when I myself was an adolescent. In high school, I was activities leader for a number of social groups. During summers between college years, when I studied psychology and sociology, I worked in summer camps supervising adolescents and bunking with them. My fascination with them grew. I developed a special interest in juvenile delinquency and spent my two years of graduate study toward a master's degree in social work studying about and working as an intern with highly delinquent female adolescents, their parents or guardians, and the courts. I went on to practice with families and children of all ages as a licensed psychologist, licensed social worker, and certified marriage and family therapist, each of which enriched my broader comprehension of adolescent issues.

My Ph.D. dissertation in developmental psychology and clinical evaluation centered on adolescent peers and the types, extent, and range of social comparisons in which they engage. That study was the forerunner of my work on the part adolescents play in one another's psychological development. Now, as a professor, I teach undergraduates and graduate students, most of whom freely admit they are still in adolescence, and I continue to learn more and more about adolescence.

PART I

Forces of Adolescent Development

1

Dealing with Development

Four Domains of Adolescent Growth

It is important for professionals to bear in mind that from time to time it may seem as if the adolescent with whom you are working is quite different from the way he or she was just a few days before. This perception may be due to shifting moods but may well be a manifestation of a periodic integration of the gradual change occurring during this stage of growth, when child turns into adult. As noted in the introduction, development occurs in four domains: physical, cognitive, emotional, and social. Each domain proceeds along its individual calendar. Sometimes physical growth is ahead; at other times it is behind one or more of the other three. Relative positions keep changing places. The domains are like cars of a railroad train that change places at junctions. Car A can be behind during one portion of the journey and ahead at others. To put this analogy in human terms, an early adolescent who has been taller than classmates for years may stop growing at age 13 or 14. Conversely, the slow developer may achieve full height at 16 or 17 years of age and turn out to be taller.

Physical growth is immediately visible; cognitive, emotional, and social growth are not. Growth in the latter three becomes evident in words and actions. Behaviorally, some surprises are in store. For example, she who seemed shy overtakes the "talker"; he who struggled with math may before long exceed the algebra star. These changes reflect cognitive growth maturing at different paces. Emotional growth takes place right alongside both cognitive and physical growth. It is the internally felt sensation that responds to physical and cognitive changes. As the latter two become more complex, so do emotions. Social growth can be defined as comprehending which behavior is appropriate in different social settings. It is complete when the three domains of growth are integrated and all four are combined. This type of growth evidences itself in appropriate adult social behavior.

This development process is complex and takes a long time to complete—ten years or more. Each month, each week, sometimes even each day can bring contradictions that need resolution.

Impact on the Adolescent

The adolescent does not remain immune from the impact of frequent changes. It is very confusing. The adolescent looks to peers, since they are changing too. As discussed in the introduction, adolescents seek out *similarity* to find some comfort that they are not becoming "strange" or "uncool." But they need to look at difference too. Difference offers new data with which to compare.[1] Adolescents need both similarity and difference, similarity to bring a sense of ease and difference to model possible qualities for the self they are trying to construct.

All adolescents speculate on what happens between themselves and their peer models. Whereas physical interaction is intentional and obvious, most psychological interactions of this stage are subliminal. Assessing the results of psychological interactions requires cognitive direction *and* emotional reflection. Results are registered emotionally. No adolescent finishes the process quickly. All do a lot of pondering, altering, re-altering, and re-re-altering. When they study outcomes, or when they encounter new models, they may switch to new aspirations and behaviors. The subliminal comparison processes start all over again. Adolescents may be together physically, but growth is an individual task.

A natural question to ask is, if adolescents seek to find their individuality, why do they dress similarly and use codelike phrases and innuendos and why are they eager to be in touch with one another almost constantly? The answer is quite simple: uncertainty. It is a formidable situation no longer to see yourself as you did before but to remain uncertain of who you are right now. It is even more angst-ridden when there is little clue as to what you will eventually be like. Thus, finding others essentially in the same boat who need to resolve similar, albeit not identical, growth issues is welcomed. Looking, talking, and acting alike afford a balance to an internal sense of instability. Yet, as adolescents witness one another's spurts in development, usually at times different from their own and/or not necessarily in the same direction, relationships can become far less soothing.

Then and Now in the Academic Literature

It is important to note before we proceed to explore child and adolescent development that controversy regarding how to categorize adolescence in psychology is age-old and continues today. The perception of "adolescence" as a distinct period of development grew more prominent in contemporary times during the dramatic decade of the '60s. The perception of adolescence as a stage of life to have some unease about also grew during this period of U.S. history, which saw rebellious youth acting out in unpredictable and antiestablishment behaviors. The appeal to young people of dramatic and even dangerous contrariness worried parents and elders. However, this was not the first instance in history in which youth were singled out for special attention and, in some cases, concern.

Long ago, adolescence was considered a distinct period of development. Yet for quite a lengthy period it was not acknowledged to be a stage separate from childhood. According to Rolf Muuss, an educational psychologist and author of books with discriminating synopses of major theories of adolescence, the word *adolescence* first appeared in the 15th century and was at that time "subordinated to theoretical considerations about the general nature of human development."[2]

Aristotle

Aristotle, who lived in the fourth century B.C.E., conceived of human development within three stages. Each stage lasted seven years: infancy to age 7, age 7 to the onset of puberty, and puberty to young adulthood. Translated into modern usage, the third period is what we now call adolescence, the period identified as commencing with the changes of puberty and ending in maturity. Aristotle described the nature of adolescent sexuality as "young men possessed of strong passions and a tendency to gratify them indiscriminately."[3] Today, we include both genders in our "worry sack" about adolescents and how, when, and with whom their libidinous drives are expressed. Aristotle thought of adolescence as a period of "instability," and we too worry about adolescent uncertainty, tendencies to abrupt and possibly unwise decision-making, and lightning-fast changes in attitudes and even behaviors.

Aristotle wrote about adolescents' sensitivities and their concern about fair treatment. Today, these same stressors may be expressed in adolescents' demands for "respect." Aristotle also wrote about adolescents' desire for success and concern for the future rather than the past. We call these "goal setting" and abdication of values revered by older generations. The "symptoms" may appear different, but youth transitioning to adulthood seem to express by their behaviors the same drives and ambitions seen hundreds of years in the past.

Instantaneous Creation

The theological view of instantaneous creation was espoused centuries after Aristotle and Plato. It was a philosophy of preformation, or what is on occasion referred to as a view of "homuncular man"—a child born as a little adult, in whom all systems are complete at birth. The difference between a child and an adult was considered to be quantitative, not qualitative. Children were small adults. Paintings of that period feature children in adult attire. In other words, after birth no development was expected other than the internal and physical height and breadth that was preordained. Children were expected to behave as the adults they were. Hence, there was no childhood, let alone any concept of adolescence.[4]

Rousseau and Locke

The position of the preformationists was challenged at the very start of modern science. The writings of the French author and philosopher of the 18th century Jean-Jacques Rousseau promoted his position that a child is very different from an adult and is entitled to grow freely rather than being restricted as an adult would be.[5] Perhaps the most serious actual and forthright challenger to the doctrine of homunculism was another philosopher, John Locke (1632–1704). Locke took the position that at birth one arrives as an empty slate—a *tabula rasa*. He regarded *experience* as the source of development—of what we know, what we think about, and what we have to offer.[6] How the child becomes adult and what kind of adult he or she becomes depends on what his or her experiences have been. Here, we see antecedent thinking of 20th-century behaviorism[7] and operant conditioning.[8] Although the positions taken by Rousseau and Locke were radically different from each other, since Rousseau followed a stage view of development rather than the Lockean philosophy of tabula rasa, neither believed that a child was merely a small adult. Rousseau accorded adolescence a unique stage, as had Aristotle.

Modern Time in Adolescence

G. Stanley Hall is widely acknowledged as the father of modern adolescence. He bridged the gap between the philosophies of his predecessors by connecting them to modern science. Hall concurred that physiological factors are genetically determined (but do not arrive complete with birth) and emphasized that they come to fruition in a gradual unfolding growth (and are not a product of experience alone). The latter view left him open to a later challenge by disciples of tabula rasa.

Hall presented his model in a series of groundbreaking lectures at Clark University in 1908. The lectures, based on a book published in 1904, marked the first formal psychology of adolescence. At last, there was a formula to follow in understanding behavior clearly demarcated as uniquely adolescent.[9] Hall's model perceived of adolescence as the fourth stage of growth, as opposed to Aristotle's view of it as being the third stage and Sigmund Freud's identification of adolescence as the fifth stage.[10] Hall's fourth stage was preceded by infancy, childhood, and youth. All these theories were similar in setting the onset of adolescence at puberty and establishing that it continued until psychological maturity is achieved. Each identified adolescence to be different from both childhood and adulthood.

Today, little argument exists in contemporary thought that adolescence is a quite separate stage of development. And yet it is puzzling to see so many scholarly books—and for that matter popular books—that discuss children and adolescents in one relatively small volume. Children and adolescents are not the same and should be regarded and handled quite differently.

A Short Step Back in Time

Before turning to the stage directly leading up to adolescence, it is well to take into consideration mid-20th-century theorists whose work brought very important but less popularly known perspectives on development. Psychoanalyst Otto Rank, a disciple of Freud who later broke from him, formulated a theory stemming from the "birth trauma." Rank's work introduces us to the most primitive and intimate relationship between mother and child. The mother's body responds to the infant's signal of readiness to separate. Psychological growth of the child begins with resolving separation, which Rank designated as the first emotional task of the individual. Union and separation, one of Rank's most prominent themes, depicts the reality of "living"; each occurrence of union and separation reawakens emotions of the primary experience.[11] Thus, adolescents are inevitably in an extremely sensitive life-stage. An early social psychologist, Harry Stack Sullivan, contributed the concept of "interpersonal psychology." Sullivan concentrated on the influence of depth and process in interpersonal relating on development and behavior. Erik Erikson is widely known for his seminal contribution of establishing identity achievement as the adolescent developmental task. All three of these theorists devoted a lifetime of study to issues of growth and psychological development—separation from the familiar, union with new others, and integration of these experiences.

Each of these historically prominent theorists provides insights that professionals will find valuable in their therapeutic work today with adolescents. A very brief look at the essential position in Sullivan's theory is followed by a discussion of Erikson on adolescence. Sullivan's position on emotional development in adolescence is also discussed later in the chapter.

HARRY STACK SULLIVAN

At a time when cognitive theory was not yet prominent in adolescent literature, Harry Sullivan advanced the theory that *interpersonal relationships* are the essential ingredients for normal human development. If experiences are negative and arouse anxiety, social problems of immaturity, deviance, and serious emotional disorders arise. Feelings of sorrow, despair, anger, even depression may also be stimulated by inadequate responses to interpersonal needs. One's feeling happy means one has positive interpersonal contact.[12]

ERIK ERIKSON

Erik Erikson was a follower of psychoanalytic theory who departed from traditional theory to stress social impacts and not libidinous outlets as Freud's followers did. Erikson's focus on social forces in everyday life and the impact of those forces on development and behavior necessitated adding three stages beyond Freud's five. All eight stages involve the resolution of a psychological conflict; lack of resolution at one stage means that movement to the next stage will be emotionally handicapped and thus harder to resolve successfully. The preadolescent (school age) task is industry versus inferiority, and the adolescent developmental task is identity versus identity diffusion.

Achievement of identity entails certainty about one's gender and direction in life. The opposite, identity diffusion, portends the trying out of many personalities and roles; it indicates that maturity is yet distant. Satisfactory resolution of identity and the three additional stages brings intimacy in relationships, pleasure of rearing the next generation, and ending life emotionally satisfied—the perception of a life well lived. Erikson sounds two notes to which it is important that the professional be ever alert. The first is an *optimistic* one. In each crisis, under favorable conditions, the positives toward resolution will probably outweigh the negatives. The second, that each stage resolution builds strength for entering the following stage defines an implicit professional responsibility: helping adolescents *find* their unique path.[13] Special attention is well spent on the identity-diffused adolescent. Although trying out a number of alternatives for what might work in the future is a good thing to do, identity diffusion—inability to discard identities deemed inappropriate and/or continuing to look for "the perfect answer"—seriously threatens reaching identity. This type of adolescent remains "in process," avoiding maturity.[14] Erikson too warns of less-than-satisfying times in the future if adolescence is not resolved well.

Late-Middle Childhood

Development moves back and forth. It does not occur abruptly. In order to understand adolescent development and behavior better, it is advisable to be informed about the years immediately prior to adolescence. Such knowledge assists in allaying concerns when there need not be any and in raising a flag if particular age-inappropriate behavior persists over a long period.

Late-middle childhood, ages 8 to 10 or 11, is generally a pleasant time for both children and parents. For the child, it is a period when new skills are being acquired. Parents enjoy teaching children and entering into activities with them. The child is less dependent, has more information, can join into conversation, and appears interested in being a real part of the family. Children enjoy going places with their parents. Home is still the center of their life. Parents retain their reputations as "experts." Friendships are generally smooth. Youth venture out further and further by themselves, yet not too far. Children of this age delight in hobbies, Internet entertainments, stories, and movies. If there are no serious internal or external problems, life is generally pretty good for all concerned.

Physical Development

The late-middle-childhood youth does not take much note of height and weight differences, although during the latter part of this period of life bodies begin to change. All sizes are seen as natural. Children are not yet tuned in to emotional aspects of physicality in themselves and others. Males are particularly alert to those who are good at sports and those whom not to choose to join one's team. Those selected are not regarded as "early developers"; rather, they are "good at sports." Nor are there names for those who grow very tall or show beginning sexual characteristics. As females near adolescence, they become aware of beginning breast buds, but they are not self-conscious. It is not yet important. Playing with friends and going places with the family is what matters—usually for both early and late developers.

The growing distance between the genders goes relatively unnoticed. Same-sex friendships are so important that little attention is paid to how the other gender changes. Neither hair under the arms, in private parts, nor on the legs is relevant to either gender. External signals may not even be evident when most children begin pubertal development in midchildhood years, particularly when first increases in adrenal and androgens begin before age 10 for both sexes. This change involves an initial rise in hormones that occurs at an average age of 7 for both boys and girls. There is some evidence that change in hormones, with females at least, is related to an increase of girls' more intense anger over time. These hormonal changes contribute to eventual puberty.[15] Generally males turn more to books to resolve their curiosities than do females, who tend to use conversation as their educational source. And, of course, ubiquitous TV, movies, and websites leave little to the imagination.

To some extent, all youths of this age are in a no-person's land, which becomes increasingly confusing as the middle-period child transitions into late childhood.

Cognitive Development

At the very same time, all youths at this stage of development make progress in their power to think more broadly. Cognitive growth brings a greater understanding of what is happening, particularly through a phenomenon that Piaget explained as "reversibility." This concept indicates that there is a knowledge of stability and change, for example, that water under freezing conditions turns into an ice cube, and at temperatures above freezing the ice cube will turn back into water. This intellectual capacity has implications for a broader picture of social interactions and happenings. For example, attractions can turn into love, but love can also reduce in intensity back to attraction. What is *not* reversible is also understood. When people die, they do not come back to life. Very young children do not understand, for example, that when a pet dies it is gone forever.

In addition, children in midchildhood grow intellectually sufficient to comprehend volume and mass, classifications and categories, ordering systems, construction of natural numbers, measurement of lines and surfaces, perspectives, and certain types of causality. This understanding becomes part of the mental repertoire. Most basic of all is the ability of these children to begin to think expansively about what they see before them. Now they understand that objects they see may be one form but that there can be many renditions of the same object. For example, all tables are not like the one they see. There are different types of tables, but all share certain similar characteristics: there is a top that sits on legs. That is why they are all called *tables*. Thus, thought expands to other examples.

Although each object is individual, it fits into a category. Dogs can have different names and look different, but they all walk on four legs and are of a general shape. Serialization is also possible, for example, the order of numbers, 1, 2, 3. With this flexible thought, the world becomes broader and the individual's own sense of self-importance is humbled. In technical terms, these children have achieved *concrete operations*. Those who have not grown to this point yet still feel very important. They continue to see themselves as a big fish, notwithstanding the size of the pond.[16] When late-middle children conquer these challenges in cognitive development, it signifies that they are en route to mature thought. Ascertaining a particular client's level of cognitive development can protect the professional from being misled by other impressions, for example, that a client's height does not imply development in other domains.

A diagnostic tip with adolescents: if an adolescent cannot understand cognitive principles that can be linked to his or her own life, it is a cue that development may be slower than generally anticipated. This level should have been reached in most cases by age 8 or 9. Further inquiry can be initiated regarding the possibility of an organic issue or a psychological trauma. The child is not being ornery or uncooperative. He or she just does not understand.

Emotional Development

The period prior to adolescence is a quiet one emotionally. Sigmund Freud explained it this way: Unconscious sexual attractions to the opposite-sex parent and their frustrations are experienced during the phallic period (ages 4–6). They are repressed from consciousness during the latency period. Thus, during this calm period between 6 or 7 to 10 or 11 years old, children give love easily and are eager to be loved. This spell breaks with puberty, when unconscious Id desires are released into consciousness. Prior stability can go into a spin. New deep and unfamiliar emotions spin around. Emotional development takes a big, albeit complicated, step forward after late-middle childhood.

Social Development

Socially there is a lot for late-middle childhood children to learn. They practice new skills, love to play games, and find engrossing hobbies with which to busy themselves. Social relations are generally smooth and wrapped around activities. Children of this age do not really engage with the *person* of one another yet. They may attend one another's birthday parties without ever talking to the birthday celebrant. Joint relating many times takes the form of making fun of some persons or familiar things that look different from what is expected. This behavior shows a beginning understanding of norms and a tentative sense of what deviates from the norm.

Cognitive advance, physical growth, and emotional peacefulness combine to make late-middle childhood youth pleasant companions, though they often need reminding of social manners, since the level of their egocentrism is still such that what "I" wish to do comes first. Game playing is highly desired. It provides chances to show off skills and learn new ones, and it is a precursor to the comparison and competition in which they will engage in the next stage. In general, this is a time for acquisition of new motor skills and allowing affection from elders. Some parents look back on this period wistfully as their adolescents withdraw from such display.

Late-Middle Childhood Friendships

As long ago as 1932, Piaget reasoned that children's relationships with peers and with adults are quite different. Parent-child relationships fall

along a vertical plane: the dominator and the dominated. Child-child relations are more horizontal. The older children get, the more skilled they
are in identifying opportunities and making demands, which friends to
go with and which not to. In this way, they practice multiple perspectives.[17] Albert Bandura and Richard Walters, both behavioral psychologists, created a stir with their position that children learn through indirect
observation, nonintentional looking at peers. Their descriptions of this
nonverbal instruction of how to behave in social environments implied
an instructive source other than parents and formal schooling. Actually,
their theory was the first not-so-subtle interpretation of the power of the
peer. Their work really introduced the notion that children automatically
become one another's models.[18] In this respect, its educational impact
contradicts the notion of *free* play, that is, play that has no connections
or ramifications. Rather, the theory implies that friends are really agents
of social control. Bandura and Walters's work is particularly relevant to
the DFI view taken in this book, which is consistent with their ecological perspective on young friendships. DFI's central tenet is that age-mates
serve an evolutionary function serving separation and supporting individual initiative.[19]

Another very interesting perspective is provided by academic psychologists Steven Asher and John Coie, whose research involves child
and adolescent relationships. They suggest that friendships are quite
different from popularity: popularity provides an index of acceptance
in childhood by one's age-mates; friendships imply perceived equal-
ity.[20] The nonreciprocal nature of friendships among children before
age 8 is the quality that distinguishes the relationships between these
young children and those that develop later, in mid- to late childhood, when they understand reversibility, that is, "I do things for you
and you do them for me." Absence of this reciprocal understanding of
friendship may account for the often turbulent nature of midchildhood
relationships.

*A diagnostic tip: a child who is a cognitive slow developer and does not yet
understand reversibility may have a mode of playing that is sharply different from others who do understand it. Conversely, children who understand
reversibility may be looking for reciprocity from other children, and when
they do not get it, they may be confused or even feel rejected. The knowledge
that they do not have is that their friends are not cognitively there yet. It is
very helpful to the professionals to bear this in mind.*

Females of late-middle childhood age enjoy the conversation opportunities of reciprocal relationships. If an individual is behind, he or she will not know how to respond or act when reciprocity of friendship is sought. On the other hand, we sometimes find young men who prefer the friendship of females to male friendship. That is not necessarily a sign of potential homosexuality: it may be that these young men are cognitively ready to engage in reciprocal relationships but that many of their male counterparts are slower than they are in getting there. So they go to whomever they can enjoy relating to.

In sum, as developmental psychologist Kenneth Rubin and his colleagues have pointed out, "children's conceptions about friendship reflect their own transitions from the world of the concrete to the world of the abstract. What children may require and desire in a friendship develops as a function of their growing understanding of the world and in conjunction with their own expanding social needs."[21]

Late-Middle Childhood Tasks

Young children used to family customs and rules become aware of different customs and rules when they make friends. They learn standards for how to play, when to speak and laugh, and how to handle disappointment and anger. They all need to master these skills to prepare for the complex peer relationships of adolescence.

During late-middle childhood, even into the preadolescent period, children seek one another out for reasons other than game playing and learning new motor skills. They try to master interrelational abilities. They sleep over at a friend's house and use reading and writing skills to be creative together and develop original ideas. They create art, they dance, they make music. Along the way, they cue into what captures enthusiasms and what does not. They learn responsibility—preparing lessons for school, sharing chores in the household, doing favors to help out special people, perhaps short periods of baby-sitting for younger siblings, relatives, or neighbors.

Children of this age appear young. Very importantly, they are still considered children and treated as such. Sexual characteristics are generally not apparent or are only in the budding stage. Parents can freely give children hugs and do not risk stiffness or drawing away. Children of this age are full of suggestions for what the family can do. They like to be with relatives and often like showing off for them.

Most late-middle childhood children are not generally considered "sensitive timber" by parents, family friends, and relatives. Friends play more and more of an important part in their lives, and most relationships run smoothly. They are easily approachable. Emotional distancing comes with the next stage.

Approaching Onset of Adolescence: The Preadolescent Child

Because children develop from one stage to another gradually and a back and forth between the two stages is to be expected until they become accustomed to the increased demands of the older stage, professionals working with adolescents benefit from knowing about the preadolescent period. The period of transition, though in most cases not very long, is as confusing to the parent as it is to the child.

Preadolescents present themselves as youngsters who can think about matters beyond a self-serving point of view. They are able to hold emotions in rather than spontaneously display them. According to academic psychologist Doug Davis, during the last year or so of preadolescence, disequilibrium may be seen. Furthermore, Davis points out that internal stresses of rapid physical growth, sexual maturation, and hormonal change, in addition to the beginnings of sexual interest, challenge the school-age child's capacity to remain calm and collected.[22] There may also develop defiance of authority, self-centeredness, and emotional liability (unsteadiness). For males, this stage occurs somewhat later than for females.

Friendship takes a different turn as the child reaches preadolescence. In younger years, a friend was someone "who I like to play with" and who does "what I like to play." Preadolescents begin to regard friendships as a relationship and look for reciprocal initiatives such as responsibility to one another, loyalty, and mutual support. There often is an intellectual dimension to behavior at this stage. Saving baseball cards demands organizing them according to particular categories. Movie idols and their habits and dress codes require some kind of intellectual evaluation. All this behavior is part of what is termed *executive function*,[23] processes children will need to use during adolescence to think about problems and make decisions about their futures. In essence, there is a move forward toward prepeer relationships.

Another shift forward prepares preadolescents for more-intensive relationships. They practice conflict resolution with friends. Of great

importance is that cognitive advance allows preadolescents to tolerate ambiguity, both negative and positive aspects of a person or situation. The
childish need to act immediately on what is experienced is greatly diminished. Thus, on the whole, friendships move smoothly, though a down-
side emerges: dealing on a deeper level with friends is new, and often preadolescents would rather disengage than compete to win.[24] They withdraw
quickly, as subtly as possible. These getting-along actions of preadolescents
are based in increasing awareness of how others regard them. What is important is not losing status, since they become concerned with popularity.[25]

Still, there is significant contrast with the adolescent relations that are
just around the corner. There is a "strictly business" dimension to adolescent relationships that is not found in younger friendships. There is
also a notable difference in the psychological territory of the two stages.
Mid-childhood and preadolescent friendships concentrate on the present
or the immediate future (tomorrow or next week). In adolescence, peers
become important far beyond the present day.[26]

Adolescence: Four Developmental Domains

Physical Development

The actual onset of puberty often comes as a surprise to late-mid childhood and preadolescent youth, but the necessary conditions for its emergence have been developing for a number of years. Five general areas of
internal and external change have been identified:[27]

- growth spurt
- increase and/or redistribution of body fat
- increased strength and endurance due to development of the circulatory
  and respiratory systems
- maturation of secondary sexual characteristics and reproductive organs
- changes in hormonal/endocrine systems, which regulate and coordinate
  the other pubertal events

The first signs of sexual change from child into adolescent in girls is breast
budding; in boys, it is testicular growth. Puberty brings the onset of menarche in females (beginning of menstrual periods) and spermarche in
males (first penile ejaculation). Menarche and the peak in height closely
follow one another, at the average age of 12.16 years for Black girls and

12.88 years for White girls. Breast budding occurs on average at 8.87 years for Black girls and 9.96 years for White girls. The process from breast budding to mature breasts takes about four and a half years regardless of race.[28] Males typically begin pubertal development one to two years later than females. Testicular growth occurs at around age 11 or 11½, although for a small minority it can begin as early as 9½. It takes approximately three years from the first signs of genital growth and development of mature genitalia for boys to experience puberty. There may be lapses of up to five years for some individuals.[29] The most common age is between 13 and 14, the time first ejaculation most often takes place. It is fairly common to observe facial-hair growth beginning and the voice changing. Although for the most part these changes occur in early adolescence (ages 11–14), pubertal growth can go on into midadolescence (ages 15–18). This time span is a striking example of how different developmental patterns are, particularly between males and females.

Males experience a great increase in muscle size and strength. Together with other physiological changes, this change make males generally more capable than females of doing heavy physical work. They tend to be able to run faster and longer. The peak of muscular growth occurs about three months after the peak growth in stature.[30] It is a direct result of these anatomical and physiological changes that athletic ability increases so much in boys at adolescence. Girls lack a similar rise in red blood cells and hemoglobin, since these are brought about by the action of testosterone.[31]

Pubertal events do not remain hidden for males. Some adolescent males suffer embarrassment with appearance of facial or other body hair or as voices change or "crack" along the way. Since about 40 percent of all boys experience some transient breast development, professionals must be alert to this possible worry. Most adolescent males do not know this growth is transient and become very anxious. They may prefer oversized tee shirts. Of even greater concern to males who are learning to control their sexuality is occasional, uncontrolled erection, possibly in public, and guilt over masturbation. They may be concerned as to whether these developments are "normal." Being alert to psycho-emotional responses to physical facts of development is part of the job of professionals.

Physical growth has a lot to do with a positive impact socially. With the exception of the embarrassment some early adolescent females suffer because of the attention their breast development may receive from male peers as well as from older males,[32] looking older physically tends to be advantageous as far as social status is concerned,[33] as well as for psychological development.[34] Far more study has focused on females than on males, notwithstanding some researchers who consider the impact of spermarche to be as significant as menarche is for females. Alan Gaddis and Jeanne Brooks-Gunn, psychologists whose research area includes physical maturation, have surmised that secrecy about spermarche is very likely due to the connection between ejaculation and masturbation.[35]

SENSITIVE ISSUES

The experience of puberty is still cloaked with relative secrecy to many if not most freshly minted adolescents. Furthermore, although it is natural for youngsters to compare themselves with age-mates on sexual matters, too, in early adolescence they seek similarity, not difference. Thus, an immediate result of the changes of puberty can be unease with oneself and a tendency to hide information from others, even peers. That is particularly true for "out of sync" puberty—spermarche or menarche that occurs very early or very late—when one's difference is heightened. Since maturing breast development is visible in females, females are more open to their female peers, and even to their parents, about when they got their first period than are males about spermarche. For males, sexual maturation, except for facial pimples and hair or its absence, is a more private affair, except in the locker room, where it cannot be escaped. Nonetheless, adolescents of both genders keep sex private from peers for a sufficiently long period of time until they can safely assume that most of them are no longer children sexually. At that time, although they know that others are similar, there is a general, but silent, consensus that no one really understands what this new status means or what to do with it.

Matters of sexual exploration are particularly sensitive and often are not raised with parents, even those who make themselves available for such questions. Except for an occasional article in the popular press,[36] there is a dearth of studies that follow adolescents from puberty into adulthood, and those that have been done are primarily short-term-impact studies,[37] with few exceptions.[38] Hence, parents get little useful information, and adolescents get little relief from concerns about penile growth or how small their breasts are at an early age or the question of whether they will ever stop growing at a later age.[39] If such issues are not set aside, they may enlarge into real worry or an unhealthy preoccupation.[40] These issues need sensitive handling and adolescents need proper information, such as the four-year length of time for breast development to be complete. Since a risk exists that curious or worried adolescents may seek or have already sought information or direction from the wrong sources, sexual matters should be as important in the therapeutic session as are other concerns. Not treating them as such would be akin to not discussing food with an adolescent with a growing appetite. Both are basic, instinctual needs, highly important to adolescents.

A therapeutic tip: whether an adolescent has experienced the changes of puberty is an area of questioning that must be handled sensitively, and inquiries on this subject are best raised well after the middle of a session if there is evidence that a positive relationship is developing and matters seem to be going well. Such questions must be paired with a clearly understandable reason for asking them. Otherwise, they will be experienced as personal intrusion, which adolescents do not easily get over.

A further therapeutic caution: professionals need to check their own approachability on these sensitive topics, and if there is even the slightest discomfort in dealing directly with the adolescent about them, professionals should seek consultation or alternative planning.

Cognitive Development

Many scholars consider there to be three levels of knowledge: (1) *declarative knowledge,* which refers to everything someone might know about something, essentially what the facts are; (2) *procedural knowledge* of what to do with declarative knowledge—it is not enough to know what the facts are, but one must also know what to do with them; and (3) *conceptual knowledge,* in which one knows what something is, what to do with it, and why one would do it that way.[41]

The highest level, conceptual, is important in understanding adolescent thought. It arrives after the adolescent has practiced the first and second levels sufficiently long to feel solid with them. Sometimes, it is important for the professional to obtain information about the adolescent's level of cognitive development and whether there is similarity or difference from the level of most of his or her peers.

STRATEGIES TO DETERMINE LEVEL OF COGNITIVE DEVELOPMENT

Assessment of physical, emotional, and cognitive growth affords the professional a strong tool for understanding behavior. Knowing the level of cognition allows the professional to understand plans and behaviors that otherwise may be misunderstood, as in the example presented in the introduction.[42]

To determine the level of cognitive development of an adolescent, questions can begin at the least complex level and move up. For example, begin with "Name the streets in your neighborhood that run north and south and those that run east and west"; go on to "Why do we need to know the directions?"; then to "Why might that be useful?" Further questioning might frame the inquiry in a peer mode, for example, "When you go out with your friends, who are the ones who know how to get around the neighborhood?" or "Which kids have ideas for where is a good place to go?" or "Who knows where a good place is to go and how to get there?" And then following questions may move toward a comparison: "Are most of the kids able to do that?" Then questions may move toward comparisons that bring self-evaluations: "Can you keep up with them, or are you having trouble?" "Do you think you are way ahead of most kids?" "Why do you think that?" Simple questions such as these assist in arriving at adolescents' level of cognitive development and then assessing whether they operate at a level where they can keep up with peers or are far ahead or below them.

PROGRESSION OF COGNITIVE DEVELOPMENT

Jean Piaget and his disciples worked to uncover the course of cognitive growth—when and how cognitive development takes leaps forward. At birth, newborns enter the world equipped to learn. *Sensory* learning is immediate, since the neonate has eyes to see, ears to listen with, fingers that touch, a nose that smells, and a tongue that tastes. All our lives we continue to learn through these five senses. Within a short time, motor learning also begins: moving arms and fingers to get to things and legs to get to places. Piaget termed the combination of these skills *sensory-motor* learning, the first of three stages of cognitive growth. Infants learn by moving about. Neural excitement from touching the places that arms and legs reach conditions the individual to continue contact with the immediate environment. Growth is not accomplished through passivity; it requires "acting on the environment."[43] Stimulus deprivation retards development.[44] Development during a remarkable first year of life brings an important cognitive advance: unseen objects come to exist in memory.

Correctly experiencing the world is the result of a decentering process. The newborn arrives psychologically egocentric, an *emotionally based sense* that all objects, including people, are part of the self, the center of it all. Three periods follow of incremental cognitive decentering to an eventual understanding of oneself as but one person in a very large world. The first period, resolved at 7–8 months, is described in the preceding paragraph. The second, described earlier as the period of *concrete operations,* finds resolution between 6 and 8 years of age. Mid-late adolescence (15–17 years of age) brings sufficient maturity to the nervous system for the third resolution, *abstracting on the abstract,* which allows for formal operations, the level of solving problems using concepts rather than only what is observed.

Thus, older adolescents think differently about the world than younger ones do. They communicate using concepts such as love, bravery, jealousy, selflessness, and aggression, thus inviting complex discussions, for example, about defining civilized behavior, what democracy is, or the meaning of history. Along with this development, adolescents experience an expansive new sense of self-power. Yet because these skills are new, sometimes they are overestimated, and an adolescent who is trying out expanded thought may cause trouble. But the greater danger is that adolescents are insufficiently stimulated due to lack of opportunities to operate in new and challenging environments, which enables them to achieve advanced thought over that of their younger years.

MORAL DEVELOPMENT

The ability to deal with actions from a moral perspective is displayed in concert with the development of the cognitive domain. With achievement of sufficient cognitive advance to know oneself to be just one part of a large world comes a number of other advances. First, there is a reduction in egocentric thinking—viewing oneself as the center with others revolving around oneself—which brings a less rigid evaluation of right and wrong, with allowance being made for others' behavior that is simply irritating. Second, there is ownership of an ability to consider whether a logical reason exists for not accepting rules and authority or for accepting them. Third, reasoning can be applied to friendship-group norms: Is there reason to set aside one's own needs and desires for someone else's? With adolescents' increasing insights into the "calls from within" themselves to succeed at being a member of a social group, and even of the larger community, comes adolescents' ability to understand altruism better.[45]

ASSESSING COGNITIVE GROWTH

Consider the case of two youths, both basketball players. Although they are the same age, one is five feet six inches tall and one is six feet tall. Clearly the chances of each being a high scorer would be far more equal if there were a negligible height difference. It is simple to reason that the taller youth will be the higher scorer. Although cognitive differences are not as obvious to the eye as height is, cognitive growth too is discernable; it is just harder to spot, since it is expressed in language that communicates thinking. Furthermore, there exist different styles of encoding, retrieval, decoding, and integration, not only differences in understanding the concepts. Three principles are essential to bear in mind:

- Cognitive understanding grows over the period from infancy to early adulthood, normally reaching completion in late-middle to late adolescence.
- A supportive, even benevolent environment is necessary for cognitive growth—an environment where others get involved in providing trips to new places, close or far, new vistas, new experiences, and new words and concepts in verbal exchanges.
- It is possible for growth not to reach its full potential if conditions discourage experimentation, expression, and exposure to the environment.

A bit of back and forth with a client can be valuable in informally assessing his or her cognitive level. Bearing in mind these three principles, devising simple tests to assess cognitive level is worthwhile. With mid-childhood, preadolescence, and even early adolescence, it can be fruitful to use drawings, as in one of Piaget's classic experiments: display a long and thin water glass and a short but wide one, both filled with four ounces of water. If the client answers correctly that the glasses contain the same amount of water, then he or she understands volume and is no longer caught in the concrete, by what is seen, but has begun to abstract from what is seen. Older adolescents can be asked to respond to a question about love; if the response includes mention of an abstract concept, then they have most likely achieved the last stage of cognitive growth, abstracting on abstractions. For example, a client may be asked, "Does the term *love* bring up any other thought in your mind?" If the client answers, "a house and kids," then he or she is still abstracting on concretes. If the client says "fidelity" or "loyalty," each an abstract concept, then he or she has conquered the final cognitive task, formal operations.[46]

AN ALTERNATIVE METHOD

A second way to assess a client's level of cognitive growth is to ascertain how he or she applies cognitive processes to an existing knowledge base, as described by James Byrnes in his article on adolescent cognitive development.[47] Examples of cognitive processes to be applied are the following:

- reasoning: deductive, inductive, decision making, and problem solving
- encoding: forming a mental representation of a situation
- learning: getting information into long-term memory
- retrieving: getting information out of long-term memory

When you examine the reply, what should be determined is not just whether the adolescent can answer the question but how effective the answer is. For example, when you ask why a client selected a certain color dress, Susie might answer that her best friend is wearing red and they wanted to look like twins, and Mary may answer that red is a symbol of courage, which is a good thing to feel within you when you are in a strange place and do not know if you will be welcomed. Clearly, both girls understood the question, but Mary placed it within a conceptual framework. Her response accounts for personal strength and shows both reasoning and encoding. One can assume she has encoded past experience into long-term memory and retrieved it before her statement. It is also plausible that Susie has encoded into long-term memory what she has seen and reacted well to, seeing twins dressed alike. She has retrieved what she has seen, demonstrating the process active in concrete operations. The difference is that Mary has also done problem solving—how to handle a potential problem—feeling uncertain in a strange situation. Susie most likely will eventually reach Mary's level, but until then, there is a vast difference. This difference affects which adolescent peers each selects to spend time with and learn from. This example make clear how a solid theoretical base from which to draw clues to the developmental status of adolescents assists proper diagnosis and skilled therapeutic progress. Without such a base, outward appearance or chronological age alone can mislead.

A third assessment tool depends primarily on how closely the professional listens to adolescent responses and questions as they talk together in session. With close attention, it is possible to assess how well adolescents can articulate what they do know, if they know what they do not know, and if they are definite about everything or open to questions about what they express in order to learn even more. Not only does this approach yield an index of attitude and curiosity, but close attention also reveals the complexity level of their words, thoughts, and questions.

Far more than just physical attraction brings people together. Being able to converse on the same intellectual level also attracts. It offers opportunities for a kind of shorthand conversation: not too much needs explanation. Telling jokes can be a clue. If two adolescents laugh deeply at jokes of similar complexity, most likely they are at the same cognitive level. The level of cognitive growth an adolescent has reached underlies why older adolescents not only have more knowledge but also know how to use that knowledge more effectively. Because during the process of growing up, each adolescent has his or her own individual travel itinerary, professionals must be familiar with which stops have already been reached and which are yet to come.

A therapeutic tip: it is important to remember that youth grow up on their own schedules. The important matter is not the schedule of their development but whether they are stimulated and assisted in making the most of that development or whether there is a heightened risk for a temporary or permanent retarding of growth. Professionals should try to ascertain which of the two situations prevails prior to designing therapeutic plans for PAL group therapy or a different modality.

Emotional Development

Adolescent emotional development follows a complex and intricate path. Its process is noticed in variations of mood, ups and downs and abrupt calm, only to be followed by more of the same until adolescent growth tasks are resolved. Although many psychologists have offered fascinating formulations of the process, the interpersonal psychology of Harry Stack Sullivan, advanced years ago, captures the dynamics of the preadolescent period, oft-times regarded as a form of early adolescence. Sullivan, discussed briefly earlier, saw the "chum" dynamic as crucial. Although the very deep emotions that preadolescents feel toward their best friend are free of lust, the relationship signals the beginning of the end of childhood. Although preadolescents do feel hurt strongly, they also love strongly, and it is an unselfish love—sensitivity to what makes the chum, or friend, happy. They reap great joy in furthering whatever the friend wants. It seems a divinely innocent period of emotional freedom, perhaps unlike any other during the life span. This perspective on the chum may be seen to reflect aspects of the psychoanalytic model, in which repression of sexual instincts is strong in the latency stage. Sullivan goes on to surmise that without an opportunity for deep emotional experience with a same-sex best friend or chum, the ability to find satisfying, mature, deep relationships is highly impaired. Consequently, Sullivan considers *intimacy attainment in preadolescence* the developmental task of that period.[48]

But Sullivan's approach does not characterize the period of adolescence as altogether benign. He argues that since emotional growth is related to excitation from the genital area, when adolescents' desire is no longer emotional intimacy but lustful there is a collision. In early adolescence, uncertainty about what to do with these feelings may rock the adolescent. Before adolescence, emotions were fair play, but in adolescence, genitals imply an unworthy lustful social self and bring difficult emotional times. Sullivan suggests that there is work to do on the self to move the arousal of sexual feelings to an acceptable part of the self. Sullivan suggests that inability to resolve the conflict between wishing to feel secure and feeling lustful may wind up in a feeling of loneliness. Growth can only proceed to the next step when this conflict is resolved. Professionals need to be sensitive to the intensity of conflict. Preadolescence is different. It involves strongly felt desires for a one-to-one relationship with someone of the same sex, but it ends with an eruption of genital sexuality, namely puberty.[49]

Sullivan stresses the affect of *interpersonal* relationships on the end of adolescence. Adolescence ends when lustful needs merge with needs to share emotionally in mutual tenderness and intimacy. Sullivan does not seem to consider domains other than the emotional, except for his position that all partially developed aspects of one's personality have already fallen into place when this integration occurs. He concludes that only then does the individual find a vocational goal and embark on adulthood.

A PROCESS APPROACH

The work of Erik Erikson, a major figure in adolescent emotional development discussed earlier in this chapter, differed from Sullivan in his emphases. Most readers familiar with his work will recall that although he recognized strong sexual needs rising from unconscious repression in adolescence, he placed greater emphasis on adolescents' peer groups as a place for *tryout and feedback* than on peers as substitute love objects.[50] Other excellent formulations of emotional growth in adolescence can be found in the literature.[51]

Social Development

Mature social development involves knowing how to act in socially appropriate ways, determined by the setting and the persons occupying it. Social environments range from homes to educational institutions, religious institutions, entertainment venues, health care institutions, business offices, government facilities, and more. Acceptable behavior ranges from freedoms taken in one's own home to various degrees of restraint out of the home, sometimes differing even in similar institutions. For example, behaviors in a Baptist church may differ from expected conduct in a Catholic church. Behavior in a movie theater is unlike that at a baseball game. Dressing for a day at the beach is poles apart from dressing for a wedding. The list could go on, but it can be summed up with a very important qualification: this type of learning continues throughout life.[52]

The quality of an individual's social performance is dependent on the level of completeness of each of the other three domains of growth. At full development, occurring at end of late adolescence, the individual is capable of displaying appropriate expression and control of emotions and can grasp the purposes and mores of the setting. Also, he or she has sufficient physical stature, strength, and skill to navigate the physical setting. *Each and every social response draws from the three other domains.* Upon maturation, individuals have integrated the four domains of development and display appropriate social behavior tailored to the social setting. B. F. Skinner, the world-renowned psychological scientist, contributed to the literature a model of how a behavior becomes part of an individual's repertoire. According to Skinner's model of operant conditioning, a behavior is repeated if it is positively reinforced. This formula is applicable to social behavior. As an example, the reward for *behavior A* could be as seemingly insignificant as a smile. If each time or most of the times *behavior A* is repeated, it brings smiles, the reward over time reinforces reappearance of the rewarded behavior, assuring its continuance as a feature of one's personal style. However, if a frown, not a smile, appears each time the behavior is repeated, reward will not experienced and the behavior will not be reinforced. Eventually that behavior will be dropped.[53]

Integration of the Four Domains

The social domain of development integrates the other three domains in their outward display. The level of integration differs according to the individual's level of maturity. A simple example: A 5-year-old child may cling to her parent when she enters a relatively strange adult's home (emotional). She may not answer a question because she does not understand its meaning (cognitive). She may be too short to sit at the adult table and resist sitting elsewhere (physical). She sulks (emotional with social display). Fast-forward to the child as an 18-year-old. She extends a hand for a handshake upon entering a home to which she has been invited (emotional comfort and a cognitive understanding of the context). She responds to a question about whether school meets her expectations by answering yes but is also informative about her reasons (emotional and cognitive). She is seated at the adult table (physical) and is comfortable conversing with adults (cognitive and emotional). Furthermore, she offers to help carry the heavy plates and compliments the hostess on the meal (social). The four domains work well independently and together, and others are impressed by a "grown up" individual who would be a joy to invite back.

Incomplete Domain Development

It is impossible for the professional simply to observe adolescent behavior that is clearly inappropriate, or even antisocial, and determine with certainty in which domain or domains the adolescent is underperforming, except for physical growth. To gather additional information, the professional must do the following:

- Consult referral information, specifically the history of physical growth, to determine if there are reports of injury to the body or an exceptional number of hospitalizations. If this information is not present in the record, ask for it verbally.
- Use simple tests such as those illustrated in this chapter to determine whether the domains have reached normative developmental level. If little or no information is gleaned from the tests, seek information from a specialist in the domain(s) of concern and/or from an adult familiar with the adolescent's history. Be sure to have permissions signed first.

- Inquire of the adolescent and then of parents and family whether there has been trauma of any kind. As a beginning strategy to start the discussion, it may help to relate benign examples of what others have experienced. If the adolescent volunteers descriptions of events, even tentatively, follow through with more investigation or authentication.
- Converse with colleagues and/or superiors as to next steps.

The Domain Perspective and Practice

Professionals should envision adolescents who come to their offices for help in two ways: (1) as they appear and (2) as an outward representation of four domains of growth operating together. Completing an assessment of the level of development of each domain can set the behaviors, unfulfilled aspirations, and difficulties brought to professionals within a realistic framework of chronological *and* developmental age. The information gained becomes the cover page of the road map for therapeutic intervention, which should be far more instructive than a singular view based only on what is seen and expressed.

Information Updates

The adolescent stage of growth seems to be just one big question mark for many parents and even some professionals. Adolescent behaviors are fascinating and fleeting, only to be followed by the next round of behavior, which is again uniquely fascinating and fleeting. And so it goes.

Yet there is frequently new information that can be helpful to professionals and parent alike. In addition to those sources professionals access in peer-reviewed journals, popular-press reports can be quite fascinating and may shed light on troubling behaviors, which can then be further explored in the literature. For example, in regard to the often-asked question of why adolescents stay up late at night and then need to sleep late, a recent article in the press reported findings of a scientific study by researchers at Bradley Hospital in Providence, Rhode Island. Their work disclosed that adolescent sleeping rhythms are different from those of children and adults: adolescents are *alert longer into the dark hours and sleep during light hours.* Furthermore, other studies suggest that the first few hours in schools that start around 7:30 a.m. are lost learning time and recommend that schools open two or three hours later.[54]

The suggestions that the unique body rhythms of adolescents be taken into consideration when scheduling activities for them seem simple, but they are based in an exploration of outward behaviors that manifest *adolescent physical domain* needs, as described in this chapter. In addition, adolescent cognitive functioning is gaining an increasing amount of attention from neuroscientists. A major publication reported a finding on stimulants to brain excitation that speaks directly to adolescent comparison behavior.[55] This ubiquitous adolescent behavior is set within the theoretical context of adolescent development and behavior in the next chapter.

2

Dynamic Functional Interaction (DFI)

A Revisionist and Sequential Theoretical Model of Adolescent Psychological Development and Behavior

The Basics

Dynamic Functional Interaction (DFI) is the theory on which the practice model of this book is based.[1] DFI theory offers explanations for common problems we see in adolescents today. Its concepts explain the processes and dynamics of growth. According to DFI, problem behaviors are defensive actions, which occur when the psychological growth tasks of adolescence become too difficult and painful. Practical applications of DFI frame the diagnostic model of defensive glitches, diagnostic protocols, and PAL group therapy presented in later chapters.

Dynamic Functional Interaction describes and explains the functional purpose of most adolescent interactions and how adolescents push along their quest to reach maturity and attain identity. DFI lays out the psychological motivation beneath the surface behavior and details the moving force—comparative acts—a more extensive form of social comparison.

The developmental task of adolescence is to leave childhood and enter maturity. The corresponding psychological task is to achieve a sense of identity anchored in comfort with one's gender and knowledge of the direction one wishes to take in choosing a vocation or career. In simple terms, individuals achieve an understanding of themselves in love and in work, the basic Eriksonian definition of identity.[2] This goal is accomplished only by the adolescent's own effort to decide on self-elements.

The Dynamics of Achieving Identity

Comparison

Adolescents use social comparisons with peers generally within their various peer groups to gather information they need for the growth and development work necessary ultimately to arrive at their sense of identity. They use the findings of their comparisons to put themselves on a range with others and to assess who they are better or worse than or perhaps similar to. They do this over and over again for many long years on hundreds, if not thousands, of characteristics and talents until they find real answers to questions about themselves. These answers help them decide realistically what characteristics fit with the type of person they wish to be, who they want to befriend, their career/work goals, and who they want to mate with.

Adolescent Conformity and Intuition

Adolescent conformity has a far different purpose from adult conformity. There is a decisiveness connected to the adult form: it involves a commitment of sorts. Adult conformity serves order in the greater society, expressed for example in observing laws and customs of the nation, city, and community. Adolescent conformity is different: it is related to the needs of the developmental stage and does not involve commitment for any time beyond the immediate present. It is fueled by a preconscious internal imperative to be with one's peers in order to mature.

Adolescents are attracted to many groups, not just one or two small ones. A peer group is only a small part of a Peer Arena, which has many groups under its umbrella. There are groups in school, on the street, at concerts, and in lots of other places. It is in these various groups that the greatest percentage of psychological growth action takes place. That is why adolescents need many peers from many groups with whom to interact. And one of a number of reasons that they need to conform is to continue to have access to this fountain of information.

Adolescents intuitively know that they have to be very careful about relationships, or they may be rejected. If they are rejected, they lose direct access to peer models and to what they themselves can copy, imitate, or reject. So they operate with extreme care. An interesting picture of adolescents' interactions is disclosed in findings from a study of 11 adolescent discussion groups of 6 males each. In the verbal exchange, only 18.5 percent of all statements made over a 30-minute period were disagreements.

Agreement was expressed in 70.3 percent of the statements.[3] Of great interest is the 11.2 percent of statements that presented another voice, the "yes, but." This phrase allowed one to raise a question but not register a formal disagreement. It was *not* agreement but, rather, a very cautious dissent.

A second, very different example of adolescents' interaction is at concerts, which attract thousands of adolescents, often at a hefty expense. When adolescents are questioned about the music or the dancing, their answers are frequently minimal, unless the question changes to "Who was singing or dancing?" and especially if it is "Who was there?" Then chatter is often unstoppable and can be expansive in descriptions of personal characteristics and behaviors, specifics of dress, actions, missteps, romance, displays of physicality, and who spoke to whom and when.

Attendance at major concerts no matter the expense is a good example of *surface-structure behavior* and *deep-structure motivation*. Surface structure identifies the concert as a place all the kids are going and therefore an event that one wants to attend. The deep-structure motivation is what fuels the intensity of the desire to *be there*. This motivation is one way adolescents accomplish getting to as many peer attachment others as possible to look, listen, and compare with. The drive to be together with peers has been perceived by worried parents and community figures as "blind obedience to peers." This statement is in fact half right: it is obedience, but it is not blind.

Theory Applied to Practice

Freud's theories offer good examples of pragmatic application of theoretical concepts to practice. Aspects of his theories are among various antecedent literature from various fields that constitute DFI's theoretical foundations.

Freudian Structural Theory

Sigmund Freud's *structural theory* details the way the psyche is organized and operates to effect behaviors. It posits two levels of awareness: the Conscious level, of which individuals are aware, and the Unconscious, of which they are unaware. Freud theorizes three structures, Id, Ego, and Superego, which operate within the Unconscious and essentially govern most behavior. The Id is the seat of instincts and desires. The Ego is the arbiter of conflict between the Id and the Superego and controls motor functions. The Superego represents what is morally correct and thus functions as a conscience does. A simple example of these structures' joint operation is the desire to buy a chocolate cake (Id), despite an intention to diet and the directive to stay away (Superego). The decision to buy a cookie is directed by the mediator (Ego). This back-and-forth governance of behavior takes place without one's conscious awareness. Occasionally, these unconscious operations rise to consciousness, for example, as "slips of the tongue" or in psychoanalytic therapy through free association or analysis of dreams.

Anxiety of different degrees is stimulated by unconscious conflict, primarily between the Id and Superego. Anxiety can be relatively benign, of which we may or may not be aware, or so intense and unbearable that in order to relieve the psychic pain defensive behaviors are adopted. Although for the most part anxiety is of a sort that individuals can control, it is capable of affecting daily functioning if the defense mechanism becomes so strong and rigid that it controls the person, rather than the other way around.[4] For example, in Shakespeare's *Macbeth,* Lady Macbeth's defense against overwhelming anxiety about her complicity in the murder of the king manifests itself in obsessively washing and rewashing her hands.[5]

Freud's Developmental Theory

Freud's corollary work and the second of his two basic theories, *developmental theory,* sets five stages of development: oral, anal, phallic, latency, and adolescence. Each stage involves the resolution of a developmental task. Incomplete resolution, not working out the tasks of the stage with an acceptable measure of success, results in being in a weakened position to take on the next stage.[6] Freud's two separate but interrelated theories are used in applied form in psychoanalysis and the practice of analytic psychotherapy.

As mentioned earlier, some psychoanalytic thinkers consider adolescence a difficult challenge. They see it as so extreme a period of upheaval as to be one of almost near-psychosis.[7] But Freud's optimism about adolescence as another chance to rework mistakes of the past would consider adolescents as candidates for psychoanalysis or psychotherapy if they are deeply troubled.

DFI Structure

DFI theory begins with adolescence. It accords even greater recognition than its forerunners do to peers as the most relevant other of the period. Its basic premise is that adolescents are one another's attachment figures and that the dynamics of their interactions stimulate development. The work of DFI's two stages, referred to simply as Stages 1 and 2, differ. In Stage 1, a temporary picture of oneself as a unique individual is worked out. The task of Stage 2 is completing and integrating the work begun in Stage 1 to identify self-elements appropriate for who "I am" and now wish to become.

Peer Arena Defined

Within the DFI model, *Peer Arena* stands for *all* peer groups with which an adolescent spends time, both actually and virtually, whereas *Peer Group* refers to only one group. *Peer Arena* refers to the composite picture of numerous adolescents assembling in many, many assorted group settings. The Peer Arena has a psychological component best defined as *the psychological aggregate of any and all peer groups, real, remembered, or imagined, in which adolescents engage actually or psychologically.* It may include within its borders not only familiar nearby friends, kids from school, camp, church, mosque, or synagogue but also kids written to, called, or even befriended on the Web. Or it may include peers merely observed. Peer models may also be found in the media, such as in movies, television, or on the Web, where a flick of a switch or a click of the mouse invites in adolescents. Screen images take on an influential reality, sometimes as real or more so than a human. E-mail and text messaging on cell phones have revolutionized sources of communication and contact.

DFI's Peer Group Clarified

A peer group, on the other hand, usually numbers under 15 individuals, adolescents comfortable in one another's company. Generally they are of a similar age, live nearby, and attend the same school or others in the same neighborhood. They share compatible goals and interests. A peer group can also include a best friend. It is a cohesive group and somewhat exclusionary. Peer groups exist because of special interests such as socializing, athletic teams, individual sports, arts and crafts, religious activities, theater, and band. Each peer group is one of various groups that make up the Peer Arena. When the term *peer group* is used to refer to more than one group, it can be very confusing, and although that is an improper use of the term, it occurs frequently. Because *Peer Arena* encompasses all peer groups in which the adolescent participates, regardless of time or location, professionals need to look beyond the school or neighborhood.[8]

DFI's Peer Arena Dynamics

Adolescents do not just get together in peer groups. What they do goes beyond what can be observed: there are psychological activities that get started as they gather. They automatically engage the *comparative act.*[9] Intuitively, they inspect one another very carefully from tip to toe. One at a time they examine details of appearance, clothing and style, abilities, talents, deficiencies. They pay close attention to opinions and attitudes expressed. They recognize who is creative and who is dull and what the topics of interest are. Just about everything that can be observed in other human beings is noticed. How much they observe varies according to how much time they spend reacting to verbal and nonverbal responses of the rest of the group members.

The next step is for the adolescents to compare characteristics of their own with those observed and to judge their respective worth. To make this judgment, they engage in as many types of comparison as they need, three of which are unique to adolescence and are explained along with the other comparisons later in this chapter. Particularly when alone, each adolescent thinks deeply about what he or she has found.

Between all but a very few adolescents, the dynamic is not competition but *comparison.* This subliminal mental activity generally continues for 10 years or more until enough information has been collected and sorted through to complete a sense of identity: comfort with one's gender and a direction to follow in life. In essence, *the Peer Arena is adolescents' reference library.* Their attachment others, their peers, are the articles, newspaper, books, and media in this library. Thorough reading requires investment of a lot of time and energy.

Adolescents respond emotionally to findings from comparative acts, which is the way the results are first brought into consciousness. When the results are very much below expectations, adolescents suffer emotionally. Some find it very hard to continue performing comparative acts, but they do. Others may choose any number of ways to avoid peer gatherings.

For example, they may be truant in school. Others stay in school but psychologically just turn off, and still others take on psychologically defensive behaviors. In these cases, the adolescents' development is impeded. Just how much it is depends on how early or at what point and in what manner they took flight.[10]

DFI Stages of Growth

DFI posits two adolescent Peer Arena stages, identifying when adolescence begins and detailing its psychological impact, what needs to be clarified for adolescents, how they go about it, the dynamic processes utilized, and when they reach their goals of maturity and identity. Although DFI is consistent with Erikson's seminal contribution on the importance of peers and of identity achievement, DFI is different in that *it deals with the process.* DFI also focuses on the nature of the process, whether it is smooth travel or an interrupted one, and potential irregularities.

Stage 1 requires interacting with numerous peers to encounter a supermarket of characteristics, talents, attitudes, opinions, and the like to select and try out. Stage 2 requires far fewer peers since many were eliminated in Stage 1's consideration of "What can I be?" Stage 2 deals with "What will I be?"

DFI theory champions the position that adolescents develop on their own internal schedule. Thus, chronological age is regarded alongside developmental age, not as identical to it. Strict timetables do not apply to adolescents' growth since changes occur in each of the four domains subject to individual variation. Thus, DFI asks professionals to focus on discrete benchmarks of growth in each domain: behavior change, body appearance, actions, and understandings. A general timetable for expected growth in each of DFI's two stages is specified as to which behaviors hint of developmental delays and which do not.

Comparing very general age norms with developmental benchmarks makes it possible for the professional to assess whether adolescents are for the most part on target or behind. DFI's context of four domains of growth, rather than a composite one, allows (1) a simpler road map for professionals to bear in mind, that is, what to expect, in which domain, and when, and (2) a formula with which to assess existence of developmental lags as differentiated from defensive *glitches.*

Comparative Act Benchmarks of Stages 1 and 2

The number, type, pace, and process of comparative acts in both stages of DFI give evidence of an adolescent's developmental age, as do the domain growth advances discussed in chapter 1. After years and years of comparing, drawing conclusions, thinking and rethinking the data and its conclusions, and trying again, eventually making more comparisons does not add much more information. The adolescent is *satiated* with comparisons and needs no more. There are two periods when comparisons become either pseudosatiated or satiated.

Stage 1 and Pseudosatiation

The first and most intense experience of satiation comes at the end of Stage 1, the primary Peer Arena period. Generally around the 11th or 12th grade, the adolescent has decided on enough elements to construct a temporary self structure. But the adolescent does not realize that this self is only temporary. What the adolescent feels is actually first-stage satiation, or *pseudosatiation.*

Pseudosatiation is fairly easily recognized: it is distinguishable by the declarative inflection of the tone of the adolescents' comments. The comments are not interrogative at all, and many times the words offer advice and direction. Adolescents temporarily become overly impressed with their new sophistication. It remains unknown to them that it is but a facsimile sophistication. Some parents find them barely bearable in their certainty about almost all matters. The message of comfort and certainty the adolescents send to themselves is of an established self structure with no need for additional comparisons. In reality, the adolescent possesses a pseudo self structure composed of pseudo elements. Before too long, the deep-structure development-driven motive to grow, the adolescent imperative, will stimulate new comparative acts. Some attributes and attitudes will stay, and others will drop away and be replaced. All will need to be integrated. But for now, at the end of Stage 1, this certainty of a pseudo self feels good.

At this point, somewhere around age 17 or 18, an emotional calm reassures both adolescent and parent. Since adolescents are now thinking abstractly, their questions and observations have more depth. They can be overheard talking more seriously, alongside their absorption in the latest fad. When parents notice a decided difference, it is clear to them that their child is maturing. This is a benchmark of the end of the primary Peer Arena period (Stage 1), and although it does mark the end of Stage 1, by no means does it end psychological adolescence. Stage 2 is next.

Stage 2 and Authentic Satiation

Stage 2 begins with this calmer person with calmer friends. Stage 2 may last from four to six years, depending on the decisions that are made. Reassessments and rethinking take place. The supermarket of choices is replaced with the specialty store. Who one is and what direction in life one wishes to follow have been whittled down to far fewer choices. Now, comparisons are made only with others who express similar interests or future plans. These are the relevant peers now. The attachment is less emotionally intense and more cognitively directed. Comparative dynamics of Stage 2 test out which Stage 1 self-elements fit with maturity and future planning.

Peer groups making up the Stage 2 Peer Arena are few in number, smaller, and more thoughtful. Now, adolescents' functional comparative task is directed to finding answers to how to get where they wish to go and estimating their position relative to others like them. New similar others become attachment others for purposes of Stage 2 needs. The presence, information, and attitudes of these attachment others bring more complex food. As "future" takes on more resonance, private, deliberate comparisons can become filled with anxiety as the immediate takes its proper place as part of life, not the whole of life. Increasingly greater emphasis goes from immediate to future life matters: lifestyle, career choice, and before too long future mate. This is the business of Stage 2.

The similar other of Stage 2 is different from the Stage 1 security-oriented peer selection. Now, similarity of interests is the deciding factor. Thus, a type of comparison that was little used earlier takes on importance: Dissimilar Other comparison. Comparing with the dissimilar reinforces just who really is very much like oneself. A second type of comparison that was rarely used in the earlier stage takes on a far more serious aspect. Comparison with a Goal not only assists in judging where others are in relation to a common goal but entails finding out the particulars of others' goals. It stimulates the adolescent to assess whether his or her own goal is well thought out and comprehensive or falls short of others' goals. The third comparison type of high importance is comparison with the Positive Instance. How one ranks in this comparison differentiates whether a career can be successful or whether their attributes or talents are at the level of an avocation. Additionally, and very important, the continuation of comparisons sustains the attachment need. Even almost-mature adolescents need to feel the security of attachment figures—their peers.[11]

DFI Concepts

DFI brings to the literature many new concepts that are of special pertinence to practice and that will come in quite handy to the professional working with adolescents. When adolescents are together, group forces get set into motion, including (1) the adolescent dialectic, the pull away from childhood toward adulthood, (2) stand-in elements that act as a stabilizing force until they can be supplanted by one's own choices, (3) comparative acts, the most ubiquitous psychological dynamic in adolescent group interactions, and (4) three types of social comparisons unique to adolescence that, when added to five other types, offer a portrait of how adolescents use comparisons.[12]

Adolescent Dialectic

When adolescent peers gather, a composite adolescent dialectic is set in motion.[13] Adolescents' desire to gather together is bilevel. The overt reason—for example, "I want to go to the ice rink"—is a *surface-structure action*; this is what the adolescent understands as the reason. The real reason is subliminal and unknown; it is a *deep-structure imperative*. As pointed out earlier, the former reason stimulates conscious action, in this case going to the rink; the latter reason is unconscious. The force of the unconscious motivation is acted out through a developmental imperative to access growth pictures and later compare and evaluate them. All the while, the adolescent dialectic swings back and forth between adulthood and childhood, with the former based more on cognitive processes and the latter seeking a return to emotionally simpler times.

The effect of each individual's adolescent dialectic being gathered together with those of other group members results in the emergence of new forces. The most fundamental of these forces is the Peer Arena group effect, an adolescent cousin of Gestalt psychology, which advanced the idea that a group is more than the sum of its parts.[14] Thus, in adolescent groups the combined psychological imperatives to grow coalesce as a stimulus to functional comparative acts.

Stand-In Elements

Particularly in the beginning years, adolescents are psychologically far from a temporary self-concept that gives them some sense of stability. Just as adolescents do if they run out of money, they borrow from peers. They identify with what they like in others and implant it as their own. These are temporary stand-in elements that stabilize the empty spaces in the cognitive structure left by borrowed parental self-elements that they now reject. They proceed to try out these elements for fit. For example, they may try out dancing or singing; they sing or dance and gauge audience response. Simultaneously, they evaluate performances by others and compare. With time, as they select cognitive elements that fit them, they borrow less and less, since there is less empty space. Yet, although the pace is slower, the process is intensified in Stage 2 and is not discontinued until all self-elements have been selected.

Comparative Acts

As we have seen, adolescent comparative acts differ from adult comparisons directed toward *refining* attributes in an already-established self. Adult comparisons are targeted, not diffuse, and accomplished quickly. That is not so for adolescents, who are *in process* of finding a self. Consequently, the comparative-act process for adolescents is more complex: (1) it requires evaluating the outcome of each comparison and combining the evaluations together to make a final estimate on the overall quality of the self at this moment in time; (2) thus, adolescent comparisons are carried out on practically everything—characteristics, talents, opinions, every aspect of appearance, personality, and so on; (3) the series of evaluations and reevaluations and the decision-making on whether a characteristic fits does not happen quickly; (4) the perceived response of the group weighs heavily in the ultimate decision to retain or drop each element; and (5) each comparison and evaluation is repeated over and over again until a decision on its quality and functionality is settled in the adolescent mind. All in all, this is a process that takes a lot of time—and energy.[15]

Although comparison findings carry emotional impacts for adults, too, a striking difference is that adults possess a self that absorbs the emotional bounce. Adolescents have no firm foundation to balance disappointment.

Adolescents use eight types of comparison in their comparative acts,[16] three of which DFI introduces as distinctive to adolescent decision-making. DFI defines these types along with an abbreviated version of the function that each serves, as each is used for a different psychological purpose. In the list in the following section, the three types exclusive to adolescents are listed just after the other five.

Some comparisons are customarily used in Stage 1, and others in Stage 2. Hence, which type an adolescent selects to use can provide insight into how far along he or she is in development. Together, the eight types also serve as a valuable resource in detection of defensive glitches.[17] The analysis of what types of comparison an adolescent is using may be carried out directly with the adolescent, with a sensitivity to timing as to his or her readiness. Supplementary protocols found in later chapters help to elicit additional information or clear up uncertainties in the analysis.[18]

Types of Comparisons

Each type of comparison mentioned in the following list serves a different purpose. All advise adolescents on how near or far they are to what they have selected to make comparisons about. For example, Upward comparison yields information about others appearing in high rank in a specific topic, for example, tennis, algebra, hair style, or humor.

- *Upward*: a superior condition, attribute, or achievement
  Serves self-evaluation and achievement orientation by providing information on the chances of attaining the characteristic itself or of attaining it as part of a cluster of characteristics necessary to achieve a specific goal
- *Positive Instance*: the ultimate condition, achievement, or attribute, characterized by a quality of rare attainability (e.g., Hollywood star, Olympic athlete)
  Offers opportunity to compare with the most outstanding, the person considered the highest example of the characteristic under consideration; is functional to understanding how much work lies ahead to reach that point; will help adolescents decide to go for it or look for more realistic goals
- *Downward*: an inferior condition, attribute, or performance
  Serves self-evaluation and/or defensive needs for ego enhancement—to feel better about oneself; is used with people regarded as less qualified; is used in an effort to balance findings made from people regarded as more qualified, thus keeping a more accurate

perspective about one's attributes as related to others; when over-used, may indicate that the adolescent is hurting and needs to feel better, which requires further inquiry

- *Similar Other*: a parallel or like condition, attribute, performance, point of view

    Serves need for self-validation with another who thinks, feels, and looks like oneself

    Together with Upward and Downward comparisons, this type of comparison is very popular. It serves two very different purposes. The more common reason is to feel more comfortable because there are others like oneself. The other reason is an aspirational one: "Are these others really like me, or do I wish to select new interests or behaviors?"

- *Range Establishment*: the best and worst possible positions on the continuum

    Establishes high and low boundaries to create a parameter for comparisons; affords a broad picture of others who share the inter-est, talent, physical characteristics, and the like; can assist in a deci-sion whether to attempt to be "one of them"; can result in (1) sat-isfaction or dissatisfaction with oneself, (2) a conclusion about the appropriateness of the aspiration, (3) seeking other comparison ob-jects to achieve a better comfort level

The following comparisons are specific to adolescents far more than to other age groups.

- *Comparison with a Goal*: the end point, beyond daily pursuits

    Provides information about how far it is to reach an intermedi-ate or end-point goal; becomes far more frequent in Stage 2 as the adolescent nears maturity; is also used with a person perceived as having achieved the ultimate goal of maturity

- *Satiation of Comparison*: an abatement of the need to compare, which reflects an internal resolution of alternatives

    Affords closure on whatever aspects of self one has chosen, and comparison with others is no longer necessary; is detectable in ado-lescent speech, which is far less interrogative and in most cases uses declarative sentences; hesitancy is gone since all types of necessary comparative acts have been completed and the adolescent feels very close to, if not already at, identity achievement. Although an adolescent with a defensive glitch may appear very certain about something, the tell-tale sign that this certainty is a deception is inflexibility. Satiation has not been worked through as one's own but is psychologically copied from others.[19]

• *Dissimilar Other*: a condition, attribute, performance, or point of view unlike one's own

Strengthens ownership of selected self-elements through finding others who represent characteristics that do not fit one's own picture of current or future self; plays an important role in resolution of identity: in order to know who one is, it is important to know who one is *not*.[20]

Note: Satiation and Dissimilar Other are more frequent after Stage 1, once adolescents find themselves on a more stable base. Dissimilar Other can also be useful at the very end of Stage 1, when adolescents are assembling their temporary self picture. This temporary self picture is reworked in Stage 2, when adolescents make decisions about permanent self-elements as they near maturity and integrate a sense of identity.

Stage 1 Adolescence and Comparative Acts

PRAGMATIC USE OF COMPARISONS

Adolescents use Range Establishment comparison to place themselves on a continuum with regard to a characteristic of choice. The worth and the functionality of their talents, abilities, and opinions is assessed using Upward, Downward, Similar Other, and Positive Instance comparison, which advise the adolescent where he or she stands relative to peers: better, less than, equal to, close to, or as far from as one can possibly go. Adolescents think about which goals are achievable for themselves and which are most likely suitable to others who are *dissimilar* from themselves, who may be in some ways enviable and in other ways not. Of vital import to bear in mind is that adolescents do not engage comparative acts just once or twice; rather, this dynamic is almost continuous in Stage 1 and is very intense in Stage 2.

A PRAGMATIC EXAMPLE: THE CASE OF ALAN, AGE 14

Alan comes from a family of high achievers—two older brothers and his parents. Yet he operates far below what test levels show he is capable of. Analysis of his comparisons with school and neighborhood peers displays a strange pattern of Upward and Downward comparisons, primarily

Upward. No Similar Other or other types of comparisons were made. A natural question is, Why?

Upward figures—individuals whom Alan recognizes as higher achievers—may reflect aspirations. Downward figures bring emotional soothing and/or enhance the ego. Lack of Similar Other comparisons could indicate little attachment to peers, which would render similar others irrelevant. Lack of attachment might make for a good initial hypothesis, but it is necessary to look further.

A simple chart for assessing adolescent comparison activity was used in Alan's case. The chart is constructed by entering types of comparison in the left column and frequencies of use along the top row. Separate each type of comparison by drawing a line underneath it. Sum the frequencies for each type used. When a chart is used in an actual examination of an adolescent, it may be helpful to have an attached sheet with comparison types and definitions for a quick peek, but care should be taken not to peek too often. This simple analysis can provide a clear picture of comparisons engaged by the adolescent, and new areas of exploration may be opened up.

It would have been possible for Alan's therapist to find natural openings in conversations about school, teachers, friends, and even home or leisure to insert a question that may elicit comparison information. For example, in conversation about school work, a question might have been asked such as, "Do you think you are as good as or maybe even better than any friend?" But the therapist did not follow this route.

Instead, several other possible routes for further investigation with Alan were drawn:

1. Does he enjoy a fantasy of being on a par with the Upward comparison objects, despite the reality of his poor academic performance?
2. Is he under a good deal of external pressure to succeed in high places because all his older siblings are high achievers?
3. Does the disparity between his low level of academic output relative to the estimated high level of his abilities bring him a lot of attention that might mitigate all the attention given to older siblings?

Alan's therapist reasoned that Alan's customary frequent references to the values, directives, and influence of older siblings indicated that he was not as attached to peers as might be expected at his age. Had he been connected, he would have compared himself with similar others or with a person who represented the positive instance of any number of desired traits. Clearly his comparison interests had firm boundaries. He was not ready to risk. With this evidence, the professional searched for more information about his level of maturity, including whether Alan was pubertous or not.

At age 14, some males have not yet experienced puberty. Such was the case with Alan. Hence, the need to loosen emotional ties with family was not as compelling for Alan as it would have been. It is also possible that puberty had arrived but that Alan had not shared this fact with others. In either case, Alan would need to get used to the fact that he was reaching puberty. In the meantime, identifying with older brothers afforded him fantasized similar others. The side benefit was that it made him feel safe enough to be the little brother who entertained his family with playful behaviors and got loving feedback.

An alternative hypothesis could also have been pursued but was not. Was Alan's overt aloofness from his age-mate similar others based in uncertainty? Was he too afraid to compare with age-mates and come out different? Could he have feared he might be alone in his question of whether others had experienced spermarche? He might also have been ashamed and afraid to find out how far behind the others he was. With this new context in mind, the professional would be wise to broach the impact of puberty in a very gentle way, for example, by inquiring whether Alan has been comfortable in asking anyone at all about ejaculation and growth of the sex organ. A no answer would not necessarily indicate problems but would speak to the power of "not being different" at this early point of development.

An adolescent such as Alan may be a candidate for a defensive glitch,[21] perhaps one of overattachment to an older person as a means to avoid peer attachment and involvement. From this perspective, early analyses of comparison charts described earlier turn out to serve preventative intervention.

Closure on Identity

It is important for professionals to distinguish satiation of comparison from closure. Closure signals finalization, whereas satiation is not permanent; rather, satiation is satisfaction of the hunger to continue to search and examine. Barring a major psychological insult, closure at the end of Stage 2 occurs naturally after satiation. A period of consolidation, getting used to a postadolescent reality, needs some brief period to process. Clo-sure occurs when true identity is experienced within; then, comparative acts are finished. Social comparisons are occasionally engaged by adults, as discussed earlier, to serve specific purposes in continuing to refine and update oneself, but these comparisons do not constitute construction of a self, which is the task of the adolescent developmental journey.

Impact on Involved Others

When schoolteachers participating in a continuing education class on adolescent growth and behavior are asked which grades they least like to teach, they almost universally respond, "seventh and eighth grades," the beginning years of Peer Arena Stage 1 adolescence.[22] This response is based in an intuitive recognition that schoolwork and teachers rank a far second and third in importance to early adolescents. Most of their atten-tion is on one another. Teachers are aware that something is going on, but they generally do not really understand the dynamics involved. The early postpuberty years, especially the first and second years, are usually inscrutable to others, especially to the family.

Professional Responsibility

Special situations negatively encumber interpreting comparison find-ings accurately, for example, failing eyesight or a high level of anxiety. Whether from physical impairment or preoccupation, adolescents can miss a lot of important feedback, some of which may be positive. Or they may exaggerate negative feedback. Special-needs adolescents expend a good deal of energy in meeting physical, mental, or environmental needs and in psychologically handling others' reactions to them. Hence, they work with depleted energy relative to their healthy counterparts. Profes-sionals need to be especially alert to the increased vulnerability of these adolescents and to guide them. When professionals protect adolescents from their findings, it is a shallow kindness; it deprives them of their right to cope and to grow. Many, if not most, of them can "manage to manage," if given sensitive and proper professional care.

It is often overlooked that findings from comparative acts can be restor-ative: they are not always difficult but can bring comfort too. They do not always stimulate pain but can soothe it too. In fact, this hope may very deliberately underlie an adolescent's search. One early adolescent's account of how he purposely used a comparative act provides perspective:

> During a conversation about whom one might compare oneself to, a 12-year-old adolescent explained what *similar* meant to him and how it influenced what he wanted to find out through comparison: whether any of his peers' fathers were in jail too. He was searching for validation of self, since it was difficult for him to have other kids know that his father was in jail while no one else's was. If another kid was in the same situation, he believed it would make him look not too bad. He would no longer be the only one subject to ridicule. There would be others like him, similar others.[23]

DFI provides the professional with tools to understand what the world of adolescents center on, how they try to negotiate it, how much energy is required, and the dynamics involved in this lengthy period of growing up.

3

Societal Designations:
Adolescents Who Are Minorities

Being open, free, and welcoming is not easy in early and middle adolescence, the point when adolescents first move away from guidance of parents to seek their own individuality. It is an emotionally unsteady period. Adolescents' preference to be with familiar age-mates and new ones who look and act similar is not a lack of openness. Rather, it reflects a developmental need for equilibrium. Being with others like oneself supports self-security and balances new uncertainties that arise on the road to psychological and emotional self-sufficiency. At this point in developmental time, most adolescents prefer being with others of their own gender, with only occasional forays to try intergender friendships. This same hesitation or discomfort is generally also attached to others who look different or are from different cultural backgrounds.

Professionals need to understand that this behavior is not a response to particular individuals. Later in the adolescent process, when the growth tasks of early and early middle adolescence are resolved, others who are different are sought. At that point, the need for exclusivity with similar others is greatly diminished. Once adolescents complete the initial necessary decision-making on self-elements to be included in a Stage 1 "temporary self," a *developmental imperative* stimulates them to seek out others who model *both similar and different* attributes to enrich those they have already included. As discussed in the preceding chapter, eventually, after further adding and subtracting self-elements, these mixtures make up the Stage 2 full self of the new adult.

Labels Exist for Everyone

Adolescents generally identify as members of specific racial or ethnic groups, religious groups, or other types of groups, and sometimes labels derived from visible characteristics are attributed to them. Some are complimentary, some not. Division by label advantages some and disadvantages others. Adolescents, particularly younger adolescents, copy what they hear. Increased cognitive development will afford them the ability to comprehend fully that different external physical or social characteristics do not mean a different set of internal dynamics. As we have seen, all individuals develop in the same sequence and grow up by similar routes. This is notwithstanding race, ethnicity, and religion. All adolescents attach to peers, pursue the same developmental task of settling on one's identity, and strive to reach psychological maturity. They suffer the same doubts and fears about what they will grow up to be. And all risk flight to defensive glitches that stand in their way of reaching identity and maturity.

Before the 1940s, few texts were devoted to race and race relations. Since then, literature has appeared detailing differences, advantages, and disadvantages.[1] Today, fields of study on race and ethnic relations still grow in number, providing hope for increasingly valid understanding. But impasses do remain.

Today's Dilemma

Immigration preferences based on national origins were removed in the United States in the mid-1960s. From that time forward, the U.S. population became increasingly diverse. As of 1994, immigrants had come from over 140 different nations.[2] Latin Americans and Asians made up two-thirds of recent immigrants. The largest Asian groups were from the Philippines, India, and Vietnam. Built-in dilemmas attach to a society with fairly liberal immigration policies. Although most people consider this trend a positive one, it can confuse the early period of the adolescent search process.

Earlier periods in U.S. history offered simpler models. Less variation made for clear social prescriptions of what is best and after whom to model oneself. In the 21st century, adolescents usually find similar others in school and in the neighborhood, particularly in segregated neighborhoods. Similar and nonsimilar others are accessible on Web sites such as MySpace, Facebook, and YouTube. For adolescents, the diversity can be fascinating but also confusing and, for some, frightening.

Being with similar and nonsimilar age-mates brings new questions. Among them are "What must I be like to please my own ethnic group or to please the groups unlike my own?" "What will happen to me if I make friends from a combination of these groups?" As they consider these issues, new concerns can arise: "Will I find a group that likes me, or will I be all alone?" "Will I cut myself off from those I love best?" "Will I destroy my culture?" "If I give in to the other culture, will I destroy my self?" "If I combine two, three, or four of my communities, how can I interpret this decision, or live it?" At this point, other worries emerge: "If I get too complex, will there be anybody—or enough of a group—like me?" "And yet, in such a diverse country with so many models, how can I just remain simple?" Emotions come into play: "I am confused. I am angry at demands made by my own and other cultures. If the others weren't here, life would be easier." In some cases, action alternatives can arise: "I will strike out at others unlike myself. I don't need them here. They spoil it all. I don't feel happy. I want to forget it all and feel good." Professionals need to be aware that conflicts such as these rage within some adolescents trying to grow up. Adolescents are confused by these conflicts. They are struggling in their own way to be "good" people. Yet they are also dealing with developmental imperatives from within.

The society of youth reinforces openness. Being closed is seen as old-fashioned. Freer choice on matters of race, ethnicity, and sexual preference have been added to religious choice. These potential movements away from traditional values customarily upset elders concerned about adolescents' premature decision-making.[3]

The Professional's Challenge

Envision a caterpillar changing into a butterfly. The adolescent is neither the caterpillar nor the butterfly; adolescence is the changing part. Adolescents are caught in a web with two sets of forces: (1) attraction to similarities versus romance with difference and (2) pressures to resist attraction to difference versus conflict over not embracing difference. Prior to adolescents' achieving the highest level of cognitive growth, formal operational thought, race and ethnicity have little social or economic significance to them. Inclusion or exclusion depends a lot on appearance, making the football team or a class office or being cool. The social and economic importance of race and ethnicity takes off in late high school with entry into Stage 2 of adolescence. At that time, some characteristics and abilities in others begin to be regarded as valuable to future success.[4]

Both genders in disparate countries display acute awareness of what age-mates plan regarding their futures and how near or far these plans are to their own intentions. Research findings from studies in both hemi-spheres of the globe support the universality of middle/late adolescents' high interest in one another.[5]

The professional must strive for an atmosphere of emotional and intel-lectual openness to keep adolescents free to express conflicts over sen-sitive social issues. One's own biases need to be understood. Two major categories of professional bias may exist regarding matters of inequitable political, economic, and social conditions or opportunities: (1) overiden-tification, being overly attuned to the challenges a minority adolescent faces, and (2) underidentification, the opposite dynamic, in which there is not enough empathy.

Diligence is required to differentiate between adolescents' authentic anger over certain issues and a defensive glitch. Extreme and ubiquitous social outrage over injustices in society should be suspect for defensive glitches. The "outrage mask" during adolescence can cover such a glitch. A risk is that this type of glitch can be erroneously attributed to rebellion, a familiar rationale for opting out of the hard psychological work in Peer Arena comparative acts. This glitch is most likely to occur in later adoles-cence, the secondary Peer Arena period, when adolescents become more aware of social issues as they get down to brass tacks about their futures.

This later stage adolescence can be a stressful time for some adolescents from minority populations. Opportunities for nonminorities may be seen as an unfair disparity when a minority adolescent's ability and preparation are equal or higher. Some minority adolescents may react with outrage. In the extreme—and this reaction is what defines a defensive glitch—such a reaction may cover intense fear of further lack of opportunity or may cover a cognitive certainty that dreams will never be met. Others can turn their outrage inward into hopelessness and despair. There is a risk for ei-ther type of reaction; therapy should be sought for such adolescents.

Both minority and their White counterparts in lower economic classes are vulnerable to confusion and sadness when they compare themselves with their more privileged adolescent peers. The question "What chance do I have?" lies at the base of their observations. Professionals counseling these adolescents, as well as middle-class Asians, Blacks, and Hispanics, must bear in mind that most often the lives of these adolescents are quite distinct from those of Whites. Though these groups may mix naturally during the day in school, nighttime is different: then, they live as racially, ethnically, and economically discrete communities. Social realities today echo the perspective of mid-20th-century urban theorists on how and when these peoples mix: a*ssimilation* by day, *ethnic pluralism* by night, *ethnic conflict* day and night.[6]

Adolescents who lack resources are among those who consider giving up. Some are seen in our offices asking questions such as "Why grow up at all?" and "Why not live for today?" Professionals charged with diagnosing and treating adolescents who utilize these defensive rationales as a way of coping with raging anger or deep sadness will help them benefit in an atmosphere open to discussing the inequities the adolescents perceive or experience.

Cultural Variants

Certain minority adolescents disregard the guidance or assistance offered by loving family members and devoted teachers who are attuned to the lurking dangers in unequal schools and economically depressed neighborhoods. Current literature includes description of Black adolescents' attraction to the "street," much to the dismay of elders.[7] Puerto Rican adolescents can be torn between the street and family, which may account for increasing loss of family unity and closeness and which runs contrary to the customary Hispanic obligation to family as primary.[8] Chinese children are often expected to behave as adults and not to speak until spoken to, and aggressive behavior and sibling rivalry is not tolerated.[9] In lower economic classes, more minority adolescents take on responsibilities early to help meet family expenses than do their majority White counterparts.[10] Some Mexican adolescents resent that family poverty requires that they work after school in rural locations or on city construction sites at substandard pay rates. They feel anger as they compare with their bosses' children, adolescent peers who go to fine schools and own desirable material goods.[11]

Part of a professional's arsenal is to find out where the patient *is* from the time he or she first enters the office. Becoming acquainted with the adolescent's home conditions, the physical and social environment, is part of that "where the patient is." For example, a professional who learns that Andreas is starving, need not ask about cultural conflict. Instead, the professional needs to recall how hunger affects functioning from the first day of life and begin a restorative process.[12] Or if Sylvia sleeps in a small room with seven others and only three beds, how can she be expected to have sufficient energy to figure out new ideas in math class? These are the pragmatic realities that professionals need to address first, to the degree that resources allow.

Minority Parents and Issues of Growth and Comparison

During the high school years, adolescents' cognitive growth brings complex thinking that alerts them to social and economic inequities, even unseen ones. Minority parents may wish to shield their adolescents from discussion of these realities. A professional may have to negotiate a meeting of the minds about the ultimate benefit of adolescents' understanding their realities and parents' right to raise their child as they see fit. What neither therapists nor parents control, however, is adolescents' comparisons, including those regarding environmental realities. Minority adolescents from poor neighborhoods see and hear and compare and contrast their own conditions with those of peers. Professionals may wish to express to parents that these comparative acts are natural and stimulate growth.

A logical question for the professional working with minority adolescents to ask is whether the problem behavior stems from a clash of cultures. A contributing factor to the behavior might be parental hesitation or unwillingness to let go of long-held cultural positions, for example, the need for a chaperone to be present at each date, as is customary in some Latin households, as well as in others. Is such a custom appropriate within a specific culture? Yes. But between cultures? Generally not. Another contributing factor could be a matter of "politeness," a cultural value that is being violated by the adolescent. For example, some cultures historically place a high value on ancestor worship, as in some Asian cultures, but the adolescent may be less mindful of it. It cannot be sufficiently stressed how important it is for professionals to search out potential cultural aspects of discord before raising questions about intra- or interpersonal problems, either recently emerging or longstanding.

Another factor relates to academic "parent-pushers." This kind of pressure placed on adolescents is not restricted to any particular cultural background, minority or majority. As with other issues, it is the *extent* of the pressure that determines whether it is benign or problematic. But there may be a fundamental cultural conflict at work if a majority value conflicts with that of a minority. For example, a Western stress on individualism and self-determination may lead to conflict with or from home-oriented cultures that emphasize strong parental oversight on decision-making. Familial fallings-outs can be seen through the rubric of "cultural conflict." On the other hand, such conflicts can be framed as similar to a phenomenon in adolescent cognitive development: egocentrism. The societal counterpart of adolescent egocentrism is *cultural egocentrism,* which implies an overemphasis on the mores of one's own culture and a lack of sufficient respect for the validity of customs other than one's own. This sort of worldview can make it difficult for someone to accept the values of differing cultures, and the maturity level of such an individual can imitate that of one still caught in psychological egocentrism.

Professional Sensitivity to External and Internal Conflict

Cultural disturbances between generations are best regarded as a period simply to be lived through while the two sides learn, grow, and mature by themselves. But such conflicts are not to be ignored. It is not unusual for late Stage 1 or early Stage 2 adolescents to wage war on matters that are strange to their minority family. It would be a mistake for professionals to consider this behavior rebellion. If such behavior comes to the attention of professionals, it may be a good idea to attempt either a therapeutic or an educational intervention. For adolescents, an ideal vehicle may be a PAL therapy group with others who are dealing with or have dealt with cultural conflicts and family turbulence. Parents may benefit from openly discussing matters of concern, for example, discussing romantic relationships between adolescents from different backgrounds in a group with parents from a variety of cultures. Parents would then find themselves doing what their adolescents do all the time: making comparisons and evaluating findings.

If the professional detects that an adolescent has a serious individual problem—involving the loss of a tenuous sense of one's own self, stimulated by the threat of loss of familiar cultural prescriptions—the professional may want to suggest an appropriate treatment therapy or guide referral to a specialist. Deep problems can indeed be masked by antiminority or antimajority actions and words.

There is some question as to the extent to which adolescents express their own prejudice or express prejudices they hear from others. For the most part, adolescents are not aware that their bias about others who are different from themselves can actually be a disguised expression of their own confusion or conflict about aspects of themselves. The bias is probably a developmental artifact that is active prior to adolescents' completing assembly of the self-elements that form the self structure, which is generally in an unresolved state until near end of Stage 2. It is common to mistake this artifact for prejudice.

Adolescent Pragmatism and Ethnic/Racial Realities

Adolescents intuitively feel a need to accentuate the self-elements they wish to retain. Once they near the end of Stage 1, they can risk dropping behaviors that foster similarity in favor of being distinct. It is at this time that minorities who look and act quite different begin to appeal to adolescents. This early period in late adolescence, which approximates the end of high school for most adolescents, is from a developmental perspective an active time for intergroup relating. Contemporary adolescents are pragmatic. They intuit that their task is to claim an identity in a culture that appears to reinforce change, not constancy. Thus, identity must have a great deal of *flexibility*, a quality that anthropologist Margaret Mead discussed in her 1928 treatise on the process of education.[13]

In late high school, similarities and differences become more important as adolescents confront competition for entry into favored adult roles. Adolescents begin to ponder how far specific attributes or combinations of attributes can take them—and how far they can take others. For perhaps the first time, the people with whom they compare themselves also become potential *competitors in life*. The covert or overt feelings of ethnic and racial difference become more serious as adolescents reach the margins of adulthood.

Varying family and social conditions affect adolescents' direct route to a vocational or career direction. Some may drop out of high school at age 16 only to find that their employment opportunities are limited. Others have their youth shortened through teen parenthood, which brings responsibilities of caring for a child and can cut short freedoms as well as preparation for one's own future. Some adolescents become responsible for quasi-parental duties at home or work part-time for financial reasons. For adolescents, these situations often give rise to *within-group* cohesiveness based in resentment of others previously regarded as like themselves but now seen as privileged or "soft." But resentment can also be directed toward other ethnicities or races, which is far safer emotionally for the adolescent than running the risk of alienating an in-group similar other.

Misdirected Hostility

EXAMPLE 1: ROBBIE'S STORY

Robbie is a 16-year-old Puerto Rican male who would rather hang out on the street than do schoolwork. He is the fifth in a family of six children in which both parents hold two jobs to keep the family going. The grandmother also had parental responsibilities until two years prior, when she suffered a stroke, making it very difficult for her to stand without support. She needed more help from Robbie because the older siblings worked after school or headed their own families. Robbie was not helpful for too long. He liked hanging out on the corner, a spot where most of his socializing was very successful. Arguments with parents and punishments were not effective in convincing him to change his behavior. Eventually, his mother had to take an additional part-time job. Resentment toward Robbie grew along with his abdication of family responsibilities. His mother withdrew from supervising him at all and invested her energies in the youngest child, a daughter, whom she saw as her eventual substitute. Robbie was a slow cognitive developer. Thus, he could not comprehend how economic stress ate away at his parents' patience in dealing with him.

Anger at family rejection stimulated Robbie to more street behaviors and eventually to some drug dealing; he met youth of his same ethnic background who he felt were similar to him except for their fancy clothes and food, their hair cuts, and the fact that they had enough money to buy stolen cars. Cut off from former friends and criticized by parents, these delinquent youth had only one another. Robbie began dealing drugs. He found targets for his anger, which turned into prejudice, in the Scotch-Irish youth who were his drug customers. They had the money to buy and do whatever they desired. They were White, not people of color who were "targets of prejudice." Actually, his Puerto Rican cohorts also had plenty of money, but because Robbie needed them psycho-emotionally, he could not bear anger toward them. He could not forgo intimacy with his group of similars in ethnicity and in background. In fact, they joined him in anger at the Scotch-Irish young men and hurled insults at them. The mutual hatred of others increased their own group unity.

Robbie was a very angry young man. Since he did not do his part to lessen the pressures from the family's declining financial circumstances, he no longer received the emotional rewards he was used to. He felt devalued and rejected. Being young in both body and mind, he chose to heal himself through feel-good substances that he procured for himself and for others to whom he wanted to be similar and of whose group he wanted to be a part. He bought the clothes and other possessions that the group also had. By doing so, his comparative acts revealed him to be not lesser than but equal to his friends and to his "wealthy" customers. But because it is hard to blame oneself for behaviors that are actually against one's own conscience, such as theft, Robbie projected the disgust he felt toward himself out and away onto his customers, those very others who paid him the money he wanted. His friends joined him in directing insulting slurs at the Scotch-Irish privileged kids, and their actions reassured him of the correctness of his own, increasing the sense of group cohesiveness.

EXAMPLE 2: KAMEISHA'S STORY

Kameisha, age 13, was the oldest child in a middle-class African American family. Her complexion was darker than that of the rest of her family. Although she was a natural-born child of her parents, she harbored the mistaken illusion that she was adopted, since she was the oldest child and her complexion was different from both her parents and her siblings. Kameisha attended a large school with many classmates. From a very young age, she preferred friendships with dark-skinned African American children. She perceived them as her only authentic similar others. Shortly following puberty, Kameisha's best girlfriend, Dolores, a dark-skinned person like herself, began to date a light-skinned African American male. Kameisha counseled Dolores against him, claiming she knew from others that he was a ladies' man and would soon drop her. Nonetheless, the romance continued. The more Kameisha's anger at both members of the couple grew, the more her mood fell.

But it was not easy for Kameisha to acknowledge her anger; it was not based on tangible evidence of any negative wrongdoing but was the wounds of replacement. Just as Robbie did, Kameisha projected her anger onto an outside racial group: feeling like a third wheel, she chose to berate Asian classmates. Asians were "just plain no good—and uppity for no reason at all." She was irate over their in-group allegiances, and she did not consciously recognize her own in-group preferences. She perceived that the Asians' prejudice against other racial and ethnic groups was excessive, and it was too much for her to bear. Her comparative acts revealed to her that she was on the same level in school subjects as Asian females she despised. She chose to dismiss findings that their level surpassed hers in certain areas, such as their graceful dancing, which received more attention and praise by others than her type of dancing. She ridiculed their home-tailored conservative dress and their trouble with pronouncing the letter "r" and railed against their closeness to parents and family. She declared them unworthy of a chance to rise in the social ladder because they were definitely not American enough.

Thus, Kameisha, who saw no prejudice in herself, projected her own disappointments and Downward comparisons onto two groups she had regarded as Upward comparison figures: African Americans of lighter complexion than she and Asians. She could tell no one close to her about her anger against light-skinned Blacks since among them were members of her own family and the boyfriend of her best friend. So she selected a scapegoat, Asians, against whom she could rail safely out loud. In fact, Kameisha envied the Asians' grace, handmade clothes, and closeness of family—just what she herself did not have and obviously longed for. The route she found to contain her disappointments and deep sorrow was to strike out against Asian classmates. This prejudice toward a group other than her own was the person others saw.

Prejudice and Discrimination

EXAMPLE 3: ELIZABETH'S STORY

Elizabeth, age 17, a Latino student beginning her freshman year at a university, had recently settled for herself that she was lesbian. She was going to turn 18 within the month and was not quite ready to "come out." Her parents did not know yet. Furthermore, she did not want to introduce herself at the university right off the bat as a lesbian. But it was hard. When she went to freshman-week parties, young men hit on her, and she felt she had to cooperate to keep up the charade. She needed to be more certain of her similarity with lesbians.

Elizabeth felt in transition and frameworkless, just as she had in early adolescence. She felt it strange that this phenomenon was repeating itself in this new environment where she thought she would feel free.[14] Rather than raging against lesbians who had resolved their own sexual preference and were impatient at her delay and pressing her to come out, Elizabeth resented those who had no sexual preference issue to resolve: heterosexuals, particularly female heterosexuals. She considered them spoiled, conflict free, flaunting sexuality with males, and free of self-introductions with an implicit "I'm sorry but you should know I am a lesbian." Perhaps hardest to bear of all, they risked no abandonment or loss of love from parents and family as she did.

Elizabeth chose to believe that being a conflict-free heterosexual meant free passage without suffering. Heterosexuals would not see the job discrimination that lesbians face, which she feared might restrict her own ability to work in scientific research as she desired. "Oh, cruel heterosexual world" reached almost mantra proportions. She was very troubled. The more troubled she became, the more she lashed out at others she "used to be like." Clearly her conflict was beginning to manage her rather than the other way around.

Elizabeth was having trouble resolving her own conflict: should she claim her lesbianism, which might subject her to unfair societal discrimination that might affect her professional life but also might enable greater social ease in her personal life? Needing to find relief, she made a target of the part of herself she was disowning. She projected her discomfort with her own sexuality outward and assailed those who were comfortable with theirs.

EXAMPLE 4: EDWARD'S STORY

Edward was a Chinese American university student beginning his second year of study in an Ivy League school. His first year away from home went smoothly. He achieved according to his own and his family's expectations. He made friends among all groups and made it a point not to spend more time with Asian students than with others. He was nominated for student leadership posts in his second year. He returned home for summer break between freshman and sophomore year and gained employment as a summer accountant in offices of a nearby, successful Chinese restaurant chain for which his mother worked as a cook. Upon return to school the following fall, he was assigned to share a dorm room with Raj, a student from India. Raj and Edward got along very well. Raj, too, was a serious student who planned to take an advanced degree in finance and join his family's computer-analysis firm, founded at the beginning of the computer revolution. Raj's friends from Mumbai were also interesting and likable. Edward's comparative acts revealed all of them to be at a similarly high level of ability as his own, and they all planned for an international business career. But as the semester progressed, Edward became irritated by small matters, he did not enjoy student activity posts, and increasingly felt lower in mood. Alarmed, he contacted student counseling services and began regular treatment for "mild depressive syndrome."

The counselor became concerned by the impact of the family situation on Edward. Edward's older sister was rebellious and going out with Caucasian young men, to which the family and Edward objected. They were concerned about how they would maintain their culture if their youth deserted them. The counselor and Edward spent many sessions delving into Edward's feelings. As winter break grew closer, Edward's condition incrementally worsened. Well-intended support from Raj and his friends did not help. The treatment plan was amended to allow for more frequent outpatient therapeutic visits. Going home was out of the question since family conflict was becoming stronger and stronger. The counselor wanted Edward as far from the home situation as possible, though it was inevitable that his parents would need to be contacted eventually.

Because the attending therapist had a prior scheduled vacation, an interim therapist was assigned. The interim therapist spent a short time on Edward's concern about the family conflict, the deteriorating home environment, family finances, and Edward's gratitude to his parents for scrimping to send him to this Ivy League college for a really good education.[15] Then the professional asked about college peers and social activities. It was not difficult to engage Edward in his use of comparative acts and what the findings seemed to be telling him. Edward did talk about his peer history, his wonderful high school years, his even more exciting first year at college, and his fondness for Raj and friends. But he could not understand his sadness: "For someone as bright as me, why can't I figure it out?" was a refrain that ran through his comments. Deeper feelings were hard to get at. What eventually broke through the defenses was suppressed anger at his parents for being poor with no contacts. In essence, Edward wanted what Raj and his friends could expect from their wealthy Indian parents. Comparative acts revealed their abilities and achievements as no better than his, but their future prospects were brighter because of these advantages. Edward was unable to face what he felt, which was manifested outwardly as depression.

Like some others, Edward might have directed anger at social inequities for Asian minorities, which yielded wages good only for life on the economic edge. Or he might have cried out about a cruel society in which selected groups are privileged. Instead of doing those things, he trusted his own abilities to rise above his disadvantages. Cognitively, he was mature enough to know that his family were good people and sacrificed to do the best for him. Yet emotionally he was angry. The angrier he got, the greater his guilt toward a family who sacrificed everything for him. He was too ethical to spring free by blaming society for its discriminatory practices in opportunities, hiring, and education. Unconscious guilt transformed into a depression, which crippled his pursuit of his life dreams.

Handling Adolescent Vulnerabilities

The factor common in each of the preceding four examples is the tenderness of adolescence, a raw and vulnerable period of life. This tenderness, experienced in varying intensities throughout the adolescent stage, needs care. Frustration or hurt over "not being understood," or being "ignored," "underestimated," or "undervalued," strikes deep. Among alternative release strategies is projecting pain onto similarly vulnerable others, including racial, ethnic, and sexual-preference others. This sort of internal conflict is not always resolved silently; sometimes it can be mollified or purged by screaming it out. Others become targets, and as we have seen, favorite targets are many times those who look different or who are different. Insults are sometimes self-protecting, as when they are directed at others whose very difference is intriguing, in an attempt to destroy those attractions that stimulate unbearable internal conflict.

Practitioners may find it useful to adopt with adolescent clients a more comprehensive approach to racial/ethnic relations by focusing a comparative-act lens on behaviors that on the surface appear to be responses to societal inequities. At this stage of life, adolescents may well be distressed about findings from comparative acts. A client who also is suffering the sting of social inequities and personal injustice may intentionally or unintentionally manipulate professionals.

Professional Responsibility

Professionals working with adolescents bear an ethical obligation not to promote clients' favorite social issues as part of their professional service, even though it may be hard to withstand a natural impulse to identify with wrath over the inequities of disadvantaged groups. Otherwise, the professional may "get lost in the field" and "become partner to the client's defenses."[16] When working with adolescents from minority populations, research about their racial/ethnic group assists the professional in teasing out culture-specific dimensions of their issues and in understanding the impact on adolescents' development and current functioning.[17]

Within this context of practice with adolescents from diverse backgrounds and their relations with peers familiar and unfamiliar, the following insight may resonate: "Diversity takes on its variable meanings through the concrete details of our daily lives, public as well as private, and not by proclamation in an abstract theory or simple slogan."[18]

4

Societal Designations: Adolescents Who Are Gay

The preceding chapter looked at the impact of minority status on the adolescent experience. This chapter focuses on adolescents of one of those minority groups, those who are homosexual or still working out confusion about their gender identity or preference.[1] Such adolescents are found in all majority and minority groups. Notwithstanding their differences, it must be remembered that each is first and foremost an adolescent.

A shift in attitudes in the first half of the twentieth century influenced the *Annals of Psychiatry*'s designation of homosexuality as a category of mental illness. Currently, homosexuality is not listed in *The Diagnostic and Statistical Manual of Disorders* used by the psychiatric and psychological community to define and set criteria for categorization of mental disorders.[2] The research on homosexuality is not yet extensive and has generally dealt with the contextual impact on social, emotional, and behavior problems. Although the literature has become richer since the 1970s, more scholarship is necessary to enhance our understandings of the origins of homosexuality and of social influences affecting nonheterosexuals during the important period of adolescence.[3]

Adolescents with unresolved issues about homosexuality generally are not open with their feelings or questions. Whereas heterosexual adolescents easily find similar others among peers fairly soon after entering adolescence, uncertain adolescents often hide their homosexuality, making it hard to identify similar others and gain their support. Thus, for quite some time, these adolescents bear confusions alone. Furthermore, they fear that their secret will be exposed even before it has been resolved. Like all other adolescents, they respond to internal imperatives to observe peers closely and become the target of similar assessments. Additionally, junior high school and even most high school personnel are rarely forthright about this type of dilemma, thus providing these adolescents little opportunity for consultation.

Earlier chapters have stressed that resolving identity requires physical and imagined interactions with as many attachment peers as possible to access attributes, actions, and opinions that can be modeled for one's own growth work. Expressions, dress, activities, and types of friends are tried out and can go from being adored to crashing and burning and then being immediately replaced by others. Eventually families get used to altered opinions, attitudes, and loyalties and accept these behaviors as "being adolescent." But the situation is different for gay and lesbian adolescents. In their early stages of indecision, they are not free to try out being homosexual publicly. Sometimes, the furthest they can go is to mimic popular stereotypes humorously—"Be entertaining. It won't get taken seriously"— and then observe reactions.

Gender Identity and Gender Preference

Working out gender identity and working out gender preference are not the same. Gender identity involves a sense of being a male or a female. Gender preference relates to the gender of a sexual partner or love object, sometimes referred to as sexual orientation. For example, a person's gender identity may be female and gender preference may be for male or female. Or gender identity may be male and gender preference may be for female or male. If a person's gender identity is male and gender preference is for a male, that person is considered to be gay. If a person is female and gender preference is for a female, she is considered a lesbian. A very small minority identify as bisexual; for such people, preference for a sexual partner can be either male, female, or both.

When adolescents feel sexually attracted to the opposite gender, they join the majority. When their attraction is to the same gender, they join the much smaller minority. Some, primarily those in the latter category, often need to try out others in both sexual categories in their search for who they are. The importance of correctly arriving at this basic ingredient of "who I am" may be better understood with the example of a coil, introduced by the educational psychologist Edmund Purkey to describe an individual's attributes. In Purkey's model, attributes considered central to an individual are near center of the coil, immediately after unchangeable aspects of self: race, age, and gender.[4] A person's temperament may also be included in this center.[5] Other values may also be placed at the center of an individual's coil, such as religion, ethnicity, and culture. Making changes to values at the center of the coil is a major undertaking. Doing so—to the extent possible—might cut off a person's essence. Gender identity would most often be placed at the core. Gender preference is not at the core but is almost so, very near to gender identity. Gender preference that is still in progress of being resolved by a person might be at any distance from core, depending on the significance of gender preference to the person at the time.

Distorted Comparative Acts

Nonacceptance of homosexuals by their adolescent peers has a heavy impact on their comparison findings. Feedback that homosexual adolescents receive from heterosexuals, verbally or nonverbally, is often negative, or of the Downward type, rather than positive, or of the Upward or goal-oriented comparison types. Homosexual adolescents sense these conclusions from their peers and may experience them as insulting, thus influencing their self-evaluations on other of their attributes, opinions, and ambitions. A serious hazard exists here, the probability that at this tender, uncertain age these adolescents will accept what they hear and see from others as entirely accurate. This threat is grave, since such perceptions may warp future plans and even discourage efforts to excel in ongoing personal, social, and achievement goals.

The difficult growth issues with which all adolescents tussle can become exaggerated for adolescents who are homosexual. As for all other adolescents, these issues for homosexual adolescents include adjusting to physical changes in their bodies, visible and invisible. But homosexual adolescents search in what feels like a virtual desert for the comfort that finding similar others brings. They must also simultaneously bear the impact of the "imaginary audience" phase of cognitive development, in which they feel themselves to be at the center of everyone's attention.[6]

There is good reason to be worried about adolescents as they think and rethink the ramifications of coming out. Evidence exists that most adolescents who come out to parents do so around age 17. Sadly, such youth are sometimes subject to abuse at home. Four times as many homosexual as heterosexual youth attempt suicide, and two and a half times as many frequently fantasize about committing suicide but make no attempts.[7] Although incremental progress is being made in research on this topic, a lack of sufficient data about how early professionals should be on the alert for such danger signs impedes their efforts to be available to these adolescents and in easily accessible settings.

The Price of Difference

Resolving development issues is a much lonelier process for most homosexual adolescents than for adolescent heterosexuals. Although it is true that such resolution is fundamentally a one-person task, similar peers are badly needed both to soothe uncertainties and to discuss common issues with. In the extreme of the absence of similar others, defensive flight away from frustration, anger, and pain becomes an attractive option. The choices for gay, lesbian, and bisexual adolescents are the same as those for heterosexuals who can no longer withstand the heat of comparative acts. In an effort to relieve tension or feel independent and adequate, they may choose to adopt an easily available defensive glitch, which also stops development short.[8] For homosexuals, the flight patterns and glitches are often related to where they can finally find some escape, no matter the cost.

Strategies That Can Work

Fortunately, the internal drive of most homosexuals to work, grow, and reach maturity is stronger than the motivation to escape. They do a lot of watching and listening. Some hide their sexual preference from others and try to *pass*. So as to be diligent about the charade of keeping their homosexuality secret, one aspect of passing is to deny oneself opportunities to be with similar others. The case of Carl, who tried his best to pass, is illustrative.

Example 1: Carl, Age 17

Carl, who grew up in a far-midwestern state, spent a lot of time in his upstairs room on the computer. He told his parents he had a lot of homework to do, but actually he was communicating with women in chat rooms. Every now and then, he would set up a date and then cancel it. On occasion he would carry through with the date, but only if it involved a number of others, not only one woman. The date was always a sexual encounter.

Carl did socialize with groups of teens his age. Secretly, he was disturbed and very confused because he felt sexually attracted to both males and females. When the internal pressure to hide got stronger, he decided to tell others he was interested in Margaret, a youngish, less mature agemate. They became a couple, but within a short time matters went downhill. Others understood: "Relationships are hard to manage." As Carl reached the end of his senior year, prom time came, and a female class member invited him to accompany her. Carl accepted. She became sexually aggressive in the wee hours of the morning, and he cooperated. He wanted no one to guess his confusion.

Summer between high school and college freed Carl to travel to a resort area. There he stayed up late and was approached by a male. This short liaison acquainted him with where gay males gathered. He told himself he would go there again to "experiment," but Carl encountered a problem he had not counted on. His fantasy was that once the sexual-preference matter was resolved, all would be well; he would have friends and continue on with normal life. But Carl was surprised to find that resolving matters required more than that. He continued to *act* heterosexual, and it was getting harder for him.

In adolescence, though sexual preference is a large component of who and what one is, it is not the only one. Carl's understanding broadened. He learned that gender preference makes one like others in one respect, albeit a major one, but not in every respect. It was not until he enrolled in a large eastern university that he encountered sufficient others to afford him a wide variety of comparative acts, not just about gender identity and preference. These others included homosexuals at the LGBT Center. Enough others went there that he was able to find Similar Other, Upward, and Downward comparison figures, and he was also able to engage in Comparison with a Goal. Some of those he encountered were quite different from himself, even though they were all gay. Carl had at last found himself a Stage 1 Primary Peer Arena. Carl's story stayed happy: he confirmed his homosexuality and was out on campus in his sophomore year.

Now that Carl was publicly gay, he concentrated more deliberately on his future and on looking for gays and straights who were more like him. He reasoned that were he to remain at the same university for graduate school, he might well find others even more like himself (Stage 2 Secondary Peer Arena). Or, if he were to move, he would be well advised to search out other large, cosmopolitan campus settings. But he was a long way from that decision. He still had a road full of comparative acts to travel.

Eventually, Carl partnered in a satisfying relationship with a male one year younger. Carl's home in the far Midwest was thousands of miles away. When his parents visited, he guarded his secret, keeping away from gay friends and avoiding the LGBT Center. But his mother's intuition told her that she needed to talk with her son. They talked, and she was accepting but suggested that the news be kept from his father a while longer until Carl was very certain of his sexual preference. She agreed to help him when the time came.

Carl's mother would need time before she was ready to talk to her husband about their son's sexual orientation. It is not always easy for parents to take in this information. Parents generally look to their own genetics and attitudes for a clue, but it was hard to figure out why Carl became gay. In the general society, it is not hard to ask individuals why they grew up *heterosexual*, yet societal inhibitions make it very hard to inquire why they grew up *homosexual*. Furthermore, if people are asked to define what a homosexual is, they do not answer in a word or a sentence. Labels, however, represent an oversimplification. Not all individuals display consistency of sexual feelings, behaviors, and identity; some experience considerable fluidity in their sexuality throughout their lives.[9]

Carl and his partner broke up in senior year when Carl was accepted for graduate school at a university near home. He had become less and less attracted to his partner, who he felt was less mature than himself. He needed a different kind of relationship. It would be with a gay male, but similarity was no longer necessary. At his more mature point of development, more defined needs directed his preferences. He wanted a goal-directed partner. The graduate school did not need to be as large as the undergraduate school had been, when he experienced needs for similarity and diversity. Now, in Stage 2 (secondary Peer Arena) adolescence, he looked for diversity within similarity—in this case, those interested in making their life in the arts. Carl planned to pursue a graduate degree in music performance. Because he wanted to be within driving distance of family, he would enroll in the best music school within 500 miles of home but near a big city. When he did move, his mother had done some spade work before he arrived, telling Carl's father of Carl's sexual identification.

Difficulties

Maturing does not necessarily decrease adolescent homosexual needs for reassurance and comfort. In fact, products of development such as increased emotional and cognitive flexibility and savvy bring two mysteries to the forefront: not knowing why one might be gay or lesbian and not knowing whether one wishes to be. The dilemmas continue to be confounded by two additional problems: not knowing who else may be lesbian, gay, or bisexual and fear of others' negative perceptions of homosexuality.

Negative opinion, difficult at any age, is particularly disconcerting when piled on top of one's own confusion and concern during a long period of change. Relationships with attachment peers fluctuate according to one another's needs. Lesbian, gay, bisexual, or transgender (LGBT) youth become particularly intuitive and even more prone than heterosexual adolescents to fear rejection. Unfortunately, the personal intrusiveness of direct inquiry makes studies on this question rare, but findings from a study of high-ranking high school students support the difficulty faced by LGBT adolescents: 48 percent of the students admitted prejudice against LGBTs.[10]

Acknowledging Homosexuality

There is little information on the number of adolescent homosexuals or on those struggling with their sexual preference. The question is more than a statistical one; it is also one of definition.[11] Yet in the relatively limited studies of lesbian and gay youth, adolescents who self-identified and committed to homosexuality tend to have positive attitudes about themselves. Those who identified as bisexuals or as still in the process of exploring their sexual identity had more negative attitudes.[12] This finding could be attributed to several factors. The most logical is that such adolescents' midway status leaves them even more alone and therefore unhappy. Hence, finding sufficient numbers of others with whom to compare and evaluate oneself is quite difficult for adolescents who are confused about whether they may be bisexual. Regarding the declared lesbians and gays, highly regarded social psychological research studies suggest that once one makes a decision, one is more likely to find reasons why that decision is correct.[13]

In the late 20th century, research explored the question of when homosexual feelings rise to awareness. The still-undeveloped field has reported some interesting findings: self-labeling generally occurs at age 14, four years after subjects initially become aware of same-sex desires.[14] A second study found that lesbians and gays coming out at age 16 had also experienced their first same-sex attraction at about age 10.[15] On the other hand, concerns continue to exist about self-identification at younger ages. Since personnel in settings that cater to youth under age 10 generally are not geared to handle issues of sexual maturation, they remain ill prepared to deal with frustrations of young children who also find no outlet for understanding at home or in the community.[16]

Competing Pressures for Minorities

A special problem for homosexual youth arises for those who are of a racial/ethnic minority population. These adolescents must learn to be part of at least three separate communities, each with very different and often conflicting values: the majority race/ethnic community, one's minority group, and the lesbian and gay community, which is primarily White.

A study by Edward Morales, a sociologist, found that although each community provides access to important resources, all tend to devalue the homosexual part of youths' identity.[17] In African American families, in which these negative attitudes are well grounded in African American history, few homosexuals declare themselves.[18] It is somewhat easier for women because they can "hide" within the extended family structure of many African American families, whose organization often involves women living together and raising children. The case of Joyous illustrates the uncertainty and aloneness of an adolescent struggling with gender identity and preference and living within an extended family setting.

Example 2: Joyous, Age 20

Joyous, an African American female living in an Atlantic-seaboard city, was 13 years old and in seventh grade when she was first referred by the school for psychological therapy. Her schoolwork was below grade level, she was withdrawn, and she did not participate well in class. Her hair was cut very short in masculine style, but she wore a bow on one side. She wore no makeup and was of muscular build. Her appearance was of a masculine-looking female. Joyous told close peers that she was a lesbian but needed to keep it secret from her family, which included her parents, five siblings, a grandmother, and an aunt and her son.

Joyous's mother was easy to get along with. Given the number of dependents still at home, both parents worked overtime to support the family and came home well after dinner. Joyous was troubled about her lesbianism. If her brothers ever found out, they would make fun of her. She was one of the boys in this family, but unlike them, she liked to help with the cooking and cleaning. In this way, she identified with her mother. The best day of the week was Sunday, when she went to church with her parents and could see her new lovers out of the corners of her eyes. She was not "in love" with them; she liked their company better than the sex, but they were older and wanted both. It did not seem to Joyous that they had problems being lesbian, but then again she decided maybe they did not really think about it the way she did. Although she had been carefree about her sexuality in the beginning, lately she had begun to wonder if it was right or if she was a bad person.

For a 13-year-old early adolescent, Joyous's behavior had for the most part been typical. She looked and listened to practically everyone and tried out attributes she liked. She played out expected sex roles on the one hand but experimented with homosexual desires on the other. She was aware of her own confusion.

By the time Joyous was 15, she was working after school from three to six o'clock as a girl Friday in a financial firm. She did not like it very much, but it was fun to be in a fancy setting. She got to see her female lovers during the week when no one was home, and she had money to treat them with. Nobody knew about what they did. They shared the secret.

TRYING TO BE STRAIGHT

Eventually, Joyous went to a clinic for psychotherapy and worked on not looking gay. She told the professional that she wanted to look more like a girl. First, she lost weight, started wearing lipstick, and actually turned out to be quite pretty. She was more careful in her dress. At age 16, she found a boyfriend who lived an hour away in Washington, D.C., and tried to make a go of being feminine. The boyfriend had a good job and was regular at it. Sex was okay, sometimes quite dissatisfying, but he was a nice guy and they went places on his tab. She really wanted to be like her parents and older two brothers—"normal and married." By the time Joyous was 18, she was slender, pretty, feminine, and engaged to be married. She thought she was happy. She was aware that she had little ambition because she did not know what she was good at, not realizing that she had been too scared to make the comparisons that would have helped her decide. She planned to take on a full-time girl-Friday job when she graduated the following year. Robbie, her fiancé, promised to work hard at his good job and asked little more of her than sex.

Thus, at 18, Joyous's models were not her age-mates but her parents. There is no indication that she made attempts at connecting with attachment others. Rather, she was satisfied first with two female lovers and then with the serious male suitor. None was really satisfying to her, but her life revolved around them in sequential fashion. Joyous was trying out the feminine role, including a heterosexual relationship. She was trying her best to fit in, but it was not working. Her resistance was expressed in having no real vocational plans. It was as if she was allowing others to sweep her away.

HAUNTING CONFLICT AND FALSE STARTS

Then Joyous met Lara. Lara worked for a client of the company that Joyous worked for. Lara was beautiful. She also was a writer. Lara was five years older than Joyous and coming out of a relationship in which she was the mother to her female lover's baby daughter. The lover was jealous of how much attention Lara showered on the baby. Sex went out the window, and the relationship ended.

Lara said she loved Joyous because she was so beautiful. Joyous had not made quite that assessment of herself in the few comparative acts in which she had engaged.[19] Actually, she stopped comparing because finding others like herself was almost impossible. After meeting Lara, Joyous was so disturbed that she went back to the clinic. She did not know what to do regarding Robbie. In psychotherapy, she discovered that Robbie was her answer to being normal, straight, and respected. If she could be okay with that relationship, she could be a successful member of her own family. But her passion for Lara, though under control and unexpressed, was plaguing her.

Joyous was not joyous. Her physical self was battling with her cognitive self. Cognitively, she knew where others found safe contentment, but she could not be like them. She had miles to go before there could be any joy in her life. Recognizing her aloneness and fondness for her parents, the professional helped her decide to come out to them. They took it well and surprised Joyous by joining Parents and Friends of Lesbians and Gays (PFLAG), a society of others dealing with similar issues. The decision to join was hard for them because they risked being the only African American members, because of the general intolerance of homosexuality in their close community. In fact, Joyous would never have dreamed of recommending that they join PFLAG. But it meant a lot to her that they did so. The insight her parents got in PFLAG sessions led them to leave her free to make her own decision about Robbie. To celebrate, Joyous abruptly quit psychotherapy. She broke her engagement to the heartbroken Robbie, and she and Lara "married." Joyous did not go on to school but worked at her job and became a co-mother to a baby boy Lara gave birth to.

But there were troubles ahead. Neither she nor Lara had wanted sex together once the baby came. Some time later, Lara fell in love with another woman and asked Joyous to move out. Joyous was heartbroken primarily because the separation meant that she could have no further relationship with the baby. She had enjoyed seeing herself as akin to her mother.

Although Joyous was almost 20 years old, she was still deep in adolescence. She had shut down developmentally at age 13 or 14, late-early adolescence. She rode piggyback on her family, then on Robbie, and then on Lara. When her own conflict over lesbianism reemerged in her reluctance to "do sex," she immersed herself in a maternal role caring for Lara's baby. Developmentally, Joyous substituted Lara for her mother in her cognitive structure and was doing what she thought would please her.[20] But that was not enough to satisfy Lara, who wanted a mature lesbian relationship. Union with Lara resolved one set of dreams but soon brought Joyous the reality of unresolved development, incompatibility, and then heartbreak and loss. Joyous needed to take a hard look at herself.

Joyous tried psychotherapy again, and as she reviewed her history with a second female professional, she understood that she had cut herself off from her peers shortly after puberty and aborted her own development by not engaging the dynamics of her very limited Peer Arena. Instead, she jumped to a false maturity (which we will later call a False Facade glitch), which gave her some comfort by successively having "someone." Underneath it all she had been escaping from facing her painful conflict: desire to be and fear of not being straight. Her first two liaisons with other young females were actually preliminary sex play. What she did not know was that in heterosexual development some early homosexual activity often occurs. Sometimes it is a brief part of a best-friend relationship.[21]

Unaware that her sexual relationships at age 13 might have been natural, she tried heterosexuality with Robbie and found the sex part unpleasant, not recognizing that it could be quite natural not to be ready yet for heterosexual relationships. Even becoming close to some peers at her job in a casual way increased her fear and confusion. She felt increasingly inadequate. Joyous found a way out by depending more on her False Facade.[22] Feigning maturity, she captured the heart of Lara. Her therapeutic work brought her to recognize that this relationship served two purposes: (1) she could claim lesbianism within a "sisterhood" of two women living together and raising a child, and (2) by doing so, she could escape the rigors of the Peer Arena. Joyous's playing mother outweighed her desire to be a lover, and Lara asked her to leave.

Joyous went on to learn that she had failed on two counts: (1) fleeing from the Peer Arena because comparative acts were too hard and (2) not completing adolescence and feigning her adulthood. At this level of understanding, the therapist began gently to suggest Peer Arena Lens (PAL) group therapy (discussed later in this book). Notwithstanding Joyous's chronological age, she was still an adolescent. The therapist explained that together with peers who also were experiencing setbacks, she could resolve her issues. But Joyous did what she had done before: she abruptly ended contact with her female therapist. Discussing gender issues in PAL group therapy was too hot a topic.

Before too long, Joyous did seek out a male therapist to work with. She advised him what she considered was the core problem: gender *preference*, not identity, since she claimed maturity. Hopefully, the new therapist would discern her lack of understanding as to what achieving full and complete identity involved, clue into her self-destructive actions to put a patch where she perceived the problem to lie and to change life course when it failed, and then assist Joyous in working toward resolving her adolescence and advancing to true maturity.

An Unfortunate Misperception

Joyous elected to separate out *gender preference* from the other issues she needed to resolve before she could successfully reach identity. Unfortunately, the struggle was so deep and unguided that she also foreclosed achievement of the other part of identity: the work of one's life. Such was not the situation in the case of Carl, who worked on both gender preference and vocational direction. Professionals working with adolescents would be wise to be ever alert to adolescents' getting stuck in only one aspect of identity resolution. All adolescents, regardless of minority or majority group and sexuality, have parallel adolescent tasks of resolving both identity elements, love and work. Self-imposed temporary or permanent delays, referred to in this formulation as defensive glitches, can destructively serve to avoid the pain of the challenges inherent in maturing. Professionals need be well versed in the causes and behavioral manifestations of these kind of glitches, a subject to which I turn in chapters 6 and 7.

5

Parenting Adolescents

It may be strange to think of home as being a haven for adolescents. It is more common to think of home as the place adolescents consider full of restrictions, rules, and limits. In reality, it is both.

Along with dramatic changes of puberty in the four domains of growth comes the psychological need to individuate and discover one's own identity. As we have seen, age-mates become peers and attachment others, highly relevant as models of personality, talents, behaviors, character, and life-style choices. Parents and elders have exhausted their attachment currency. Indeed, one growth task of adolescence is to rework top-down relationships with parents. It is not infrequent that adolescents' sense of urgency about this task makes for clumsy handling.

But parents are more practiced in life and know that their youthful offspring lack sufficient experience for the decision-making and challenges for which they now claim to be fit. Parents' protective instinct remains in place, and there may even be some intensification of their efforts to avert the children's mistakes. There is a good chance that disagreement and conflict will be frequent. The dilemma for parents is not really letting go but knowing when and how to let go.

Understanding the Impact of Pubertal Change

Pubertal change has a two-pronged impact on adolescents. The first one that is seen is the personal impact. It is important for professionals working with parents to raise awareness of the mind-boggling impact of pubertal change on their adolescents' sense of themselves. Physical change is visible, but equally dramatic emotional and cognitive development are not. Early-middle adolescents confuse physical change with maturity since they cannot visualize the other domains that are also in process. Thus, they operate on a mistaken assumption, leaving them open to even more confusion and mistaken assumptions. These adolescents do not yet understand that many years are required to become mature and to make wise decisions. Parents who are guided in understanding this misinterpretation will be more equipped to tolerate their adolescents' unrealistic assertions of ability and judgment.

The second impact of pubertal change is on parents. They need help to accept that the others who are *relevant* for their adolescents have shifted and that they as parents no longer occupy center stage.[1] This information is not easy for parents to cope with. Some may have more trouble with it than others and may benefit from a professional's objective empathy about what they experience as *loss*.

In essence, parents can use a new perspective to deal with a transforming person. They must know that their adolescents' needs change as he or she continues to integrate new development, and they must realize that on any given day brand-new needs may spring up. They also need to learn the skills of thinking flexibly so as to live with an adolescent who is no longer a child but not yet an adult. Four different domains of growth need to mature. Some develop fast; others are slower.

Parents need time to rework old habits and accept a slip every now and then. The task is complex—weaning oneself off a *basic* instinct. Those who parent younger children also need to master this skill while maintaining the oversight that the younger children require. Achieving success in this two-task expectation may at times feel the equivalent of a full-time job. Not all parents manage it easily. It takes time.

Newly minted adolescents are consumed with themselves as they learn to be separate persons. They are too young to have mastered a correct sense of their place in a large world. So caught up are they in their own new world that they have no space for realizing that their parents are in transition too. In fact, adolescents can be quite insensitive. So parents or mates turn to each other or to friends for counsel. At times, it is the blind leading the blind. Some do receive words of wisdom and even an occasional shoulder to cry on from contemporaries, but seldom do Western adults allow others to be privy to the depth of their uncertainties. Ironically, both parent and child struggle with transitions. For adolescents, it is learning how to handle power; for parents, it is letting go of it.

The popular culture both helps and hinders the work of parents. Modern adolescents master new technologies and informational and communication opportunities. They communicate with local and virtual agemates and models in various e-formats. Just as the times are changing and complex, so do parents seek wisdom in changing along with the complex realities and conditions for raising adolescents well.

When a child reaches adolescence, parenting tasks go into reverse. Protection needs to be replaced by guidance. New words must be mastered and supplant others as part of the basic repertoire. Adolescent parenting requires *switching* from telling to recommending, advising, and suggesting.

The content of this chapter is useful for professionals working with parents of offspring who are following a normative course, with those whose adolescents have become worrisome, and with those parenting adolescents with physical or mental problems or disabilities. Diverse concerns become far more similar when what adolescence is becomes comprehensible. Professionals are encouraged never to let go of the facts: every adolescent except those with hormonal issues reaches puberty eventually, and each youngster also experiences psychological ramifications of this important physical event, as do parents. But there are a few concepts that each parent must remember: (1) each pubescent youth, notwithstanding physical or psychological diagnosis, has earned the right to be regarded as an adolescent, (2) each adolescent should be regarded by parents and professionals alike as an adolescent with a problem, not as a "problem adolescent," (3) for each, *adolescent* is the overarching definitional noun, not *problem*.

The Changing Face of Home Life

When children are young, a great part of their schooling takes place in the home. Parents, elders, and siblings are teachers and models. For most, formal academic education is then provided by the local public or private school system. Social education is shared with the school, for example, through group conduct, sharing, and play. With the onset of adolescence, academics continue to be a major demand, but social education is no longer child's play but adolescent work. It entails interactions that involve both outreach and introspection. Concurrently, the home as major setting for social education takes a step into the shadows, a change that may begin surprisingly and intensively, especially so in seventh and eighth grades, when learning from peers takes over. Thus, school is a large and important peer group in the Peer Arena. It is a social learning center in which comparative acts are ubiquitous. Becoming a physical member of a small group of peers or a psychological member of a large peer group or groups leads to less and less dependence on parents.

Individuation and the drive to reach adulthood is the active motive for growth. As individuation completes itself, aspects of emotional separation come with it, and the parent-child relationship reaches mature status, having gradually evolved into a lateral relationship over a long period of years. Parents can use help to understand that they are not being rejected but that their offspring are moving along psycho-emotionally, along with normative physical and cognitive changes.

As early adolescents, these newly minted ex-children give up the psychologically protective framework of home and initially feel "frameworkless" and adrift, which, as we have seen, sparks the internal imperative to attach to peers. This unique type of relationship can no longer be contained within a definition of friendship; the relationship is one of *peership*, which means that each individual is driven by an identical task to individuate and mature into an adult. Each goes at it alone, but all intuitively understand what the other is working to resolve. Peership does not compete with an adolescent's relationship with parents; it lives right next to it.[2]

Developmentally Driven Moods and Behaviors

Adolescent psychic pain and moodiness is not attributed to parental actions or to the agonies of an unconscious need to separate from them.[3] The pain is connected to disappointing findings from comparative acts in which adolescents engage when peers interact in one or more of the many peer groups that constitute each adolescent's Peer Arena. What should be stressed with parents is that adolescent desires to be with peers stems from a developmental imperative. It is preconscious, not really understood by the adolescent but emotionally driven. Even though most parents do not understand why their adolescents' mood changes, from despair to joy or vice versa, they tolerate these new and very confusing signals. Some even try to join in activities, much to adolescents' chagrin. Aside from parents' role in filling transportation needs, most adolescents prefer peers to be their private domain. There may be other such hidden resentments, unique to each adolescent. Professionals need to be alert to the various types of masks adolescents use from time to time to cover their real feelings, which will remain undetected by professionals who insist on attributing most, if not almost all, adolescents' relationship problems with parents to some manifestation of rebellion.[4]

THE CASE OF OLIVIA, AGE 15

Olivia King's parents wanted to give her something special for her Sweet 16 birthday. She was a lovely young lady, polite, well mannered, and courteous. She did well in school, striving to meet the standards set by older cousins and by one of her older brothers. Since she was the youngest child, one would expect that she would be spoiled, but she was not. She was not nearly as demanding as other teens the family had heard about or as her big brothers were.

The King family was not as well off as other families in the private school where Olivia was a scholarship student. But Mom sewed very nice things for her, and Olivia always felt like she fit in. Because of the many joys and few troubles Olivia brought Mr. and Mrs. King, they saved from the time she was 13 to surprise her with a trip to Disneyland for her 16th birthday. They planned the trip for a long weekend for financial reasons and so Olivia would not miss too much school. They surprised her with the news one week before departure, but instead of rapture, Olivia lowered her head and said nothing. Where was the joy? The excitement? The hugs and kisses and running up to her brothers to tell them the news?

Before too long, Mr. and Mrs. King learned the cause of the unexpected reaction. Several weeks prior, Olivia had been invited to a sleepover for eight girls in celebration of a classmate's 16th birthday. She was allowed to go and had a swell time. All the girls were having sleepovers, and she hoped that the invitation from a very popular classmate would bring her other invitations too, and perhaps there would be enough girls to invite back for her own sleepover party. She thought sleepovers were a lot of fun; you heard so much stuff about everyone else when it got to be after midnight.

Olivia's plans for her own birthday sleepover were taking shape in her own mind. In fact, she felt lucky that her birthday fell on a Saturday, a perfect sleepover night. She was going to invite one or two girls with whom she felt most comfortable, even though they were "a lot richer." She had not mentioned the party to her parents yet because she knew it would cost a lot of money. Now, all her plans would be ruined. Her parents had bought the tickets and paid all that money for them and for the hotel. She did not want to tell them, but she did not want to go. She wanted her own party, but there would not be enough money for both. A party might go a long way toward making her "one of them," not an onlooker. No matter how smart she was, the crowd always seemed to be looking for other qualities. And, apparently, maybe she had some of those too. She had planned to cement that impression. She liked those girls a lot.

Because Olivia was not overtly rebellious, she did not meet the common definition of a rebellious teenager. Her parents neither saw nor felt a change in her attitude toward them. She was not wild and contrary like Andrew, the older brother, nor did she mope around like Ralph, the younger brother. And she was not selfish like her cousin Rhonda. Therefore, her parents assumed that all was as it had always been. Hearing that the marvelous trip they had planned did not mean as much to Olivia as a Sweet 16 sleepover at home stunned them. And it hurt. These parents needed to come to terms with a new reality: Olivia's relationship with them had changed, although not in outwardly obvious way. Although in retrospect the Kings concluded that their perception of their relationship with Olivia had been too perfect to be real, they had been enjoying it and did not make the realization at the time.

So when Olivia's parents told her about their plans for the trip, Olivia was quiet for quite a while, and then a tear dropped, and then more and more tears. And finally her Dad got the information out of her. Now, they were being asked to share Olivia with her age-mate counterparts, indeed, to place them in a rank far above their own. It seemed puzzling. Why? Mrs. King became inflamed. Mr. King masked his feeling of rejection by tinkering with a leaky kitchen fixture. Olivia cried and cried but then suggested that she could work in the summertime and pay her parents back the loss of the hotel deposits. She even volunteered to stay at her aunt's house, and her cousin Rhonda could go on the trip in her place. But she would not abandon her desire to stay home and have her own Sweet 16 sleepover. It was the first time the Kings saw "this part of Olivia."

The extent of the Kings' puzzlement and hurt was such that they contacted a local family service agency. They wanted to avoid the school's knowing that all was no longer "perfect." The objective of the professional with whom the Kings met was to help them with the rejection they experienced and then to work with them to identify cues that Olivia must have given them about her "growing up." A refrain that Olivia's parents repeated over and over again was how they never expected this behavior from her. Reasons for their emotional blindness could be manifold, but one thing that became clear was that they might have wished to see no changes in their relationship with their daughter and so remained blind to them until this very dramatic surprise. As the discussion continued, Mr. King put his finger on how their devastation might have been related to a prior disappointment in Andrew, the oldest son, who suddenly quit college and never met "his potential." Olivia was such a pleasure compared to Andrew. Up until this incident, Olivia had renewed their own faith in themselves. Or so they thought. Family therapy with Andrew was suggested to the Kings if sessions with them alone did not suffice to soothe their wounds from their experience with Andrew and allow Olivia the freedom to be adolescent.

Parents, fresh out of the caretaking stage, feel robbed of the relationship time for which they have worked so hard. The Kings needed help with managing the emotional pain of raising a developing adolescent.

Adaptations of Parenting

Pain hurts, no matter the circumstance or eventual benefit. It may be helpful for professionals to cast pain of disappointment or perceived rejection as *reorienting pain*. Parents also benefit from hearing that this degree of intensity does not last forever and that their prior positive parenting has laid a foundation to help them get through it.

Ironically, the Kings accepted "rebellion" of their son Andrew far better than they accepted Olivia's birthday preference, which they experienced as rejection. They read Olivia's preference as a desire to replace them. The Kings had taken pride that Olivia had never rebelled, but now they considered rebellion better than replacement. After all, they had heard that all parents are rebelled against, and they were proud to be an exception. But what they perceived as Olivia's rejection of them seemed so much worse. As they told the professional with whom they worked, "Think about it: isn't it far easier to bear something that happens to all parents than a personal rejection?"

The Kings' feelings were natural. Preference for *A* over *B* is a competitive loss for *B*. On the other hand, rebellion is not a win-lose situation at all but a phenomenon. One's accepting a social phenomenon such as rebellion can be seen as doing what everyone else does. Viewed in this way, the individual's ego, or sense of importance, is not attacked or belittled. Yet according to the DFI model, what the Kings interpreted as Olivia's desire to reject and replace them was *not* a hit at all. Rather, it was a parenting *achievement*, an outward verbal manifestation of a natural process—Olivia's desire to be with peers at all costs. The underlying growth purpose of this desire is for adolescents to get relevant information about what counts and about how they rank in relation to everyone else. The opportunity to acquire such information far outweighs the fun and good times offered by parents.

The Kings needed help to get to a deeper level of understanding about how and why adolescents' transition from child to adult changes their interaction with parents. It cannot be communicated to parents too many times that adolescents' advance in strengths, skills, emotions, and cognitive interpretations need to be tried out with others *like themselves.* This understanding is hard for parents to assimilate because they have invested so much of themselves into the rearing of their child.

Deceiving Pictures of Peer Life

Pictures parents get of adolescent peer life can be confusing, if not deceiving. It often appears to be full of good times, laughter, and constant conversation. The seriousness and functional character of group exchange is not evident and can be totally misconstrued. Intense involvement with peers is misunderstood as frivolous. Hence, based on limited observations, most parents understandably feel it merits limited time.

Most adolescents have few clues, if any, that being with peers is an essential stepping-stone to growth. Their uniquely adolescent social relationships that do not adhere to any formal rules foster psychological growth. Since logic does not become part of adolescent exchange until the late period of adolescence, until then, they may freely express various viewpoints, some of which may even be contradictory. Adolescents can adopt positions with as much vehemence as they did to contrary views only minutes before. Peers have no need to attach permanence to anything expressed. Since the Peer Arena is a reciprocal arena for tryout, changing one's mind is acceptable. Furthermore, adolescents express ideas to get a handle on how they will go over. Is it popular? Effective? Admired? These sorts of assessments are the "business" of the peer group.

Yet parents often demand that matters make sense and are often put off by the nonchalance of their offspring. During adolescence, parents and adolescents time and again exchange views in something akin to two different languages. They feel trapped, but because they need to save face, arguments ensue, and hostilities can build while the basic points that started discussion get lost in negative emotion.

Once parents get some hint that peer interactions are about matters very important to their adolescent, it may be easier to understand why adolescents reserve energies for school and other settings where peers gather.

BURT, AGE 17

Burt usually wears jeans and a tee shirt, but one Saturday afternoon after many uninterrupted hours in his second-floor room, he came into the kitchen wearing jeans, a suit jacket, shirt, and tie. Surprised, his mother asked him why he was dressed up. He avoided a reply. Later in the evening, he came down in jeans and a tee shirt and a tie with a Windsor knot. The following Monday, he left for school dressed in pants, shirt, jacket, and a tie with a Windsor knot announcing that he and a friend had decided to have a "formal day in school."

Burt's actions offer some hint at the way adolescent growth and development takes place in the company of peers. Egocentric youth are adept at reserving their energies for settings that they intuit as having the greatest potential for learning about themselves. Thus, an outward appearance of "anything goes," as in Burt's case, belies the serious individual psychological business going on within the adolescent. And home becomes a place to take a rest from serious thinking.

Significance of the Peer (Friend): My Friend Might Be Me

The place that friends occupy in the hearts of adolescents is not at all confusing to the adolescent, but it can be very confusing to parents and family members. This dynamic causes lots of problems between parents and adolescents. Adolescents' attitudes about particular friends often changes from week to week, and talking with parents about friends can be a real danger zone. It is most important that professionals understand what lies underneath these changing attitudes so they can work with parents to help them do better with such issues.

First, early in adolescence, adolescents begin to identify with peers. Adolescents become angry if parents do not think much of or criticize one of their friends. Why? Because adolescents unconsciously experience the criticism as an attack against themselves: "My peer is me." An adolescent's identifying with a peer, or an aspect of a peer, offers the adolescent internal stabilization. Adolescents have little, if any, consciousness that this new aspect of their persona, a particular characteristic, or a talent is copied from that of a valued peer. As the adolescent matures, this identification reaction is neutralized. Nevertheless, it is important that professionals translate this complex unconscious dynamic for parents: Go slow about peers. Measure your words. Understand the power of a comment.

The developmental reason behind adolescents' identifications with peers is that at rather early points in the two-stage process of growth, but ongoing to a lesser degree throughout development, adolescents abandon their childhood frame of reference and thus seek to relieve the discomfort of the feeling of being frameworkless. To tide them over a period of uncertainty, adolescents unconsciously identify with attractive attributes of other adolescents and psychologically adopt them into their cognitive structure as their own. At some point, after trying out the particular attribute, opinion, or talent that they have borrowed, they evaluate whether they like it. If they have borrowed from someone who also has a number of other attractive attributes, they may identify with the person wholesale.

For example, Patrice has a wonderful voice, which Eloise admires. Eloise identifies with Patrice, allowing her to believe that she too has great singing talent. She tries her voice out and experiences it as quite good. She thinks about a career as a vocalist. Patrice, in turn, identifies with Eloise's sense of humor, and by psychologically absorbing Eloise's humor into her cognitive structure as her own, she feels skilled at catching nuances of someone else's humor and believes she is funny. When Patrice visits Eloise, Eloise's parents are so appalled that their daughter likes this loud and almost vulgar person that they even demean Patrice's voice. They tell Eloise to look for other friends. Eloise becomes furious and overreacts, quite out of concert with her usual cool personality. Of course, what Eloise's parents did not understand was that their daughter identified herself with Patrice and that in her mind Patrice's voice *was her voice too.* In fact, Eloise had signed up to try out for the lead in the school musical. Thus, on the day of Patrice's visit, Eloise's parents unknowingly insulted their own daughter.

An example such as this one can aid professionals in enlightening parents about the complex functions that peers serve for one another. It may also reduce parents' confusion about some unlikely friendships that their adolescent values. These friendships are usually time limited, but they serve developmental comfort and try-out purposes.[5] In addition, this type of discussion opens the door for parents to relate their own confusing examples.

Basic Guidance Tasks of the Professional

Guiding parents who are concerned that their adolescent is suffering with serious problems needs sensitive handling. Professionals should bear in mind that the most important first step is to explore with parents whether the problem may in fact be a defensive glitch or other type of serious problem. The following guidelines may be of general help: (1) Be sympathetic to parents' concerns and recognize their unease about the future of their family. Listen carefully to their perspective on the problem. There is always information that a professional can obtain only from parents. (2) Offer a clear explanation of what it means to say that the child turns adolescent and starts a journey to maturity. To clarify, explain as simply as possible the DFI two-stage course of adolescence and the general growth path. (3) Explain what the search for identity is all about. Simplify using examples. An effective strategy is to encourage parents to think of their own adolescent experience, which will help them connect with the fact that adolescents do sometimes falter. (4) Assure parents that you are there to assist them. Express your respect for their efforts, and do all you can to communicate your understanding of their frustrations and worries. (5) Explain the function of protocols, that they assist in eliciting information important to resolving issues of concern. (6) Encourage them to be frank, which will speed the way to providing them tips on parenting and thus help their adolescent.

It is very important that parents be advised of the other family members you plan to see. Take the opportunity to ask them to recommend additional others to talk with and why. Do your best to give them confidence that you will value their suggestions. Encourage them to call you immediately if their adolescent engages in any action they consider seriously dangerous or wrong. On the other hand, suggest that they also try to hang in there for a while, since change takes place slowly at first. Suggest that they call you if they are finding it difficult. Finally, ask them sincerely if they have any further questions, and answer the best you can. In addition, consult with colleagues or supervisors about how the information and examples in this book may be applied to specific problems that parents bring.

The Peculiar Position of Adolescents' Parents

Newspapers and periodicals are full of information about the preferences, actions, confusions, and aspirations of adolescents. They make for dramatic eye-catching articles, pictures, and even movies and TV series. Much less attention is given to the accommodations that the parents of adolescents must make. When adolescents have grown beyond the familiar child-oriented parenting style, some parents feel like displaced persons. Furthermore, a confusing inequity exists. No longer do parents carry the unequivocal authority or power that parents of toddlers and young children have. Yet they are held responsible for the actions of their adolescent. In contrast to the easily recognized contributions of parents wheeling strollers or teaching young children skills or how to play sports, adolescent parenting is almost invisible.

Ironically, parents are in a similar position to their young adolescents. Initially, they also lack a framework. Professionals can help by acknowledging the skills that parents have developed over years of nurturing and concern for which they now experience no outlet.

Over half a century ago, in an article on parenthood, the psychoanalyst Therese Benedek proposed a prophetic conception of parenthood as a developmental phase. She stressed that processes activated in becoming a parent greatly affect the execution of responsibilities connected with that role. For parents whose fragile and weakened sense of competency are threatened by talk of their adolescent's individuation and any type of separation, Benedek took the position that reassurance therapy must be built in to any type of therapeutic intervention.[6]

Treating Transitions as Successes

Current views of the function of parents and peers to a great extent still reflect the cultural lag between outmoded customs related to an adolescent's development and the expansion of the varieties of travel, communication, and information acquisition. Our society's mores and traditions with regard to adolescence also lag behind our understanding of developmental transitions. Parenting has moved from being homebound to supporting an adolescent's growth and development wherever it takes place. During adolescence, practically all growth and development occurs in the various settings of the Peer Arena, the diverse groups in which peers congregate. In this setting, the adolescent needs always to be "on"—trying hard not to be rejected so as to stay in the group. The stakes are great since, if an adolescent is rejected, then he or she loses access to the growth materials modeled by age-mates. Adolescents sense internal signals to join in, be admired, and be careful all at the same time. Home is an important support base where parents stand ready to be an informational source, to offer guidance and advice. This new arrangement between parents and former child is natural and appropriate.

As we have seen, this transition away from an adolescent's need for active parenting must not be considered rejection. Rather, it is a necessary transition about which professionals need to update parents. They need to advise them that from early adolescence on, their offspring begin to take command of their own ship. The object is to guide the ship to Port Maturity. This passage is located in the adolescent Peer Arena, where necessary development takes place through psychological interaction, as well as physical, with many different types of peers. The Peer Arena model of development should be anticipated in the same way that weddings are anticipated and celebrated as a developmental transition. "Adolescent transfer of functional energies into Peer Arena membership heralds successful closure for the parent on the *active* sequence of parenting. A helpless offspring has been husbanded into biological maturity and guided through initial socialization. Membership of a child in a peer group is considered a milestone of passage."7 Hailing this transition to Peer Arena membership reinforces successful parenting. Parents' concern about their adolescent's competing loyalties to parents and peers might be dispelled if the transition to peers is interpreted correctly as movement forward.

As parents internalize mental congratulations when they see their adolescents transition to peers in the miscellaneous groups of their Peer Arena, home life can be a great relief for both parents and adolescents. No false fronts are required. Family members may live at a reduced risk of becoming targets of adolescents' pent-up emotions, angers, and tensions, which are held in when they are with peers. Free exchange about the day can be welcomed, understood, and supported. Home can even become a haven, a safe place, a sanctuary of sorts, in which an adolescent can regroup and get ready for the next day in the Peer Arena.

In this approach to adolescence, professionals assist parents to recognize that adolescent energies are consumed by keeping up with schoolwork, home responsibilities, and for some, a part-time job. In addition, as discussed in earlier chapters, adolescents are depleted by expending energy in evaluating findings of comparative acts and dealing with the consequences. Even so, some days adolescents will just seem happy or spend time with family and not be preoccupied with peers. Such are the confusing messages that parents try to read correctly, which is not always an easy task.

PART II

Defensive Glitches

6

Defining and Detecting
Defensive Glitches

A *defensive glitch* is a response to pain that brings a halt to the normative developmental process. The category of glitches includes a variety of defensive flights from unbearable psycho-emotional pain resulting from unexpected disappointing findings of comparative acts with peers over a period of time. The term *glitch* is apt because it implies the possibility of reversal.

As we have seen, the DFI perspective on adolescent psychosocial development defines the psychological goal of adolescent development as cognitively and emotionally selecting self-elements that together constitute a sense of self, a sense of who the adolescent is. This collection of elements represents the various aspects of the human personality, which find expression in thought, words, feelings, and actions. DFI conceptualizes this collection of elements as the *cognitive self structure*.

Adolescent Struggle

We have also seen that DFI introduces the idea of an adolescent imperative to be with peers, an imperative energized by puberty. The purpose of this drive is functional: advanced psychological development. Some adolescents do not complete a smooth passage of development that results in a positive, integrated picture of oneself. This failure is testimony to the intensity and demands of this growth stage. Most youth are expected to pass, or to excel, in school. Some also carry family responsibilities. Others work part-time. With the additional time adolescents need to make comparative acts, they are understandably exhausted by day's end. And even though comparative acts, in which adolescents engage almost constantly, have a number of steps, laypeople and even many professionals are not aware of them and their energy drain. Although adolescents are usually not cognizant of their comparing, they are indeed comparing. The process occurs automatically and subliminally.

In one study, a questionnaire revealed that although adolescents are generally unaware of how much they compare with peers, and some are totally unaware of this dynamic process, all of the subjects, 66 12th-grade males in an academically advanced high school, were able to respond and answer all questions relating to how they felt about themselves in relation to their peers in a group setting. Questions were asked immediately after a half-hour discussion on a topic relevant to 11 groups of 6 subjects each. No discussion leader was present, and the discussion was tape-recorded. The youth could choose to agree or disagree with the statements provided on the questionnaire. The following table presents a sample of the responses.[1]

Statement	Percentage who agreed
1. I was aware of whether I knew as much as the group as a whole.	71.9
2. I was aware of my relative standing throughout the discussion.	86.0
3. It felt good when I seemed to know as much or more than others.	98.5
4. I felt good when I knew as much or more than the person I felt knew the most.	60.9
5. I felt badly when the others did not receive my contribution well.	61.9
6. I felt badly when I knew less than others.	82.9
7. At various periods of this discussion, I had negative feelings about myself.	75.0
8. This was an uncomfortable experience for me at times.	96.9

Responses to the following statements provide an interesting insight into how the students applied to themselves what they heard.

Statement	Percentage who agreed
1. I learned something about myself during this discussion.	70.0
2. Recognizing attributes in others stimulated me to look at myself to see if I had them too.	98.0

Most striking, notwithstanding the painful affective response, students felt positive about the group experience and desired a second interaction experience.

Statement	Percentage who agreed
1. I was interested in finding out the views of others.	98.0
2. I would like to join another group.	90.0

When adolescents' self-importance is pricked during their self-centered (egocentric) period, generally at its height at a slightly younger age than that of the males in this group, they feel as if the whole world is aware of their failures.[2] Although those particularly vulnerable are early to early-middle adolescents, whose egocentrism is still quite powerful, it is clear that the males in this group were not immune. Yet most of them managed those feelings candidly.

Glitch Adolescents

Those adolescents who do not manage their feelings of failure are what I call *glitch adolescents,* adolescents for whom findings of comparisons continually disappoint and for whom deep questions of self-worth grow and grow. They stay with what makes them feel good, or at least what makes them feel better. They do not always recognize what they are doing. To parents, elders, or friends, they appear to be overdoing something, such as a hobby or time spent on a cause or with another person. They are actually manifesting glitches, which are found in a range of degrees of seriousness. Many glitch adolescents will eventually need psychological treatment.

Psychological treatment may have been offered to such adolescents previously, but in the past they may have refused it. At a severe point of self-disappointment, especially if it also leads to deep self-concern, the treatment option becomes more attractive. Professionals who examine why the glitch exists need be aware that adolescents cannot always relate the precise reason for their behavior. It is a task of therapy to discover the real reason. Adolescents are capable of denying even to themselves that they are fearful and looking for some peace. Down deep, there may be a glimmer that their behavior is based in disappointment, frustration, or even anger. What they do know is that what they are doing makes them feel better than the way they felt in their recent past.

People in older age groups will also frequently deny a problem. Friends and relatives are often concerned about the excuses that loved ones make for escaping reality. For example, some people deny that they feel physical pain in order to avoid going to a doctor and facing a feared medical opinion; others claim that smoking does no harm to their lungs in spite of clinical evidence to the contrary. These attitudes are contrary to common sense, but when fear is great, denial is a favorite flight. Professionals often find that when they point out "scientific information," it does not help much. For adolescents, there is a further complication: except for older adolescents, who are near finalizing their development, most have not yet conquered their egocentricity. Since they are still incapable of holding too many variables in mind at one time, they do not *really* understand the potential consequences of a plan in the way older people do. Thus, they are inclined to take for themselves whatever defense is easily available. They have no way to know what price they might pay in stunting their growth or negating the growth they have already achieved.[3]

Unique Histories

Each youngster arrives in adolescence with a different ratio of psychological strengths and weaknesses. This ratio is the result of hereditary and environmental factors, including trauma.[4] Youth who enter adolescence psychologically sound have usually had strong home support and little trauma. Most of them probably had some problems but successfully worked them out. This type of adolescent brings a firm base to the academic and interpersonal challenges that frequently arise before the psychological work of the stage is completed. Adolescents with a troubled base are most vulnerable to disappointing outcomes in substantive comparisons between themselves and others, though they do have a chance of being Upward-comparison persons because of their observable physical features or personality characteristics. Some adolescents use their own strategies to deal with the dynamics of the day; for example, in early adolescence and even beyond, some pour their hearts out into diaries or journals. Nevertheless, adolescents continue to feel a strong need to hear and see more in their comparisons with peers. Early research documented that one-third of all statements in half-hour conversations between adolescents contained comparisons of others.[5] Several decades later, two research assistants recorded the popularity in peer settings of a new means to communicate experiences immediately: cell phones. At two separate locations on the main enclosed walkway of an eastern college campus on two different days, 21 percent of approximately 300 students who walked by were talking on cell phones within a one-hour period.[6] Through such avenues as these, and through others, during the course of adolescence individuals revise prior notions of their abilities, capacities, talents, and personal worth.

It is difficult to factor in the toll that a troubled background takes on an adolescent, each of whom is busy enough redefining almost everything.

Self-questioning becomes the name of the game. Later, tasks of Stage 2 also kindle comparisons on future planning and goal setting, including education and occupation. If an adolescent perceives that others see him or her as lacking, it is difficult for that adolescent to deal with. When adolescents manifest a glitch and are admitted to PAL group therapy—as described later in this book—one goal is for them to earn a sufficient balance of expectation, humanity, and respect from group members to strengthen their fallen resolve to make it in a community of peers.

Prior to Glitches

In order to be able to correctly recognize a glitch, professionals must have the knowledge to diagnose the adolescent's developmental position in each of the four domains of development. The following case is illustrative.

Roger, Age 14

Roger is in the eighth grade in a central-Midwest capital city with a population of 600,000. He loves athletics and has been a good student, but his academic work has dropped off in quality in the past year. Although he is nice looking, his physical development appears behind the majority of the other males. Hence, although his performance at individual sports such as biking or tennis was at an acceptable level, team sports were his downfall. He tried a number of positions but always fell short. So when coaches allowed players to pick teammates, he was one of those chosen last. Everyone liked him well enough because he was quiet and did not offend, but the impact of his poor team performance disillusioned him. Soon his near obsession with his team performance used up a lot of spare energies, and it spilled over into lowering the quality of his academic work. So his perception of himself sunk lower and lower.

Roger's parents were worried about him. They too were quiet and gentle people, shy like Roger. They felt it would be good for him to see a male professional, and he was assigned to Mr. G. Roger's opening statements to Mr. G. related his low rank in athletics. Mr. G. listened closely and very seldom interrupted Roger, who seemed to need to vent and share his stories. But there was an interesting omission: he said nothing about academic work; he spoke only of his failure at sports, giving example after example. Mr. G. noted that this was all Roger seemed to care about.

Notwithstanding Mr. G.'s efforts to encourage Roger by stressing other qualities and interests, Roger's need for self-punishment won. His mood went lower and lower. Mr. G.'s diagnosis of Roger was Dysthymic Disorder due to increasing disillusionment about his athletic abilities.[7] Yet Mr. G. did not consider Roger's athletic abilities *as compared to* those of his peers. It was as if Roger was an island alone. Mr. G. recommended medication for his young client. So Roger started out on medical assistance very early in life.

Unfortunately, Mr. G. was not versed in developmental theory. He missed one very obvious developmental domain, the physical. Mr. G. did not discuss what he saw before him: Roger's smaller-than-average, slender frame. He spoke with Roger only about the disadvantages of being short. He was so intent on the sports problem that he saw Roger simply as an *"adolescent misfit—sport ability deficient."* In addition, Roger's vocabulary should have been a clue to his stage of development: he still used concrete, not abstract, examples, and he was very literal. But Mr. G. missed the cognitive signs that Roger still had a way to go to reach an advanced cognitive level. Furthermore, Mr. G. had no information with which to judge whether he was dealing with an adolescent or a child; for example, he had not inquired whether Roger had experienced a wet dream or whether he knew what that meant. Had he inquired, he would have learned that Roger's sexual fantasies and locker-room comparisons of penis size were confusing if not traumatic to the 14-year-old adolescent. Physically, Roger was way behind and very worried. Tales of sex with girls scared him, and worst of all, the locker-room comparisons in which he came up short were reinforced on the sports fields.

The fact that Mr. G. was not developmentally knowledgeable, an orientation so essential to dealing with growing adolescents, left him with no clue about Roger's egocentric state. In Stage 1 adolescence, adolescents hold an exaggerated view of their own importance and thus feel that others are preoccupied with them.[8] They are certain that all their qualities are evident to everyone, including their deficiencies. Hence, Roger felt that his inadequacies were evident to everyone. To Roger, others saw no one and nothing but him. Unfortunately, Roger's story did not turn out well. He went on to become addicted to cocaine.

Comparison Cues and Cognitive Development

The types of comparison adolescents use are also a source of important cues to their level of cognitive development and particularly helpful in understanding how adolescents who have taken flight into a glitch interpret their peer environment and their place in it. Do they think of peers as only those in their immediate environment? Or are peers perceived as part of a larger world? The latter view reflects a more advanced cognitive level. Is the adolescent feeling pain because of a limited view of only a few others his or her age? This same question can be asked if the adolescent has a larger view of their world, but at least the professional would be operating in the correct cognitive ballpark.

Adolescents' point of cognitive development also affects their mode of communication. Understanding an adolescent's level of development assists a professional in knowing whether the client can communicate about abstractions or whether he or she needs communication to be concrete, more factual. In addition, the number of variables that adolescents can hold in their mind at any one moment affects the number of alternatives that can be presented to them.[9] This information sets the scope and type of verbal exchange that can take place between an adolescent and a therapist. Unfortunately, when professionals lack knowledge of cognitive theory, they tend to make assessments of adolescents' level of cognitive growth after the fact, such as how adolescents scored in their algebra, geometry, or physics courses.

An Assessment Model

Professionals should always make developmental assessments. Such assessments provide clues as to why adolescents may have taken flight to a defensive glitch instead of working out the emotional or cognitive insult they experienced.

One way to make a cognitive assessment it is to analyze the types of comparison the adolescent uses. Very simply, if the adolescent does not use comparison with a range, a comparison whose findings supply information about his or her rank relative to others, it is logical to wonder why he or she does not want this information. On the other hand, if an adolescent has sought out this information, it offers a route into his or her self-perception. In addition, for adolescents 15 years old or older, lack of interest in such comparisons raises questions about their cognitive development. It could hint of their inability to operate on the abstract level. Looking at grades in academic subjects may be valuable in providing additional information that may support this supposition, but it may not be sufficient.

Some scholars believe that cognitive development can be taught.[10] According to this perspective, when a notion such as comparison with a range is introduced, discussed, and explained, it may jog the individual's set notions and encourage thinking about something new. Professionals might consider such a quasi-teaching approach as a further test of where the adolescent is developmentally.

If an adolescent has not reached the formal operational stage of cognitive development, the abstract stage, it is not necessarily correct to hypothesize that he or she is slow. The age of the adolescent must be taken into account: this conclusion would be incorrect for a 12- to 13-year-old. Similarly, if an adolescent has reached that stage by 12 or 13 years old, it does not mean that the youth is "bright" or "brighter" but merely that cognitive development is ahead of the other domains at this point in time. Cognitive development has nothing to do with "brain power." These traits are for the most part independent of each other.

What follows is a discussion of what professionals can gain from looking at comparisons made by adolescents. First, I analyze the comparisons made by a small group of high school seniors. These findings provide information about judging the abilities of a group as a whole as well as about getting a picture of their aspirational level. A case example follows to illustrate the diagnostic clues to a defensive glitch that appeared in an adolescent's selection of comparisons. Analyzing comparisons in this way offers a data source in order to raise hypotheses to explain troubling behavior.

Analysis of Comparisons Carried Out in a Group Setting

In the study mentioned earlier that was carried out with 66 males in the 12th grade, because all the boys had reached age 16 or 17, the researchers predicted that the adolescents would use all types of comparison with peers, based on an assumption that by that age sufficient cognitive development to think abstractly had taken place. Recall that depending on what adolescents want to find out, they choose the type of comparison that will yield the information. Once they select a specific type (or types), the dynamics of comparative acts operate quickly but need to be exhaustive before they satisfy adolescents' questions. Adolescents first compare and then evaluate findings; and then they compare again and again on one or more attributes with additional peers in a series of trials and evaluations until they become confident in the findings. In the case of the academically talented 12th graders studied, the findings confirmed the prediction that they would use all types of comparison.[11]

The findings of this study are important in illuminating the level of cognitive maturity of the participants. The top two categories of comparisons that they employed were Downward and Upward, respectively. Over a 30-year period, these types of comparison have been consistently found to be of greatest interest to adolescents between 12 and 18 years old.[12] Why? Downward comparison informs adolescents of how much better they are than their peers, and Upward comparison informs them of who is better than they are. Downward serves self-enhancing needs; Upward, aspirational ones. But Upward comparisons can also serve self-enhancement needs if an adolescent discovers early on that he or she is in the Upward comparison league. Of course, comparing with the Positive Instance (the ultimate best) is the true test. These two types together, Upward comparison and Positive Instance comparison accounted for 25.3 percent of the comparisons made by the 12th graders in the study, and 22.9 percent were Downward comparisons.[13]

Another striking finding is that Comparison with a Goal ranked third in the youths' comparisons, just below Upward and Downward ones. This finding speaks to the high interest these 12th graders had in where they stood compared to one another. Their ability to abstract enabled them to inquire about their position on the continuum, since they could hold in their mind how far they were from their goal as they pragmatically checked out where others stood. After taking note of where the competition ranked academically, they could ask themselves practical questions such as whether studying more might put them in line to win the scholarship or whether they should adjust their goals downward. As pointed out earlier, not all adolescents proceed at a common pace, but most do achieve the sort of mental abilities for abstract thought that we are discussing.[14]

In assessing just these three types of comparison—Upward, Downward, and Comparison with a Goal—the professional can glean hints as to what the adolescent in question aspires to and whether he or she feels the goal can be achieved. Meeting standards of group norms or risking psychological expulsion plays an important role in what adolescents aspire to. It exerts strong pressure. Professionals are advised to make it their business to learn what the prevailing strong school and peer-group norms are.

As discussed earlier, adolescents' appearing physically similar may confuse matters if their emotional and cognitive growth, which are not outwardly apparent, are not similar. Peers may expect others' interests and performance to be similar to theirs. Thus, some adolescents may feel alone, bereft of others like themselves. A few simple comparison protocols can reveal very important clues. For example, an adolescent's selecting a great many Downward comparisons and not many Upward comparisons, Comparisons with a Goal, or Positive Instance comparisons might lead a professional to consider whether the adolescent may be disillusioned about the chances of thinking better of him- or herself among others whom he or she sees as superior.[15]

Another finding from the study of 12th graders was that their hunger for information trumps their comfort. An analysis of one individual's comparisons shows that he made more comparisons with peers of different rank on the continuum than comparisons with peers he assessed as similar, a comparison that ordinarily brings comfort.[16] This finding provides further evidence of the pressure to achieve that adolescents feel, perhaps of a group norm such as the one in this high school of high-achieving males: study hard and get ahead.

There is little question that it can be instructive for professionals who suspect that the adolescent with whom they are working has a defensive glitch to administer some simple comparison protocols, such as those found in the chapters that follow, and analyze the findings together with the adolescent. Comparisons offer a wealth of information since they are products of intuitive actions and not entirely conscious.

Sources of a Defensive Glitch

By addressing what adolescents with a defensive glitch are finding from their comparisons with peers, professionals can discover a gold mine of clues about the concerns that stimulated adolescents' flight from interaction with peers and the comparisons that accompany it. The example of one adolescent's pattern of comparison activity is instructive in the way it provides an understanding of such adolescents' cognitive and emotional condition, as well as their flight to a defensive glitch. The example below also includes discussion of the temptation to diagnose too quickly.

Charles, Age 16

Charles is a student in a traditional school, not one for academically gifted students. Charles used five of the nine comparison options. He did *not* use (1) Dissimilar Other, which adolescents usually use after they have assembled a temporary self structure in order to escape restriction to only similar others, (2) Satiation of Comparison, which adolescents usually demonstrate near the end of the adolescent period when they have completed sufficient comparisons, and (3) Comparison with a Goal, which adolescents usually use in the ending phase of adolescence and indicates that they can think abstractly and are concerned with matters beyond the immediate. In order of prevalence, the comparisons Charles did use were (1) Similar Other, (2) Downward, (3) Range Establishment, (4) Positive Instance, and (5) Upward.

That Similar Other and Downward comparisons were most prevalent for Charles indicates that he was more concerned with emotional comfort than with achievement. Because Charles's Similar Other comparison may have been disappointing, he built himself up by looking at those he considered below him. Because he needed to see where he stood in relation to everyone, he may have used Range Establishment comparisons during classes or afterschool activities. Charles's use of Downward and Range Establishment comparisons may have buoyed him so that he either dared to compare with the "best of the best" (Positive Instance) or, if he was advanced enough cognitively, wished to see just how far he might be able to go. Perhaps in addition to his peers, he had a second comparison group in mind. He could ignore his peers as comparison figures by going above them. This condition would be like comparing with the range of college-age football players without knowing the degree of talent required to be on top: so he would compare with a Heisman Trophy winner, the player selected as the best of the season. As one last try with those around him, Charles returned to comparing with his peers using Upward comparison, which is usually used with someone in one's own group or like oneself. Then, Charles quit comparing. Either the findings on his Upward comparisons reassured him or satiated him (actually a pseudosatiation), and he wanted to stop there and enjoy the feeling, or he was disappointed. If the latter, was he so disappointed that he was a candidate for a defensive glitch? It is too early to jump to this diagnosis. It is best to entertain another hypothesis before assuming such a serious problem so early. Charles may have been so confused that he was behaving with a randomness that required additional investigation.

This possibility of random comparisons disturbed the professional who treated Charles, Dr. Angelis. Her hypothesis was that notwithstanding his outward cooperation, he poked fun at the task and selected comparisons at random. She also entertained the possibility that Charles's disappointment in himself convinced him to *stop comparing*. She wondered how often he stopped himself.

Initially, findings from the comparison analysis caused Dr. Angelis to consider the possibility that Charles had a Veiled or Loner glitch (discussed in chapter 7) with substance abuse, since his comparison patterns appeared illogical, as if there were confusion or fantasy thought. But Dr. Angelis knew that a professional should first consider additional areas to investigate to assure proper hypothesizing and eventual diagnosis— for example, by examining school records, referral information, and information from family. Once Charles was diagnosed, Dr. Angelis would have consulted with her senior colleagues to determine whether he was a candidate for PAL group therapy or individual therapy. If there was suspicion of a defensive glitch, referral to the appropriate specialized therapy would need to follow immediately, among which might be PAL group therapy.

Vulnerable Adolescents

Some adolescents are kept from dynamics of comparative acts not because of defensive flight but because of some type of denial of access to the Peer Arena. They are deprived of a full fundamental and essential developmental experience: the opportunity to form an adult self-structure in the same way almost all their age-mates do. Hopefully, there will be other aspects to their lives that stimulate development and in some way make up for the deprivation. Four categories of adolescents may serve as examples of who is vulnerable.

1. Restricted Adolescents

Restricted adolescents are not in contact with sufficient numbers of age-mate peers, through no fault of their own but rather because of their conditions or situations. Fortunately, nowadays some relief is available from media and computer resources through which these adolescents can view virtual age-mates. Comparative acts can be carried out at least in some limited way. But such virtual comparisons are by no means a route to satisfying these adolescents' attachment needs. They are left frustrated, having no daily contact with lots of peers and not regarding themselves as a member of a peer group, let alone of the many peer groups open to age-mates that together form both the physical and psychological Peer Arena.

Among such restricted adolescents are those hospitalized or in home or institutional care with a chronic physical illness. Some children's hospitals make valiant efforts to bring such youth together as often as possible. But true similar others are hard to find, since illnesses differ, and these adolescents' primary similarity is thus *illness*, a negative self-attribute. Even so, this limited contact brings some relief to the pain of lacking attachment others; at least these adolescents do not feel totally alone and are able to compare characteristics, abilities, and opinions to some degree, albeit a very limited one.

2. Geographically Isolated Adolescents

Rural youth are a good example of geographically isolated adolescents. Notwithstanding the efforts of communities to build district junior and senior high schools where possible, these adolescents lack easy access to large numbers of peers on an informal regular basis. Thus, they suffer lack of opportunities to gather in groups for walks or just a chat on the corner, let alone membership in many groups making up a Peer Arena. Findings from my research with city and suburban adolescents revealed an average of 24 settings where adolescents gathered together or met one another, including afterschool groups and community and neighborhood locations.[17] Geographically isolated adolescents do not enjoy this array of opportunity to choose unique dreams and goals.

3. Unusual-Looking Adolescents

Unusual-looking adolescents may suffer from neurological or other physical problems that are outwardly observable in the way they walk or talk or in their dependence on mechanical aids. Or they may be unusually thin or obese or have a facial or physical deformity. In a period of life during which adolescents search not only for similarity but for individuality, it is ironic that those among them who appear different are avoided. But adolescents' cognitive condition of egocentrism may contribute to this insensitivity. A majority of adolescents are not yet sufficiently developed to understand the complexities of the real world or the importance of each person in it. They are caught in immature perceptions of their own self-importance.

A second factor is active in adolescents' insensitivity. The degree of remaining uncertainty they have about their own self-worth makes them particularly anxious about who their friends are and with whom they are seen. Open-heartedness and concern for others is more rhetoric than reality for most adolescents until they near the end of the adolescent stage. Unfortunately, unusual-looking adolescents lack enough age-mates to have the broad attachment opportunities that are open to their contemporaries. Professionals need to be aware of this deprivation if they are dealing with unusual-looking adolescents who are thus also emotionally restricted.

4. Adolescents Bearing Conflicting Allegiances

Another category of vulnerable adolescents is the large and still growing group who are the offspring of recent ethnic-minority immigrants to the United States. The vast majority of these immigrants aspire to make the United States their home, to carry out the responsibilities of citizenship, and to receive its benefits. They dream of belonging and anticipate the deep joy they will feel when their children are truly "American." But for their adolescent offspring, this benefit also brings problems. At the age when puberty arrives and the process of individuation toward identity and maturity begins, they wrestle with competing signals to be fully American and to retain original cultural identification—conflicting allegiances that complicate establishing their identity. On a daily basis, these adolescents must handle the clash of cultural imperatives alone and with others as they deal with the usual aspects of "adolescent overload."[18]

A General Concern

Of concern with regard to all these groups of vulnerable adolescents is the absence of enough numbers of peers with whom to compare and from whom to model. Real danger exists that these adolescents may not let go of elements borrowed from parents and adults in childhood. For adolescents that do not have contact with a large number of other adolescents, what is readily available is the option of installing a substitution of adult elements they find attractive, a strategy similar but not identical to the false maturity discussed in the next chapter. Professionals currently treating adolescents whom they suspect of developmental delay or aborted development should consider this situation a possible causative factor. It may be that in the environment of these adolescents, other options are few or do not exist.[19]

Professional Opportunities

Special care is due adolescents with few age-mates. Subtly granting them permission will encourage them to act adolescent with the professional or in therapy groups—that is, to differ, to argue, to reconsider their own perspectives, and to change their mind. This encouragement will re-assure adolescents who feel rejected in so many ways and those who are just plain underexposed that they can take a risk without rejection. The structure of the contact might well also include use of as many virtual sources and verbal examples as possible to replicate a Peer Arena experience. Use of PAL group therapy, as discussed later in this book, may also be explored. Attempts might also be made to work with parents to maximize their understanding and assistance. Group therapy with other parents might be considered. The attention that professional societies are beginning to give to these issues deserves encouragement and participation.

7

Understanding Specific Defensive Glitches

As we have seen, adolescents who adopt defensive glitches for one reason or another have found comparisons with peers just too painful to bear and have taken psychological flight. Among them are those who take physical flight in substance use or abuse. Some individuals with glitches can be readily recognized; others are well disguised. All, when chronologically mature, will risk problems in adult functioning, including relationships and employment, though often problems will not be significant until a crisis arises. They also have not learned, through continuing comparisons and deliberations about the findings, which attributes carry intrinsic value and which do not. They will remain psychological adolescents, not developed into full maturity and lacking achievement of a sense of identity. Essentially, they have given up and try to make do. A glitch takes up free time to the extent that it may even interfere with good schoolwork, family responsibilities, or physical activities. Most significant, it takes time away from what adolescents need to do to grow and develop: being with peers during the period of life when most other adolescents do whatever possible to be with them. The single most defining characteristic of an adolescent with a defensive glitch is overinvolvement, possibly even zealotry.

Categories and Types of Defensive Glitches

There are 7 primary categories with a total of 13 types of defensive glitches. Each type has the potential to be fairly benign or extremely serious. Listed in an order that does not indicate severity, they are the following:

False Facade
Kid Copier
Premature Departure: 1. Time-Out, 2. Extended, 3. Forever

Early Commitment: 1. Career, 2. Romantic
Veiled: 1. Person-Dedicated, 2. Mission-Dedicated
Loner: 1. Isolated Game-Player, 2. Parallel Feel-Good Loner
The Pre-Glitch

False Facade

The False Facade glitch is the one most likely never to be discovered. It can continue through a lifetime or unravel at any time. Individuals with this glitch avoid adolescence and assume a mature face, a False Facade. Little that they do is kidlike; they act like adults. What they do and where they go never seems immature. Paradoxically, even though parents should worry about early appearance of such maturity, they are instead often full of pride. False Facade adolescents are among the few who do not get into trouble or argue much and who are comfortable in the company of older folks. They communicate well on timely topics, initiate conversation, and respond clearly. No problems seem to plague this type of adolescent, but what is unseen is their discomfort with age-mates.

The Susceptible

Which type of adolescent tends to adopt this particular defense? Those who enter adolescence with an experience of "praise overload" are most susceptible. Generally these are the children who receive overdoses of positive reinforcement for most of what they do. Not too much that they do escapes some type of praise. Hence, when puberty arrives, with its growth imperatives to cleave to new nurturers, peers, these adolescents expect praise to continue, albeit about different things in different circumstances. Yet as we know, interactions in peer groups can be far from reinforcing. Results of comparative acts range from ego enhancing to ego detrimental, often occurring in the same day.

Most adolescents remain glued to their task of forging their own identity, painful or not. No matter the stress, discontent, or worry, most stay in the game. They do not retreat psychologically or physically, and they earn maturity. But adolescents with a False Facade glitch do not have this kind of strength. Putting a toe into the waters of adolescence is painful from the very beginning, and they immediately want to run away. The pull of the attachment other is strong, but when results of comparisons yield such painful findings, they are willing to give up continuous access to the tantalizing source of comparisons. The appeal of being a "member" cannot compete with the need to escape the feelings of shock, fear, and even panic. What they feel most deeply is "I need to get out."

Outward Appearance and Activity

False Facade adolescents generally

- appear settled;
- do not conform to stereotypes of the laughing, talkative, freethinking, changeable adolescent;
- contrast with the turbulent motion of other adolescents;
- adopt a maturity that is strikingly different from the adolescent norm;
- usually are not seen with gangs of others; and
- prefer quiet activities.

The Downside of Praise

Although there may be other factors involved, adolescents with a False Facade glitch are accustomed to frequent praise and overvaluation and little objective appraisal. Not needing to deal with criticism or be held responsible for mediocre or failing outcomes does not prepare adolescents to withstand emotionally what feels like severe critique from others—or from themselves after disappointing comparative acts. Confusing and continuous changes, frameworklessness, and the frenetic pace of adolescent social interactions alarm them. They are frightened, and with no one with whom to talk about it, they quit.

They take their foot out of the water of adolescence. They do a U-turn and retreat to dependency and imitation. The body keeps growing and physical maturation is uninterrupted, so there is no observable threat to their facade. They stop registering peer data and are comfortable once more. Instead, they regress to copying cognitive elements of parents and elders on a wholesale basis. This tottering, immature aspiring self morphs into an outwardly stable, self-satisfied, and apparently successful adolescent.

The False Facade glitch makes parents feel successful. They feel that rather than having reared a contrary youth, they have become good friends with their child. Who would not be proud of this grown-up, no-trouble adolescent who defies all predictions of contrariness? Adults reinforce the pseudomaturity because they do not know the difference. But adolescents with the False Facade glitch do know: they are aware of peers in school every day, in the neighborhood, and on television, and they are confused because their attraction to peers remains. But this type of adolescent does not attach to peers but instead reattaches to parents and other elders.

A Dangerous Condition

It must be noted that those adopting this defense *do not skip adolescence.* They only appear as if they do. Actually, while the others continue to grow up, they remain adolescent but cast a mature outward appearance. Many remain adolescent in developmental level. *Cognitive* development does not reach its potential because of resistance to really dealing with disappointments and mistakes. Thinking may lay fallow for lack of exercise and challenge. They avoid figuring out how to move forward for fear of suffering humiliations. *Emotional* development is not advanced since avoiding interaction with age-mates circumvents handling anger at those who reject them or jealousy toward peers who appear more skilled. False Facades bury their frustration, save for occasional uncontrollable eruptions. Growth skills lay undeveloped like muscles that have seen no exercise.

Since False Facades' maturation levels in each domain at best remain as they were when the defense took over, they cannot cope well with the demands of life. They remain at risk of faltering in difficult situations. The default route is escape. False Facades are clever at making up authentic-sounding reasons for a quick exit or nonparticipation. Should they have little history of being detected and continue to earn positive reinforcement for adultlike behavior, the defense is supported and the empty adult survives. Development can be halted for many years, if not in perpetuity. It may turn out that the only others with a clue that something is amiss are peers, who find such individuals fundamentally different. Other than to these attachment others, the False Facade presents as admirable.[1]

Detection and Help

Since the adolescence stage consists of tiny steps through its two stages to psychological maturity, if False Facade indicators appear early enough, the professional may sense that all is not well. But if the adolescent is chronologically old enough to be in the "maturity ballpark," very possibly even professionals will miss clues to a proper diagnosis. To diagnose a False Facade, a good history must be taken from the first suspicion that all is not as it appears. Using the appropriate Peer Arena Retrospect (PAR) protocols offered in chapters 8 and 9 can assist in uncovering the deception.

If this facade goes on, perhaps even for a lifetime, someone with this glitch can feel like life is operating on empty. One can have a beautiful body, and perhaps great accomplishment, but the exterior runs on a foreign motor, not one's own. When a False Facade encounters a critical situation or a life crisis, he or she may need psychotherapy because the facade is insufficient. Crises cover a range such as domestic disruptions like a love affair or a marriage, business crises like drops in financial markets or being overlooked for promotion, and criminal behaviors like stealing or causing harm to a loved one in the heat of anger. In other words, False Facades do not deal well with painful experiences in the psychological arena. They have built little psycho-emotional strength through interactional attachment to adolescent peers, regardless of the joy or the pain of those experiences. Over the years, False Facades continue to hide from, and not deal with, life's tough realities.

Accordingly, this defensive glitch category is perhaps the most primitive of all glitches. It is indeed a paradox: the adolescent who appears so mature so early is the adolescent who is unable to grow because of a lack of attachment nurturance.[2]

The Kid Copier

The Kid Copier is a close cousin to the False Facade. This individual looks like a kid and acts like a kid but is not really a kid. Instead of managing the necessary rigors of psychological growth when the going gets tough, this adolescent copies wholesale just as the False Facade does. But there is an important difference: for the Kid Copier, the flight is not immediate; the Kid Copier engages with Peer Arena groups for a short time. But when painful results of comparisons begin to come on a regular basis and are unbearable, there is a flight to copying. But Kid Copiers do develop some, so the object of their copying is not adults but contemporaries, kids to whom they have begun to attach. Their outward demeanor, then, is not adultlike but kidlike. They do not appear different, but cognitive elements that they borrow wholesale early on undergo no examination, maintenance work, growth, or rejection. They stay linked to whatever they see as the new growth of those whom they have copied. The Kid Copier continues through adolescence to reflect the surface picture. There is no internal change. The only authentic growth is physical. Cognitive, emotional, and social domains continue unexercised and remain generally at the level they were when the glitch was adopted.

While age-mates move on to more suitable attachment peers and move out of Stage 1 to Stage 2 adolescence, Kid Copiers often prefer to be with those younger than they are, including younger siblings or relatives. Such a preference may appear unusual for adolescents of that chronological age, but when "it is family," it can be rationalized. Unfortunately, unless this glitch is interrupted, it continues as the adolescent ages, and a psychologically undeveloped youth reaches physical maturity and advanced chronological age unfit for psychological maturity. At some point along the way, Kid Copiers' "younger" state may become evident, for example, in schoolwork, social isolation, excessive interaction with younger children, interests that seem young for the age, and disruptive behaviors that display an inner awareness that the route they have taken is not working.

On the outside, since Kid Copiers act like a kid and think like a very young adolescent, they have no real interest in being with adults, as do their False Facade cousins. And adults likewise have no interest in Kid Copiers. Parents do not beam with pride and reinforce their offspring with praise. In fact, as years go on, they question why their children have no friends their own age. It becomes harder for Kid Copiers to maintain a happy countenance. Some do find a strategy that works. They assume a kidlike charm that can make them a mascot of sorts with age-mates or with parents and other family members—at least for a while.

But the attachment that Kid Copiers have to peers is half or three-quarters baked. They are attracted to peers, but the attraction is not reciprocal. Once-familiar age-mates generally cease offering friendship. Yet Kid Copiers can play an important role in peer interaction and may be valued for it: they are good targets for Downward comparison. They may even be seen as a figure for a Similar Other or even an Upward comparison, for their cooperation, good spirit, or willingness to take a small role in activities or to do the dirty work. But Kid Copiers' front is borrowed, and their inner qualities are insufficient to attract true attachment. Because this type of adolescent is not the type that other adolescents seek out, the Kid Copier will never feel the total involvement that adolescents give one another for periods of time until they find new needs and new comparison figures.[3]

Professionals may be able to identify Kid Copiers by observing their behavior. They often hang back and try to be part of whatever group they are with. Such youth do not volunteer in class, and some have an increasingly hard time with work as it becomes more complex. Since they are good at copying, they try their best at memorizing. Peers feel that there is something inauthentic about them. Psycho-dynamically, their retreat from peers may transform into retreat from challenges. Consequently, cognitive, emotional, and social growth may each show impact. It is a confusing picture because they desire to copy the achievers but their own resources become fewer as others move along. Eventually, they may come to the attention of school counselors and clinics, who need be alert to the unique pattern of Kid Copiers.

Adult Life

The Kid Copier at best can become only an adolescent in adult clothes. Whereas the False Facade has copied the cognitive elements of adults and thus gets along well in adult settings, the Kid Copier's cognitive elements are copied from adolescents. Thus, the Kid Copier manages to be accepted in the Peer Arena, but in adult life difficulties arise in sustaining new relationships, in employment situations, and even with a mate and children. Problem issues may crop up at almost any critical period. Kid Copiers look mature, but that is where their maturity ends.

Differences between False Facades and Kid Copiers

- False Facades have a history of overdone reinforcements. Kid Copiers do not.
- False Facades do not psychologically stay in the Peer Arena long enough to borrow self-elements from peers. Kid Copiers do reach this state of borrowing, a necessary stop on the way to adulthood.
- False Facades are content to maintain self-elements of adults. They do not reenter the Peer Arena psychologically or, except for school, physically. Kid Copiers are content to continue copying what their peers display. They, too, do not intensively compare or work with their findings. Hence, their attachment is limited to filling their copying needs.
- False Facades do not attach to peers. Kid Copiers' attachment is half-baked; full outreach from them to peers is occasional and thus only partially reciprocated.

- False Facades appear adultlike. Kid Copiers appear as young adolescents.
- False Facades copy adult self-elements. Kid Copiers copy those of adolescents.

Disadvantages

There are distinct disadvantages for Kid Copiers. False Facades appear adult, so peers are not interested in them. Peers find Kid Copiers inscrutable and thus a bit more complex to figure out. On the one hand, Kid Copiers act like an adolescent, but they are nearly impossible to engage in any depth, even around common interests. But on the other hand, they appear pleasant and interested. For example, if Kid Copiers hear a peer describing a wonderful CD, they buy it also. Since they bring little else to this decision and are just copying, they have no suggestions to offer in return. They do not have the goods of adolescence, only the cover.

In both cases, since the facsimile self that is constructed is not one's own, findings from comparisons do not really hurt. Adolescents with these types of glitches look but do not register the data that comparisons bring. As a result, a lot of the data they collect are disorganized and dysfunctional, and they are not able to learn and grow. Copying from many others is also time consuming, and frustration can grow in addition to uncertainty. This frustration is occasionally expressed in biting words by the False Facade and disruptive behavior in the Kid Copier.

Premature Departure Glitches

1. Time-Out

The Time-Out adolescent frequently seeks to stay home from school. This glitch is different from the need for a day or two away from school that occurs rather infrequently during any school year and can be regarded as a positive adaptive request. Responsible parents watch days out of school very carefully, although they most likely have little idea why a day out is needed. They may understand why kids would prefer to stay out of school if there are social matters that do not seem to be going well for them. But because the frequency of adolescents' automatically occurring comparative acts and their toll are usually unknown to parents, professionals may need to explain to parents the developmental work that occurs simultaneous to academic learning and assure them that limited time out for developmental work on occasion is as appropriate as time for academic homework.

In contrast to such a healthy need for a limited time-out, the adolescent with a Time-Out defensive glitch makes the request frequently, as often as two to three times a month. Such frequent requests do not indicate an adaptive movement. The Time-Out adolescent needs to get away from the roar of the adolescent crowd in order to assemble and reframe notions about a number of matters. Expressions such as "I can't get my head together" are not uncommon. Most pressing for them is rethinking the quality of self-elements that they already possess as compared to those in others that appear worth assimilating. Some need time to think about, for example, whether the elements are really them or whether adopting them is a good or bad idea. They feel that answering such questions may require more time than they have been able to set aside in a very busy life.

Adolescents do not deliberate these issues consciously. They act subliminally. Adolescents with Time-Out glitches need more time away from the Peer Arena before the crush of even more comparative acts. They wish to mull them over and to reassemble all they see and hear. Emotionally, they want time away from wounds of disappointing findings. Yet there is risk in stepping back from the Peer Arena for this sort of time-out for assessment. It can be too comfortable a relief from comparisons—enough to want *even more* time away from comparison peers.

2. Extended

The Extended glitch is a step more serious than the Time-Out one and can develop into the Forever glitch if not attended to in time. The adolescent with the Extended glitch attempts, like the others, to spend time away from peers—indeed, as much as possible. Staying out of school is especially important since the numbers of peers encountered there are so large. Usually, obtaining parental permission for a few days away has its limits. Other routes to avoidance include lies, faking serious illness, or even deliberately incurring self-harm, such as a bloody nose, throwing up, or even body cuts. Adolescents can be very creative in coming up with new reasons if the disappointment to be avoided is strong.

AN EXAMPLE: ELLEN, AGE 13

Ellen received disappointing news about her grades in two subjects. She was totally embarrassed. She knew she could give her parents excuses.

A bigger concern was what her peers would think if they found out. At home that evening, she suggested to her overworked mother, who had earlier complained about not getting time to iron or repair clothing for weeks, "If I could have the time, I would do it for you. Why don't I stay home tomorrow, or for a few days? I would get it all done for you." This type of request could send a feel-good message to parents: "Such an altruistic offer!" But since Ellen rarely made such an offer, it should have made Ellen's mother somewhat suspicious. It did not, however. Despite the glow of the sentiment, Ellen's mother had to go to work, and Ellen was too young to be left alone all day in their large suburban home. Ellen was disappointed. She needed time off desperately. School had been a nightmare since she had gotten her grades. In addition to thinking about herself as really dumb, Ellen was sure her friends would see her that way. The names of high achievers were slated for posting, and her name would not be among them. She was certain she would be regarded among the "lowest of the low." Translated into DFI terms, the subliminal comparisons would be active and would yield very bad news. Ellen needed to find a way to be absent for a while until it all blew over. This was not the first time she had done this.

Ellen would not share her concerns about herself with friends. She feared that doing so would draw even more awareness to her shortcomings. She also would not share her concerns with elders, who might laugh at her. So her anxieties were left to grow. This type of problem is generally not so difficult for adolescents who excel in many areas, but for Ellen it occurred in science and math, where success for her had been the rule. This customary strength had balanced out some areas in which she was not as successful as the others. She was devastated by this failure in her strong subjects and could think of nothing else. And things did not get better for Ellen; they got worse. She began to truant. She even ran away, though thankfully, she returned home the next day. The shock of her behavior shook the family. She was referred to the school psychologist.

DANGEROUS DISTORTIONS

A passing insult or an unexpected low performance can be highly exaggerated cognitively and emotionally. Recall the cognitive impression in early through middle adolescence of the "imaginary audience" referred to in chapter 6. Paired with "the group under the couch phenomenon"— the belief among adolescents that peers are always present to hear, see, and talk about everything[4]—the certainty is strong that faults cannot be hidden. This perception can become exaggerated if reasoned input is not available. It is crucial for professionals to be aware of the power of these ever-present unseen critics whom adolescents fear. Extreme exaggerations may lead to serious conditions that require therapeutic attention, particularly to guard against the behavior's intensifying.

In order to prevent the Extended glitch from becoming a Forever glitch, professionals need to enlist assistance from parents and elders to pay close attention to the adolescent's physical condition, to be on the lookout for any changes, and to safeguard good health. They should also be cautioned to be alert for adolescents' frequent requests for time out, noncustomary activities, spending a lot of time in their room, excessive e-mail from undisclosed correspondents, resistance to resuming a regular schedule, and sour or depressed demeanor or mood. This close surveillance requires dedication. Professional support for these extended efforts contribute greatly to parents' motivation and reduce the pressure brought on them by *feeling alone*.

3. Forever

The Premature Departure Forever glitch applies to adolescents who have totally abandoned the Peer Arena. These adolescents shut down all comparisons and avoid interactions with peers to every extent possible. When with contemporaries, they speak about surface matters—places, events, and objects but not the people involved or what kind of time they had. They appear to move aimlessly, possibly searching for settings where comparisons are absent. The isolation they crave may lead them to take risks, since the need for emotional stroking is intense, as is a need for positive recognition. Paradoxically, distancing themselves from their source of cognitive and emotional sustenance defeats the goals they long for. These are very sad adolescents. What they decide to do depends on the depth of their hurt and sadness.

Often, the Forever glitch begins with truanting. These adolescents wish to avoid school classrooms and hallways. For the same reason, males in particular stay off athletic fields. Other Forever glitch adolescents quit school altogether. Some become delinquents, either acting alone or with a group. There is emotional excitement about taking risks, so they feel a little blood in their veins. Success, even in their delinquency, may help them feel happy for a while. They often talk about what they can acquire, and they assure whoever joins in their escapade that they too will feel satisfied.

This behavior is serious in yet another way. It puts affected adolescents at risk of being attracted to a second glitch that has body ramifications, the Parallel Feel-Good Loner, described later in this chapter. All such adolescents are at risk for adopting other glitches.

Early Commitment Glitches

1. Career

The history of an adolescent with an Early Commitment Career glitch is similar to that of the False Facade. Both have received an overage of praise. Such adolescents find that peer evaluations can be at such variance from those accorded by elders that it stirs a very strong desire to escape them. Thus, they announce in late-middle or early-late adolescence that they have selected a career to follow and are glad to detail what it is. They often fall short on answering why they have chosen what they have, except perhaps that they are following a family member. They reason that this early preference gives them the rationale to stop comparing themselves with age-mates, but it is counterproductive to do so since they are not yet in possession of their own identity, which comes only after one knows oneself very well. Only then can a career be selected that fits for and with oneself. There is, however, a major difference between the False Facade and the Career glitch: although both escape early, the Career glitch adolescent has completed Stage 1 and has begun Stage 2, in which the particulars of career and personal aspirations are dissected with a fine-tooth comb. Comparisons become more precise, intense, and very serious. These comparisons have to do with matters of the future: career and mate.

Like False Facades, adolescents with Career glitches receive early reinforcements of high achievement and experience high self-worth. These adolescents fare well in Stage 1, in which comparisons are more diffuse and not specifically targeted like those of Stage 2, in which one evaluates the self for present *and future* life. Thus, although those with Career glitches do not flee the Peer Arena almost immediately in Stage 1, as do False Facades, when the going gets tough in Stage 2, they do flee. Both categories are similar in relishing seeing themselves as in a superior position. Both internal expectations as well as external ones from others—parents and older siblings, teachers, religious figures, employers, other community figures—can add pressure that contributes to the need for escape and development of this glitch. These adolescents are not equipped to cope with negative comparisons, which are so contrary to their prior self-impressions.

AN EXAMPLE: RONALD, AGE 17

Ronald needed to lick his wounds from serious overestimation of his self-worth. This was the result of his comparative findings with peers in the group of similar others—college-bound seniors, as he was. In Stage 2 adolescence, the individual has assembled a temporary self structure and has a general idea of what he or she would like to pursue in life. Studies support the idea that late adolescents have a reduced need for a large number of friends. These studies disclose that in the junior and senior years of high school cliques form that are more exclusive and include others like oneself.[5] Ronald was eager to limit his friends to those more like him. Very close examination of peers' attributes helps one calculate one's own career success possibilities. For example, assessing one's violin talent compared to others may reveal whether one ranks high enough to play in an orchestra or be a soloist or whether one must consider playing the violin as an avocation only. In Ronald's case, his interest was in physics. But his comparative findings were devastating because his academic record was far below that of his peers. He no longer saw himself as being of the same high caliber in math or physics courses as other pre-scientists in the group. Ronald also carried out comparisons with the range of others important to him so he could assess where he ranked. And he compared with some who were reaching for the same goal as he was to determine how far along they were and where he stood. In both respects, his findings were disappointing. Fortunately for Ronald, he knew no young scientist who could represent the positive instance of scientific ability—the closest one could come to perfection. Thus, he was spared yet another early disillusionment.

Others towered above his own abilities, or so he perceived the distance of their rank. Still, he persevered to compare with others of high ability on all sorts of parameters, adding data to reveal how high he could aspire in his chosen field of physics compared to others after whom he had modeled himself. These findings also shocked Ronald. He felt disbelief, then resentment, followed by fear. His poor findings were too difficult to deal with. He brought his ambitions to study physics to an abrupt halt. He shut down and decided to seek a different career.

Ronald was 17 years old when this happened—far from completion of growth and development. Had he sought professional help rather than abruptly changing career plans, the professional would have had the opportunity to counsel him to wait a few years until his cognitive development was complete to judge more accurately where his talents lay. Perhaps he was a slow cognitive developer. But Ronald had been too scared and too hurt to do anything but jump to a quick resolution of excruciating pain, thus closing out the field of his dreams.

EMOTION OVER REASON

Future pursuits and especially vocations and careers are emotionally laden for adolescents, even though these emotions are based on cognitive information. Ronald's plans were lofty—among them applications to prestigious honor societies. He abruptly gave up all his plans because of pain-filled fear that his inadequacies would be discovered. Distorted thought was the outcome: keep the true Ronald undiscovered and live with whatever was left of the myth about his high level of scientific ability.

Too much praise can be detrimental to adolescents. Expressed by those with the most positive of intentions, it distorts the reality of real achievement. Adolescents who are its recipients can have an exceptionally hard time dealing with negative outcomes of comparisons. Professionals can work with them to retain their goals, work to alter the route toward them and its timing.

Ronald abruptly announced in his senior year in high school that he would enroll in a midwestern state university to study for a degree in agronomy. Ronald came from a family with many academics. His father was a professor of European history. By contrast, Ronald enjoyed his garden, something his mother had introduced him to. He was interested in how things grow. He did well in this subject and was praised for it. His decision to stay with science, but in a field in which he saw a greater opportunity for the choice of pure or applied science, indicates that he was dealing with reality, though in a limited way. The emotions that had led him to very high aspirations were still in play. Ronald expressed an interest in cereal crops, and he planned to pursue a life of research after he received his Ph.D. He had not yet decided whether he would perform this research as an academic or in industry, though probably in industry, which could be considered an applied field. Thus, although he altered the direction of his ambition, he had not quite given up its essence. It remained to be seen whether he could succeed and how long it would take to find out.

Ronald was well on his way to adopting an Early Commitment Career glitch. Thus, he was elated that when he shared his plans, his parents were proud and his siblings excited. Relatives were delighted that he would be following the family tradition of academic pursuit. Ronald's outstanding academic record was referred to and his character was lauded. Once more, all was well. Best of all, he no longer needed to compare his abilities with anyone. He closed off. *Escape to defensive glitches is rarely a thought-out plan; they are emotionally inspired and acted on.*

Ronald was committing to go to school far away in unfamiliar territory. Although doing so would be a little frightening to begin with, he reasoned that no one he knew would go from the East to the Midwest for college. He could start all over again. He assumed his fellow students would be less talented since he saw the Midwest as an unsophisticated region of United States.

Yet he felt some doubt. It would be good to be free to be himself, but he was still haunted about how to rate himself. The initial rush of his announcement to his peers helped. He was admired for such an interesting future goal. He was the center of interest and questions. Since he was not competing for a spot in an eastern college, it seemed to him that others were easier on him.

Had the Career glitch helped him be easier on himself? So far, the answer was yes. Would it continue? Yes, for a while. How long that while lasted would depend on future circumstances, academic achievement, and adjustments, healthy or otherwise, that Ronald would make.

"ADVANTAGES" OF THE EARLY COMMITMENT CAREER GLITCH

Defensive glitches can bring some advantages in addition to the disadvantages escape from comparison findings cause. Ironically, adolescents with Career glitches, as with False Facade glitches, are lauded precisely because such individuals do not appear lost, confused, or hurting. They speak with certainty and maturity. Friends and relatives reassure parents that they have parented appropriately. Pride in their child's obvious maturity further reinforces the Career glitch choice, which unbeknownst to parents was a choice made out of desperation.

For effective decision-making, there must first be completion in growth and integration of the four domains of development. This integration yields maturity sufficient to make rational, informed decisions, not psychologically defensive ones. An Early Commitment Career glitch born out of disappointment in oneself seals oneself away from taking on challenges of higher-level courses in new fields en route to discovery of a true career fit. Yet school personnel and perhaps church and community can show pride in Career glitch adolescents as role models for age-mates still uncertain about their future career direction. All these accolades also bring silent pressure. Elders do not realize that it is precisely allowing temporary confusion to play itself out to its eventual resolution that then ends in solid career choice.

Since this flight pattern appears on the surface as a positive academically and socially, adolescents with Career glitches can become Upward comparison models. This notoriety brings popularity, supporting their continuing as a "member" physically and psychologically. These adolescents become emotionally comfortable. They are welcomed and happily free from carrying on comparative acts with peers; they turn off. The groups of the Peer Arena are now a relaxing, *fun* place to be.

Yet, underneath it all, as in the case of most glitches, something deep is missing. These adolescents secure the appearance of being one of the gang along with the initial praise they receive, but they do not feel themselves to be part of the group. The emotional pleasure of reciprocal attachments with peers is markedly diminished, if not totally gone by the wayside. Early Commitment Career adolescents are subliminally aware that they *are not* what others see.

EVENTUAL DISADVANTAGE

The Career glitch adolescent oftentimes is increasingly seen as different from others. This difference is usually attributed to how much further ahead they are. Such adolescents not only have a tendency to be more conservative in their interests but may choose to socialize with older adolescents or even young adults. Generally, their mature tastes bring welcome from members of an older crowd. Like the False Facade, they do well with those quite a bit older than they are. Yet when their age-mates become adults, once again Career glitch adolescents must struggle to keep up. They have never achieved identity.

Age-mates are particularly sensitive to the authenticity or veneer displayed by members of their age cohort. Most evident to them is one's not having the maturity necessary to discriminate between what is essential and what is peripheral to the objective at hand, be it professional, social, or in relationships. Thus, Career glitch adolescents are at risk with their fully developed peers. Furthermore, notwithstanding academic or vocational skill or knowledge, the emotional component of such adolescents is still undeveloped, and the risk is great that professional productivity will be affected by the exaggerated need they have for reassuring praise and by their inability to deal with critique, problems that can be manifested in mood swings, inability to take correction, and need to control.

Paradoxically, supposedly early-maturing Career glitch adolescents rarely, if ever, feel confident. This lack of confidence is detectable in their lack of skill at the small talk that is a customary prelude to serious discussion of the business at hand. It may be that only when an exchange is task related does the vulnerability of the Career glitch remain hidden. Professionals should keep this type of glitch in mind when they work with highly skilled individuals who have trouble keeping jobs.

2. Romantic

The Early Commitment Romantic glitch is also rooted in escape from overwhelming self-disappointment, a product of lower-than-acceptable outcomes of comparisons. This holds true not only for intellectual comparisons but for comparisons of physical characteristics, one's looks. As discussed earlier, the stronger the young person is psycho-emotionally at the onset of adolescence, puberty, the more equipped he or she is to cope with changes and with the affronts encountered.

Physical growth causes middle and late adolescents to be keenly aware of one another's physical characteristics. Comparison of these characteristics becomes highly important to them as newly experienced physical attraction develops. Romance begins to be a priority, and they pay a lot of attention to who is successful and who is not in attracting a romantic other. It is necessary to factor in this emotional aspect of physical/biological growth when working with older adolescents and those who mature early.

For some adolescents, these startling changes are relatively easy to deal with; for others, they are not. Once again, peer awareness and opinion make adolescents emotionally vulnerable as they try to become comfortable with a changing body and its outward appearance. Some adolescents gain by this focus, while others lose. Since romance is accompanied by sexually targeted comparisons, late maturers and those who do not see themselves as physically attractive can feel uncomfortable. This discomfort ranges from mild to severe.

AN UNEXPECTED OPPORTUNITY

The period of newly experienced sexuality brings another opportunity: the escape from comparison pain through adoption of a Romantic defensive glitch. Adolescents who are intensely disappointed by findings from comparative acts can be mollified by the satisfaction of an exciting and intense romantic relationship. Maintaining the romance rises to central prominence, leaving room for little else of significance. This is a Romantic glitch.

The Romantic glitch is also appealing to those who do see themselves as physically attractive but who need ego bolstering. Thus, whether these adolescents see themselves as attractive or not, they welcome attentions by an admirer whose attraction to them bolsters their ego. For some, such attention may be just enough to help them through a bad time. For others, who are not faring as well, the admirer offers an escape route. Psychologically, one can become consumed with the other; behaviorally, it may serve both soul and body to be together as much as possible to be strengthened by physical attentiveness and love. Generally, this type of glitch involves one of four types of relationship:

- Persons A and B are overly engrossed with each other. Both have Romantic glitches.
- Person A is overly engrossed with person B, but person B's emotions, though intense, do not match the same intensity.
- Person C is aggressively courted by person D. Person C entered adolescence psychologically weak and suffers from disappointing comparison findings. The immediate benefits of romantic overinvolvement emotionally, physically, and in time commitment serve person C well for psychological escape. Essentially, person C regresses to copying by identifying with the emotions of a romantic partner, person D, and inserting those emotions in his or her cognitive structure as his or her own. Thus, person C feels mature and strong.
- Person D sorely needs the overinvolvement of person C because it is ego enhancing to be adored by a person who is so good-looking or who has such an intellect or other virtues.

The Romantic glitch relationship is intense. The individuals in the couple are together almost every free moment and are in touch by cell phone or e-mail when apart. Their relationship is a constant focus, acting to shut out all other stimuli, especially those coming from comparative acts with age-mates. As exemplified by the four types just described, partners generally differ in the depth of their need for escape from comparative acts and from the Peer Arena. Yet they want to be thought of primarily as a couple. Notwithstanding this cover, professionals need be alert that the couple is made up of two individuals, each with unique needs.

THE RELATIONSHIP

The Romantic glitch relationship differs from those for which attraction is the sole basis. The Romantic glitch attachment gets its intensity from the unconscious safety it brings as immersion with the loved one blocks out the *consequence* of others—their characteristics, abilities, and goals. The members of the couple live for the moments they are together and separate psychologically from all others. Sadly, the basis of their relationship is loss of respect for and faith in oneself.

The professional, and perhaps even others, will sense desperation in this sort of relationship, which protects an individual's inability to be alone. One or both members of the couple may cling to the other. Publicly, the couple is seen together almost always. They meet with others only when they have each other's protection, and they escape comparison by turning all their psychological and physical efforts to affectionate or caretaking gestures toward each other. Age-mates may envy, revere, honor, or disdain the couple privately, but they usually accept the relationship publicly. In private conversations, some might mention the prematurity of such exclusive involvement and question the reason for it, hinting that something is amiss. Others may wish they had the same good luck.

To those unaware of DFI, the Romantic glitch may be attributed to mature passion or sexual drive. It is not usually seen for what it is: avoidance and escape.

THE RISKS

The danger in the Romantic glitch lies in how long the overinvolvement lasts and what development may be missed altogether. The professional should bear in mind the danger of the possibility of a gradual but intensifying progression that is similar to the one in the Premature Departure glitch: Time-Out, then Extended, then Forever.

The Romantic glitch is similar to the Career glitch in the public response to it. It is generally seen as natural and socially acceptable, even if a bit premature. But social acceptance coming from other adolescents is quite unique: it is rooted in reserving time for one's own psychological business; still egocentric, adolescents do not wish to spend too much time on others.

Veiled Glitches

The use of the term *veiled* to describe these glitches implies that adolescents who have them for the most part remain at a distance from others; that characteristic is contrary to what is generally the case with the False Facade, who participates in and is welcomed into the company of elders. Adolescents with Veiled glitches appear intriguing and interesting, and they involve themselves with persons or causes that are generally foreign to elders. They can also differ from False Facades in that their glitch may involve a noteworthy social purpose.

1. Person-Dedicated

The Person-Dedicated glitch is an extended, almost exclusive involvement with another person. As with the other glitches within the category of Veiled glitches, the Person-Dedicated glitch is adopted by adolescents who are in middle adolescence or beyond. The adolescent taking defensive flight to a Person-Dedicated glitch is not lauded for any personal achievement, as are those with False Facade or Career glitches. They also do not engage in antisocial or social problem behavior. Yet they have sufficient angst from Peer Arena comparative acts to seek escape. They also do not measure up to self-expectations and suffer because of it. Although their escape route is visible, it is rarely recognized as an escape. In fact, as with adolescents with False Facade and Career glitches, those with Person-Dedicated glitches earn considerable respect from certain quarters.

OUTWARD APPEARANCES

An adolescent with a Person-Dedicated glitch is very likely to be involved with a fascinating person who is quite a few years older, for example, a schoolteacher whose research absorbs the adolescent, a retired empty-nester who welcomes a youngster's interest in model airplanes, a nutritionist who has an adolescent vegetarian as a helper, or a photographer whose work is admired by an artistic youth who accepts a job as a helper. (Or, conversely and more rarely, the glitch may involve dedication to a younger person, such as after-school care for a child with disabilities.) Parents generally feel positive about their child's having what they consider to be a maturing experience; thus, many times the relationship does not make parents uncomfortable. This relationship is very different from a crush, which is a natural, time-limited infatuation with an older idol, often seen as part of the developmental schedule of emotional and eventually sexual maturity.[6]

AN INAPPROPRIATE IDENTIFICATION

The Person-Dedicated glitch, as opposed to a well-defined friendship, is identifiable by its intensity and the extreme dedication demonstrated by the adolescent, who usually has a fantasized identification with the object of the dedication. This identification convinces adolescents that their developmental process is finished; they have discovered who they are. This glitch offers psychological fusion of the adolescent with the older person as a bulwark against the pain of isolation and self-doubt. It can even go so far that the adolescent feels as if he or she has absorbed the selected person, which allows the adolescent to experience a pseudorelevance and pseudoimportance. This experience is ego enhancing for a youth struggling with ego deflation. This intense focus and identification with another person should not be ignored.

It is important to remember that identification with many self-elements of favorite others can be quite appropriate in earliest adolescence as the need to individuate begins. The cognitive structure is then emptied one by one of elements previously borrowed from parents so as not to jeopardize possession of a full sense of self. But adolescent identification with self-elements of peers is a process of borrowing for tryout only. In the normative process, adolescents immediately engage comparative acts to try out each element's function and fit. "Is it appropriate to be part of me? Do I want it to be?" These extended series of individual tryouts are quite different from wholesale adoption.

In order to satisfy the desire for true commitment to another individual, an adolescent must successfully complete the Peer Arena developmental task of achieving psychological identity. Identification cannot substitute for this task. The Person-Dedicated glitch and the Mission-Dedicated glitch (to be discussed shortly) are comparable to the False Facade in that these adolescents' overinvolvement with nonpeers protects them against the adolescent imperative to interact psychologically with peers and fulfill developmental tasks.[7]

REMEDIATION EFFORTS

In addressing the Person-Dedicated glitch, parents and professionals must make an effort to initiate a process of reducing the adolescent's contact with the object of dedication. Relevant others should be involved in this process. Generally, individuals who are the target of the adolescent's identification will be cooperative if they understand the stakes, namely, getting the adolescent back on the road to proper developmental process by interacting with peer age-mates in the groups of the Peer Arena and through the dynamics spawned by that interaction.

2. Mission-Dedicated

Another means of escape from painful disappointments in findings from comparative acts is to spend every minute possible on a cause. The cause may range from national political involvement to day-to-day human service work, or it may involve raising funds for an already-established cause or one the adolescent creatively develops him- or herself. Like the Person-Dedicated glitch, the Mission-Dedicated glitch also does not show in overt behaviors that are suspect. In fact, like other glitch cousins discussed earlier, he or she is often admired, this time for selflessness. Focus on a mission is an effective decoy, even to oneself. This tactic is quite clever in that the notion of selflessness tends to appeal to adolescents as well as to adults.

A WARNING NOT TO IGNORE

The cue to the Mission-Dedicated glitch is excessive investment of time in one activity. The nobility of the mission may successfully veil defensive flight. The professional may find the behavior of someone with this glitch at variance with more common concerns about overactive, unsettled adolescents. Nonetheless, *any* lengthy commitment of time should be suspect and raise an alarm for parents and for professionals.

AN EFFECTIVE DECEPTION

Like some other glitches described earlier, Mission-Dedicated adolescents do not appear as the conventional image of a failed adolescent at all. Yet there is an interesting contradiction that reveals the overinvolvement to be an escape route from comparative-act dynamics. The adolescent's objective reason for overinvolvement in the mission is that it meets one or more of the adolescent's values; the contradiction is that such values can exist only when one is anchored in a mature self.[8] Adolescence is the road between childhood and maturity, and values cannot be attached to a core of self that does not yet exist. These adolescents manifest facsimile values, developed to meet their own purposes.

The cause to which an adolescent with a Mission-Dedicated glitch is devoted provides a perfect reason to avoid being with age-mates, other than a few others who are also attracted to the mission. It provides a self-protective rationale to others and to the adolescent him- or herself for avoidance of Peer Arena interactions, which is attributed to the importance of the mission. If the adolescent's enterprise meets with success, he or she for a time becomes an Upward comparison figure and is very popular. In the meantime, he or she cuts off comparative acts and finds that comfortable. But when the mission nears its end, a new mission must be found very quickly in order not to endanger the integrity of the glitch.

Loner Glitches

1. Isolated Game-Player

The Isolated Game-Player adolescent seems strange to some, interesting to others, and suspect to a few. He or she does not make trouble for others, but the pain he or she feels is very deep. These youth seek aloneness to rest, and they prefer aloneness to risking peer settings, where comparative acts automatically start. They have been exposed too many times to findings that make them feel inferior and come to believe that it is better to be alone and to entertain oneself. Over time, this isolation desensitizes them to comparison stimuli.

The Isolated Game-Player Loner may select a defensive route that is reminiscent of the Veiled glitches. But in this case, rather than the total involvement being with a person or a cause, it is with an inanimate object such as a bicycle or chemistry set or perhaps a hobby or a game such as solitary chess. Of course, many people have hobbies, but what marks a hobby as a defensive escape is the degree of intensity committed to it. For the Isolated Game-Player Loner there is an overcommitment of time and energy that leaves none with which to see developmental comparison tasks to the end. Psychological and emotional development is stopped short in favor of the solace of solitary interests with which these adolescents fill their days.

With this type of Loner, another serious danger is just over the horizon. As games and tasks begin to lose some luster, Isolated Game-Player Loners are at risk for drug and alcohol use or abuse. They can eliminate any possible time for reflecting on comparisons by obliterating normal consciousness through drugs or drinking.

These adolescents may find relief from within for a time. But their thinking or reading about how drug or alcohol abuse can ravage the body can become frightening to them, notwithstanding the numbing effect of the substances. The safety that this type of Loner seeks is again threatened, just as comparison results threatened safety from pain. For those adolescents who become more serious substance abusers, there is a far less optimistic prognosis. Strongly addicted adolescents have a hard road ahead. They must take advantage of medical know-how and specialized inpatient as well as outpatient programs. For some, tragically, relief seems unattainable, and they choose suicide over life.

For those who stayed with games and did not descend into substance abuse, changing to more complex and engrossing games may work to suppress fears that arise from time to time. Professionals need to be sure not to confuse an extremely avid interest in computer or noncomputer games with healthy behavior, notwithstanding adolescents' testimony to that effect. Their illness is not gone; its symptoms are taking different forms.

2. Parallel Feel-Good Loner

The second Loner glitch is the individual who wishes to retain a connection with peers but seeks to avoid settings where dynamic comparative acts are active. This person is one who is innovative and clever and did well up until the very end of the primary Peer Arena period (Stage 1). The experience was so good for so long that he or she does not desire separation from peers; he or she wants this connection but no more pain from comparative acts. Therefore, the task of such adolescents is to find a group or groups in which they will not be confronted with negative findings as strongly as in the past.

The first challenge is to gain acceptance in a group that appears benign—comfortable and nonjudgmental. A number of groups answer these criteria. They are easily accessible, and members ask few questions. Unlike most other groups of adolescents, all that members need to know is whether the new member will join in the crowd activity. The entrance fee may be using alcohol or drugs, providing funds to pay for group activities such as dancing to popular CDs, catering to the constant need to find the latest thing, providing food and drink to the group, or after a while, procuring substances for the group. The applicant to the group need only say yes to membership and generally participate in the partying. This group environment is nonjudgmental. As long as one participates and contributes money or goods, one's qualities are not subject to evaluation. The new member is welcomed as-is. An important benefit is the anything-goes mindset. When these adolescents are under the influence, all judgments are suspended. This type of free, nonjudgmental, nonrejecting atmosphere offers an environment that feels very different from the environment from which the adolescent has escaped: it feels good.

The action in such groups is parallel: true interaction is absent, and exchanges between members are about objective facts. The exchange of information, materials, and monies contributes to supporting a fantasy of age-appropriate involvement. But the reality is that these adolescents suffer from sharply aborted development, and they risk further regression. The risk of this outcome is not feared, however, because it is not recognized. The model of involvement at work for those with this glitch is reminiscent of the parallel play of very young children, a likeness that clearly points to the level to which those who adopt this defense can regress. The Parallel Feel-Good Loner is a grave defensive glitch.

The Pre-Glitch

Now that we have reviewed various types of defensive glitches, we turn our attention to a precursor to a glitch, the Pre-Glitch, which may forewarn of potentially more serious glitches to come. This category is not as worrisome as those previously discussed, but it does require parental attention and professional consultation. Often, the Pre-Glitch causes worry, but no further action is pursued. But if it is left unattended, there is good potential for it to grow to a far more serious level.

Sometimes behavior that bears similarities to the Premature Departure Time-Out glitch is not a glitch but a Pre-Glitch. The adolescent may claim an illness, and the claim goes on too long. If such behavior is not diagnosed correctly, it may become more serious. Warning signs may be that temperature testing reveals no elevation and the adolescent does not appear sick, or there is no visible wound or specific pain, or when a headache or a stomachache is claimed, as the day progresses there are no traces of illness. The adolescent may make the same complaint the next day, and may even do so for an entire week. Yet the adolescent appears asymptomatic. With each increasing day, parents worry as to what might be going on. And well they should.

Paying Attention

An adolescent's claim of illness may continue into a second or third week. If the adolescent has yet to exhibit such behavior that includes self-harm such as bloodying the nose purposefully, resistance to food or sleep, a sour mood, untruthfulness, and other desperate means to reach his or her ends, the symptoms do not match diagnosis of a Premature Departure Extended glitch.

A professional at a mental health clinic may receive a call from a worried parent, a physician, or a school counselor. Certainly no stone should be left unturned. The behavior is clearly the adolescent's way of saying, "Look at me. I need your help." It is time for the professional to talk with the school, to reexamine the adolescent's behaviors at home with family and with peers, and to assess new findings. Parents may be asked to gather together information on their adolescent's interpersonal life. Evidence of adolescents' peer involvements may be gathered from information they provide about which shows they watch on television, about whether they have had any contact with peers during the past two or three weeks, and about whether the books or magazines they read are written for or about teens.

If the source of the behavior does not seem to be academic problems in school or arguments with age-mates, and there has been little contact with peers, not even text messages or emails, it is possible that this is a full-blown glitch of some kind. Either the adolescent fears telling the truth or is not aware of the origin of the pain that he or she is experiencing. Avoidance of peer contact is strong evidence that the adolescent is feeling rejected or disappointed and that the pain most likely stems from comparative acts with peers.

A More Serious Diagnosis

The Pre-Glitch adolescent whom I have been describing, who may desire a reprieve from face-to-face peer interactions, may be manifesting a condition that has been active over an extended time but has been masked well. But it has finally come to a head. Since none of the symptoms of the Premature Departure Extended glitch were identified, there is strong reason to surmise that this Pre-Glitch condition, if unattended, could develop into one of the two Loner glitches or perhaps even into the Mission-Dedicated Veiled glitch. None of these glitches requires much involvement with others, if any. Hence, they may be highly desirable escapes for the Pre-Glitch adolescent.

The Need for Time Alone

Adolescents' requests for "time away" from school or social activities are really requests for time alone. Such requests need careful analysis and thought when brought to professionals. Two sides of a coin are represented in the request: (1) a need to integrate information about self into a coherent whole or (2) an attempt to escape the disappointment and pain of facing the data from comparative acts. It is a weighty responsibility of professionals to determine correctly which side of the coin is operating.

An occasional request of a day or two away from peers can be an indication of an adolescent who knows how to care for him- or herself. He or she is sensitive to internal signals for rest such as unusual tiredness or perhaps turning down an invitation that seemed good just a few days before and wanting instead to read a book or play on a long-neglected musical instrument.

On the other hand, why does an adolescent in pain not just say so? Just explain what is needed and why? The major reason is that they cannot express what they are feeling. Chapter 1 discussed that learning first takes place through the senses. It is probably for this reason that Erikson referred to a "sense" of identity in his seminal work on the subject. Identity is experienced, not reasoned. A similar experience takes place as adolescents develop. Adolescents engage in comparative acts day and night. Although they are only subliminally aware of the intellectual activity, they *feel* the emotional impact. Most choose to attribute difficulties to tiredness stemming from intensive school days and view the back and forth with peers as the relaxing, fun part of the day. This response is a coping mechanism, but the truth is quite the opposite. At end of day, as discussed earlier, adolescents decode the ups and downs of their peer interactions in their Peer Arena library. Sometimes, they need to continue to deal with upsetting reruns into the next day, hence the occasional request to stay home.

Careful Diagnoses

Professionals must always look for the benign before looking to the complex. Adolescents' legitimate need for some time off is generally not on the radar of today's parents. Parents sometimes regard requests for time off as just plain laziness, or they suspect that their adolescent has not completed homework or prepared sufficiently for a test. Professionals might suggest to parents a policy of benign understanding partnered with close watch for sudden elevation or depression of mood, uncharacteristic behaviors, or extreme behavior, and for the time interval before similar behavior returns. If these behaviors continue, the professional must consider the possibility of glitches and gear diagnostic techniques accordingly. At a minimum, counseling with adolescents should encourage expression of their estimate of their relative worth compared to selected peers and should probe the reason for that estimate. If adolescents are not forthcoming, it is wise to help them along. For example, one way, among many others, of getting at just how comparative acts operate for an adolescent is to ask a question such as, "You have mentioned a few times that you and Jeannette are good friends. Are the two of you alike in any ways or different?"

As adolescents near the end of Stage 1, as DFI instructs, it is entirely possible that they may need time off to select and integrate self-elements into a temporary self structure. This need of adolescents to be away from others may occur again near the end of Stage 2, when they finalize and integrate elements into a permanent self structure. Deep thought is required to pick and choose and to group related self-elements together, and it is not an easy job. It requires time and concentration, which may need to be done away from the crowd. The need for this time is not planned; it is felt. And it does not always match the school schedule, or the family one either. It is ironic that adolescents can sometimes be seen as loafers when in fact the time they need is for purposes of an intense activity. Adolescence is generally not a period of loafing; adolescents are hard at work. When the task becomes too difficult, as this chapter has outlined, adolescents may escape to a defensive glitch. In that case, they need help.

The chapters in part 3 offer protocols useful in diagnosing the presence of a defensive glitch, and part 4 provides an overview of a model of treatment exclusively for adolescents, PAL group therapy.

PART III

The Peer Arena Retrospect (PAR) Protocols

8

Getting to Know the Adolescent

An Introduction to the PAR Protocols

Though adolescents are most focused on their peers, and on learning what is hot and looked on favorably, too many models of therapy seem to pass right over this vital piece of adolescent reality despite its ubiquity, evident in their conversations, music, fashion, and activities. Adolescents' resistance to therapy can many times be connected to its outmoded emphases on familiar family matters that miss what is on their radar, from cell phones, text messaging, and Facebook to face-to-face exchanges about the latest or forthcoming peer haunts and happenings. The DFI approach focuses from the outset on adolescents' daily concerns in order to capture their core preoccupations.

As we have seen, in the defensive glitch model of maladaptive development, adolescents may flee from engaging normative growth dynamics because they have been hit very hard by disappointments in themselves when they compared with peers. At times, they choose routes that dull their minds, sometimes routes in which they deceive even themselves. The protocols found in chapters 8–11 were developed so that professionals can speed along the process of eliciting from adolescents the type of peer-related information that is needed to piece together an initial diagnosis and detail a treatment plan.

About the Protocols

The protocols presented in the chapters of part 3 are designed to elicit information from the adolescent about what has gone wrong in their relationships with peers, so wrong as to affect their behavior and development. Or, if a defensive glitch has been stimulated, the protocols will help the professional discover how this glitch is related to the outcomes of the adolescent's comparisons with peers, outcomes so devastating that the adolescent sought relief in problem behavior. Most of the protocols are designed *for* adolescents. The exceptions are those for a few relevant others such as parents and teachers who supply information to supplement the referral history. The protocols elicit information such as what, why, and where matters went wrong in accessing sufficient peers, what the outcomes of comparative acts were, clues to the impact on the adolescent, and much more. Furthermore, the data they yield enable a diagnosis for PAL treatment planning. If PAL group therapy is deemed appropriate for an adolescent, he or she is assigned to a group that best simulates his or her original peer groups, the Peer Arena, so that very similar psychological dynamics will be stimulated into action. Joining this group forces the adolescent to relive and rework the difficult experiences that were so egregious that he or she took flight, many times into a full-blown defensive glitch. This time, the adolescent remains in the group and, together with the assistance of peers in the group and with the safety of professional oversight, reworks the trauma. Part 4 of this book provides the details of the PAL group therapy method. The protocols presented here can also be used in individual therapy, as the professional sees appropriate, but the order of use may be different from that recommended here for diagnostic purposes of PAL.

The primary goals of the adolescent age group generally have little to do with parents, beyond cleverly handling them for sufficient freedom to be with their attachment others, their age-mate peers. The best of kids do this, since they are one another's developmental food. Some do not have smooth adolescent experience and seek escape; these adolescents we often see in our offices. Later in this chapter and in chapters 9–11 to follow, 30 protocols are presented for professional use in interview sessions. They focus on peer-related comparisons and evaluations and subsequent thoughts and actions.[1] During the diagnostic phase, they yield data from relevant sources, in particular family, school, and important others in the adolescent's environment.

Finding the Right Focus

The force behind an adolescent's arrival at a mental health office is often parental concern. Or it may be by order of the court. Generally, adolescents do not come of their own accord, even if they are experiencing psychic distress. But parents frequently do not seek professional help right away either, not because they are just ignoring the problem but because they are many times unaware that the problem is real. Most parents do not really understand how very important peers are to adolescents or how adolescents assist one another to grow and develop; they see peer engagement as largely fun and games. Other than parental objections to particular types of friends or concerns about violations of nighttime curfews, problems with peer attachment are usually not discernable to busy parents. If and when their child's pain is expressed in school matters or social problem behavior such as petty crime, drinking or drugs, or other troubles, parents swing into action and haul the adolescent in to get fixed up.

Unfortunately, on the face of it, problem behaviors appear too serious to be connected to concerns about peer standing or relationships. Even on the professional side, there are a variety of reasons why many professionals prefer to use the therapeutic hour to focus on complex-sounding issues adolescents have so long been asked about: family concerns and rebellion. Popularly seen as the therapy of choice, families flock to family therapy sessions in which they work hard on family issues. This approach may make a trip to the therapist and its costs seem worthwhile to parents and third-party payers, as it is what is well known. Yet all the while, significant issues may not get broached, at least not for quite a while. Real therapeutic concern should often be directed at what appears trivial: today's triumphs and troubles, such as what happened in school, on the school bus, in the neighborhood, or at home. There lie many of the kernels of adolescent problems to come. Two examples of exchanges between loving parents and their daughters portray instances when the adolescent message was just not heard.

Katie, age 13, arrives home from school:

> "Mom, you'll never guess what happened today in school."
> "What?"
> "Joanne wore that dress we saw the other day that we thought was a party dress. I saw her in it in Spanish class."
> "Oh, well. Her parents have too much money anyway. They can't find enough to spend it on. Did your teacher explain why you missed that problem on the math test?"
> "She was busy telling us about tomorrow's test. She didn't have a lot of time. I better go up to my room and get to work on my homework."
> "When you get finished, come down early enough for dinner. I bought some really good peanut butter cookies. I think you'll like them."
> "OK."

Katie had brought home what was important to her: had she made a mistake thinking that the article of clothing she had seen the other day was not a dress that would go over big at school? Not all the kids thought it was overdone. In fact, some thought it was really cool. What would the other kids think of her for not agreeing with them? Would she be dropped from the crowd?

Katie's mother skipped right over what was really troubling Katie. Apparently, it was not her math problem at all. Clearly, that was her mother's problem. Since Katie had nothing else to share, she went to her room to think more about what happened in school.

Sandy, age 16, arrives home from school:

"Hi, Mom. I got a 91 on my French test!"
"Oh, that's great, dear. I am so happy you did so well."
"Yeah, I was about the only one who scored that high."
"How nice. You must be very happy. Would you like a snack? I bought some good peanut butter cookies. You usually like them."
"Rozzie was wearing some really cute jeans. They were trendy, but the kind of trendy in the way you like them, Mom. Remember the ones we saw at Macy's? I thought they looked really good on me. I think you liked them too. All the kids agree they are really worth the money."

By this time, Sandy knows that the way to avoid her mother's questions about what she does not want to talk to her about—in this case, that she lent her best jeans to Amanda for her trip to Florida without permission from her mom or dad, and Amanda left them on the beach—is to tell her something she will be happy to hear, that her daughter is doing well academically. Sandy manages to tell her mother about her academic prowess and also about how sensible she is about the amount of money she asks her mother to spend on clothes for her—and, by the way, how sensible her friends are too.

"Where are those peanut butter cookies? I just love them."
"I put them in the oven to keep them fresh."
"Will we be able to go shopping for me, maybe at Macy's?"
"Sure, but five minutes down the road there is another store I think you will like even better. You know, more trendy."

Katie's example describes a loving and concerned parent who just did not leave room for what was important to her daughter. Instead, she focused on what she saw as the important issue: the math problem. Katie was preoccupied, questioning her instincts about what sort of dress is acceptable at school. Her mother missed the boat.

Sandy, three years older, knew the ropes better. A sure way to soften up a parent is to bring good news about an academic achievement. Sandy did that and went on from there. But, for all her efforts, she did not win totally. Her mother did not understand that Sandy was most concerned about being like all the popular girls. Possibly because she scored so high on the test, she was worried that people might think she was a nerd. She wanted some external symbol of being cool, like the jeans that everyone had agreed were cute and worth the money. Sandy's strategy did not entirely work; she did not totally control her mother, but she came close. Her mother had her own ideas about what Sandy should look like and reasoned that just as she had guided Sandy to be at the top of the heap academically, she could lead Sandy to what *she believed* would assist her daughter to the top of the heap with regard to her fashion sense.

Such benign beginnings as related in these examples may escalate, and the adolescent involved may possibly find a defensive glitch appealing. Like parents, professionals too may miss the boat unless they have an appropriate theoretical road map such as DFI to guide them.

Overview

To date, the literature has not offered protocols that are guided specifically by a theory of adolescent development and behavior. DFI fills that gap. The purpose of the intake protocols offered here is to establish the point at which growth shuts off. Once that point has been established, the stage is set for determining a proper treatment. If a troubled adolescent shut off or escaped into a defensive glitch at a point in his or her development when feedback from comparisons became unbearably painful, was it in Stage 1 adolescence or in Stage 2? Was it in the early, middle, or end of the stage? Clues are to be found in answers to the protocols' questions. Making use of several protocols, one following the other as needed, is a good strategy for collecting and clustering clues.[2]

Use of the protocols elicits diagnostic information earlier than does the interview process without them. Each protocol has a sequence of questions that follows a purposeful pattern. Thus, DFI theory is always at professionals' side to augment their own professional instincts. Adolescents' responses to questions in the defensive glitch protocol signal signs of potential or actual defensive flight. Accompanying back-and-forth exchange may elicit other useful information.

The psychological protocols offered in this chapter and in chapters 9–11 are not intended for use with other age groups; they were developed exclusively for adolescents, family, school officials, and just one or two relevant others. Since the protocols ask the individual to look back in time, they are referred to as Peer Arena Retrospect, or PAR, protocols. The content of each protocol, or list of questions, is derived from basic premises of DFI theory.[3] The sequence of the questions is intended to elicit the desired information.

Potential of Mixing and Matching Protocols

Separate protocols are available for use with adolescents, parents, siblings, teachers and school personnel, and significant environmental others and for occasional small group use. Use of two or even more protocols can expand the professional's information about the client's peer relationship preferences, family dynamics, perceived support or nonsupport from the family, and his or her reactions to all these issues. Parent and sibling protocols are intended to elicit alternate views of identical situations.

EXAMPLE: THE CASE OF CHARLES, AGE 15

Findings from Charles's and his parents' protocols disclose a number of conflicts. Charles says that his mother does not take him to peer get-togethers, and his mother states that she does. During a subsequent interview, the professional learns that Charles, who has a leg deformity and wears long pants to hide it, would like to go to school dances. However, he cannot walk the distance to the dance and needs a ride. His mother's responses to the parent protocol (PAR-P) reveal that she takes him to every school function but does not pick him up because she goes to work early in the morning and needs her sleep. Charles's father works on ships and is away for long periods. The first adolescent protocol (PAR-A) reveals that Charles wants to go to the events, but he is afraid to ask peers for a ride back because running or squeezing into a car may reveal his deformity. Consequently, he remains at home, and his anger at both his mother and his disability grows. His anger is not limited to his mother's denial of transportation: he holds family genetics responsible for his problem. Charles cannot afford to be too angry at his mother because he is dependent on her, so he turns his anger inward and his despair about his infirmity grows and grows.

From Charles's mother's point of view, she *is* available to take Charles to the dance. From Charles's point of view, he cannot go because she *is not* available to take him home. He is angry. Examining both the protocols allows the professional to identify the disconnect. A simple straightforward question needs to be asked: "Charles, have you ever told your mother why you are hesitant to take a ride home with friends?"

Charles is still in early-middle adolescence, so DFI instructs that he is highly egocentric. He believes his deformity will be seen by everyone if he does not hide it well. Emotionally, it does not register that the deformity is not terribly important to others and would not be talked about for too long even if it became visible for a moment. He feels subject to an imaginary audience, a perception characteristic of this age group, and this audience sees all. To protect himself from more psychic pain about his difference from everyone else, he does what he can to shield himself. PAR-DG, the Phase II protocol used to diagnose defensive glitches, reveals that Charles intensively immerses himself in a research project with one of his teachers on AIDS in children to escape from more comparative acts with peers. In addition, he becomes respected for this accomplishment. So far, all is well and good, but he goes on to do more: his obsession with the project and his spending every minute he can spare on it and thinking about it when he is not working on it blocks out evaluations of comparisons with peers during the school day and after. But he does not quit school or have a lot of absences. In this way, he preserves the *appearance* of still being involved with peers of his Peer Arena, but psychologically he has left the Peer Arena and has aborted his social-psychological development.

Charles took flight into the Veiled Mission-Dedicated glitch. Together with the PAR-A (Adolescent) and PAR-P (Parent) protocol findings, some of the Supplementary protocols need to be used to elicit as complete an understanding of Charles's thinking and problems as necessary prior to entering him into PAL group therapy. The information constitutes background material for the PAL professional. The goal of therapy will be to help him back on track psychologically, so that he can grow cognitively beyond the imaginary-audience stage of cognition. With acquisition of abstract thought, he will be able to see that he is but a very small part of a very large world. All eyes cannot possibly remain just on him. With the exit of the imaginary audience, his burden will be greatly lightened.

Charles's case demonstrates how protocols can yield diagnostic information and conclusions within a very few sessions. It is very important that the adolescent patient becomes aware early on that the questioning relates to what is important to him or her. Explanatory examples of the dynamics of the PAL experience itself are found in chapters 12 and 13.

How to Use the PAR Protocols

The PAR protocols are not meant for use as a paper-and-pencil questionnaire for adolescents to fill in privately. They are fashioned to guide the interview. In situations in which interviews are absolutely not possible, the protocols can be used as a paper-and-pencil instrument, but the findings will not approach the richness of the interview model.

A modest amount of clinician choice is permitted, for example, altering which question is asked first in the various protocols. But regardless of where the protocol is started, the clinician is encouraged to follow the sequence of the questions. The protocol structures specific issues in short groupings, with a progression by design from one to another. No matter which question is the starter question, all questions listed on the protocol should be asked. The goal is to determine whether psychological growth is on a proper course, seems delayed, or is at risk and why. Questions sequentially move closer and closer to reach adolescents' interpretations of their comparative-act findings and how those findings have affected their developing self. Innovations of style, not content, are up to the clinician, but remember that adolescents are usually accustomed to the sound-bite-sequenced communication they experience on the computer and television.

The PAR protocols elicit material in addition to what is in the referral materials to determine whether the adolescent's problem can be remediated with the PAL group therapy model. Although the protocols are also useful for other types of therapy, they are most effective when supported by knowledge of DFI. Sometimes PAR conclusions do not agree with those of the referral source.

It is usually possible to arrive at a diagnosis within two to three sessions, depending on the number of protocols and persons interviewed. Using the PAR protocols facilitates a comfortable interaction between the adolescent and the clinician because the questions come from a piece of paper held by the professional: that the questions are routine and the adolescent seems not to be singled out is a subtle but highly effective difference. With reduction of anxiety, an adolescent's hesitation to respond decreases. Another very important feature also encourages participation: since questions focus on what is most relevant to the adolescent, they ring with pertinence.

Auxiliary protocols are designed for interviews with family members, school personnel, and relevant environmental others for informational purposes. *Supplementary* protocols are for further exploration of tentative hypotheses. All protocols serve as an aid, not a firm directive. Selection of which protocols to employ is the province of the professional, with two exceptions: (1) the basic PAR-A protocol should be used first with all adolescents, and (2) the PAR-DG protocol designed to assist diagnosis of a defensive glitch must follow at least two of the basic protocols.

Although it is not uncommon for an experienced clinician to begin the interview in the manner and order he or she prefers, it is suggested strongly that the order in Phase I be followed, unless there is a clear rationale for not doing so. The order is as follows: The PAR-A is the first protocol used; it is designed for use with adolescents who have *not* been identified with a specific defensive glitch but whose behavior is very troubling. After PAR-A or its substitutes or complements, any Auxiliary protocol in the Phase I collection is appropriate if it is seen to have the potential to supply the additional information needed. Supplementary protocols, which were also designed to fill the information gap, ordinarily should not be used before Auxiliary protocols. Which of these protocols are used is also open to the professional's choice, according to the objective.

In sum, the PAR protocols aid diagnosis and treatment planning. They uncover adolescents' perception of their place on the continuum between perceived success and failure as well as what their experiences have been. Some estimate can be made of when discouragement set in, what may have dissuaded continued interaction and comparisons, and the circumstances of the psychological withdrawal. The questions leave room to discern how adolescents see their own participation in causing their emotional pain and in allowing that pain to be felt so deeply. In this manner, responses to protocol questions stimulate insights into the defensive-flight type and its path.

Adolescents' analyses of why their relationships with peers have gone sour reveal a lot about how they figure out their own sadness. The range of responses can be fantasy or fact. On the other hand, strategically placed questions in all the protocols reinforce the adolescent's sense that his or her views have real merit. It may be the first time that the adolescent has experienced this sense.

Directions for Use
Getting Started: Opening Statement

The following statement, to be read essentially verbatim, is expressed by the admissions (intake) professional, not the in-group therapist for PAL group therapy. Should the intake professionals determine that PAL group therapy is not the therapy of choice, referral should be made for other mental health modalities or resources.

> Hello. My name is [name], and I see that your name is [adolescent's name]. Welcome to my office [or name of agency or clinic]. I look forward to being together. Today we will get started. I have a paper in my hand on which there are a few questions that should help us begin. They are not complicated, and we may or may not finish today. There is no rush if you have other things to talk about too. Just let me know. I am the person you will be seeing for the next two or three sessions. My purpose is to decide how we might best help you with your matter. After that is determined, we can talk together about the initial plan and who you will be working with. I will arrange for you to meet that person together with me for a few minutes a few days prior to when you begin together. [Pause] Do you have any questions? I have time for one or two before we get down to today's task.

Then, put your sheet down and say something like,

> Sometime today, I am going to read from a sheet with questions about your contacts with your friends. There is no grade you will receive. My questions and your answers are just for our private confidential use. They will not be shown to anyone else who you will not meet first. It will be just one other professional, maybe two at the most. We always like to consult with one another.
>
> I will not be able to explain the question to you. Your answers will be a big help to me as I decide how best to help you and who is the right person for you to work with next. Once I start reading, if necessary, you may ask me to define a word.

In an inviting manner, ask, "Do you have any question you might like to ask now?" Spend a short time answering it, if the question is appropriate. If it is not appropriate, say, "That question may be appropriate for another setting, but not here. I just don't have an answer for it." Then go on with the second and final part of your welcome and introduction: "You know, just before you walked in today, I was thinking about the time of life you are in, and I was reminding myself about what an interesting but sometimes very confusing time it can be . . . particularly because there are so many changes going on in oneself as well as changes in friends. [Pause] Do you find it that way?" (Normally a short answer will be given). This type of opening immediately sends the message that the professional is interested in the adolescent's world, not just in the usual discussion of family relationships or rebellion against parents.

Warm-Up

There are questions that do not appear on any protocol that can be used for a warm-up. Make them sound neutral and unrelated to anything serious. A common strategy is to start with identifying information such as the adolescent's age, school, or home neighborhood and then go on to a favorite hobby or television show. It is best for these questions not to be too specific since it is impossible to predict which questions may touch a sore point.

This warm-up period can be quite valuable in sending a message of interest in the adolescent as a person, not just someone in trouble. It can be simple. With male adolescents, often sports or hobbies are topics about which they can easily converse. Ask which team is their favorite, if they know the score of the last game, and the like. Similarly, for many adolescent females questions about hairstyle, fashion, or favorite movies are likely to get a response. Both genders usually respond to questions about music they like, famous singers, and the type of weather they like.

Unless the client is extremely resistant, a brief amount of time should be sufficient for the warm-up. Extended warm-up questions may afford time for clever adolescents to adopt strategies to avoid valid answers. They may be testing the "savvy" quotient of the professional. In cases of passive opposition, it may work to offer the option of writing responses rather than conducting the interview verbally.

Procedure

The PAR question sheet can also serve as the response sheet on which to jot notes. Numbered sheets attached to the question sheet can be used to record extended answers or longer notes, but try not to spend too much time writing.

1. PAR should be administered verbally, with short periods of time for each response.
2. Register the first response or two if the adolescent offers a series of responses.
3. When possible, all questions should be asked with the PAR protocol visible on the desk, not in the professional's hands.
4. Observe nonverbal behavior and record it on the PAR question sheet in the space under each question.
5. Enter the adolescent's affect when he or she hears each question and when he or she answers it. These are not necessarily the same.
6. Begin with the first question. You should have a therapeutically sound reason for starting later in the protocol. If you do start later in the protocol, indicate which was the start question and why.
7. Questions that are ordinarily asked first but that have been postponed until later should be asked during the same session unless a special situation exists. If there is such a special situation, record what it is.
8. Limit the adolescent's inquiries about a question to one or two to avoid invalid findings. Make your responses polite but clear and short. Try to restrict them to word definitions. Do not reply to inquiries about the intent of the questions.

Nonverbal Diary

Nonverbal behavior is extremely important to understanding which questions may have stirred anxiety. It also provides some index of an adolescent's anxiety level and personal style. Include this nonverbal diary, the first PAR protocol, with use of every other protocol:

PAR 1: NONVERBAL DIARY
Check off immediately after all questions are answered:
Approximate response speed: Slow _____ Moderate _____ Quick _____
Observable affect: Relaxed _____ Moderate stress _____ Troubled _____
    Little affect _____
Approximate number of questions originated by adolescent _____
Short summary of type of question(s)
_____

At what point asked _____
Professional's comment: _____

Phase I and Phase II PAR Protocol Information

All protocols selected from Phase I protocols—Basic and Circumstance-Specific Auxiliary protocols (chapter 9)—as well as from the larger number of Supplementary protocols (chapter 10), must be completed prior to moving on to Phase II protocols (chapter 11). Phase II protocols are designed for use exclusively with adolescents who may have a defensive glitch. Selected Phase II protocols can be used earlier if additional information elicited by those protocols is needed right away. This can be done in the same session if prior responses have been brief or if an emergency is suspected. Otherwise, schedule time for the Phase II protocols after a break or just a day or two later.

What follows is a brief description of the protocols of Phase I. The protocols themselves follow in chapter 9. They are most commonly used at the beginning of the process.

Phase I Basic Protocols

Phase I protocols begin with the Basic PAR-A (Adolescent) or PAR-AA (Adolescent Alternative). PAR-AA is used when from the outset there is concern about the possibility of a defensive glitch. There is also a third basic protocol, PAR-Aab (Adolescent abridged), of shorter length, which can be switched to if the client exhibits extreme distress in responding to the PAR-A.

PAR-A (ADOLESCENT)
To every extent possible, use protocol PAR-A prior to any other protocol. It is appropriate for the youngster whose referral indicates a deviation

from normative progress. An example would be very occasional drug use, but not drug abuse, in which case PAR-DG is used first.

If the adolescent shows extremes of behavior or distress while responding to the PAR-A, the PAR-AA (Adolescent Alternative) protocol can be seamlessly switched to.

PAR-AA (ADOLESCENT ALTERNATIVE)

PAR-AA can also be used in conjunction with or immediately after the PAR-A protocol when a defensive glitch is suspected. It does not normally allow inclusion of borrowed questions from the PAR-A *unless* the object is to examine more closely a link missing in PAR-A that PAR-AA inquiries may fill. The disparities in response between PAR-A and PAR-AA offer material for further exploration. A possibility always exists that the same questions adolescents answered in PAR-A will be responded to differently if they are part of the more focused PAR-AA questions. The appropriate response may become more clear to the adolescent. Conversely, the response may be more closely crafted, even hidden. In all cases, professionals are free to add a few appropriate questions of their own in the blank spaces following each question. These questions should be related to a response that needs more clarification. A simple example is an adolescent's mentioning eight brothers and sisters but not mentioning their gender. The question would be, "Which are male and which are female?"

Since the PAR-AA protocol explores severe resistance problems and indicates suspicion of the presence of glitches, the adolescent should be contacted as immediately as possible after the referral material is received. It may be that time is of the essence; for example, the adolescent may be demonstrating extreme and unexpected mood changes and despondency or may be acting hostilely toward a sibling. As quickly as possible, such an adolescent should be assigned to PAL group therapy or be referred for individual therapy. An adolescent in PAL group therapy on rare occasion may unexpectedly need to leave the group for a time for individual therapy sessions as part of the overall plan for PAL. An example is discussed in the final chapter of this book.

PAR-AAB (ADOLESCENT ABRIDGED)

This protocol, though rarely necessary, can also be switched to seamlessly if the adolescent has an overanxious response early in the PAR-A questioning. Since the first 7 questions are the same and the questions are consecutive, this shorter version of PAR-A can be used at a more leisurely pace. The questions may be asked again after all others have been replied to, according to professional discretion.

Circumstance-Specific Auxiliary Protocols of Phase I

Precisely because information from these Circumstance-Specific protocols is not needed in every case, they are grouped as Auxiliary protocols of choice. It would be very rare for all these protocols to be used for one adolescent's situation.

PAR-P (PARENTS)

This protocol is a questionnaire developed for the parents or guardians of the adolescent. It can be administered to one parent or both, as needed. If it is administered to both parents, it should be administered separately in order to compare responses. This protocol serves to access the parental perspective and allows comparison of the adolescent's and the parents' responses.

PAR-S OR PAR-OS (SIBLING/OLDER SIBLING)

This protocol elicits information from younger and older siblings, with a special designation for older siblings because of the general strength of their influence.[4] It adds additional family information to the growing number of perspectives.

PAR-T (TEACHERS AND SCHOOL PERSONNEL)

This protocol is used when information is needed about the adolescent's school performance, attitude, and customary affect and about whether he or she appears to be accepted or rejected by friends and other adolescents.[5]

PAR-E (ENVIRONMENTAL OTHER)

This protocol is used to gather information from individuals who are important in the adolescent's life and who are not nuclear family members or school employees, for example, a close relative such as a grandmother, an aunt or uncle, a cousin, a longtime family friend, or a scout leader who is regularly in contact with the adolescent, the neighborhood, and its milieu.

PAR-G (GROUP ADMINISTRATION)

On rare occasions, the professional may find it helpful to use a group model. Administration of the protocols in groups of four or fewer is permissible. Although there may be a risk of some group conformity when this protocol is used, the risk is negligible because the four or fewer adolescents grouped together should be unknown to one another and are considered for different group placements. Notation should be made of individuals who raise questions or need extra attention, that is, who, what, and when. Occasionally, the PAR protocols may be administered to a small group of adolescents who are seated at a distance from one another so that their written responses remain concealed.

PAR-DG (DEFENSIVE GLITCH)

Although this protocol is *not* a Phase I protocol, it is listed here because it is used directly after either PAR-A or PAR-AA in emergency situations if a defensive glitch is suspected. It is discussed as a Phase II protocol in chapter 11.

To explain the theory that directs the composition of the PAR protocol questions, chapter 9 begins with a description of PAR-A and an interpretation of its questions.

9

Phase I: Basic and Circumstance-Specific Auxiliary Protocols

When adolescents are in the admissions and diagnosis period, it is necessary to gain as much information as possible about the circumstances of their situation. This information is most efficiently elicited by the professional through use of a Basic protocol and, if necessary, one or more of the Circumstance-Specific Auxiliary protocols, which are designed to elicit information from a specific source area. The Phase I Basic protocol that is ordinarily used first is PAR-A (Adolescent), the most comprehensive of the Basic protocols.

There are some matters of clinical judgment in using the protocols. For example, practitioners should feel free to ask "why" at any point in the protocol, being careful to place the question selectively and not too frequently. Or practitioners may occasionally want to leave out questions but return to them before the protocol is completed. The entire protocol does not need to be used all at once or asked in a rapid-fire manner; it can occur as part of the conversation when in the hands of a person familiar with DFI theory and its sequence of psychological development.[1] Completion of the protocol can be interrupted for short diversions of conversation, but make every attempt to cover PAR-A completely in one session.

Peer Arena Retrospect (PAR) Basic Protocols
PAR-A (Adolescent): Questions and Information about the Adolescent

PAR 2: PAR-A (ADOLESCENT)
ID# _____ Age: _____ yrs. _____ mos. _____ M _____ F _____
   1. Have you begun to prefer to be with a lot of friends rather than just a
      few? Yes _____ No _____
      If yes, When? _____
      If no, Any special reason? _____

2. Have the types of people you are friendly with changed? Yes _____ No
_____
3. If so, how?
4. Are these friends part of a special group? Yes _____ No _____ Are they
from different groups? Yes _____ No _____
*If the responses are negative to both of these questions, ask if the subject
has any individual friends.* Yes _____ No _____
5. Has the number of friends you have now
increased? Yes _____ No _____ Why?
decreased? Yes _____ No _____ Why?
6. Do you have a lot of friends? Yes _____ No _____ Why?
7. Do you prefer to be with fewer friends? Yes _____ No _____ Why?

Questions 1–7 of PAR-A go directly to whether the adolescent prefers to
be with friends, new or old, or whether he or she prefers avoidance, as
well as whether this desire has increased or decreased. Analyses of the
responses make it possible to begin hypothesizing about whether the adolescent has entered psychological adolescence and is engaging dynamics
of the Stage 1 primary Peer Arena. Embedded in what appear to be simple
questions are clues as to whether the adolescent has begun making comparative acts, which as we have seen become more frequent during this
stage. If the adolescent shows interest in having lots of friends, old and
especially new, the protocols contain questions that ascertain whether he
or she is actively engaging in comparative acts. Appraisal of findings must
take into account the status that larger groups of peers accord particular
characteristics. In one study, for example, 732 mixed-gender adolescents
were asked to rank characteristics of greatest importance to them. Findings revealed high percentages of adolescents selecting the same attributes
and placing them in similar rank.[2] Also in these findings, even though
typing skill could be seen as helpful to getting a job, peers did not rank it
nearly as high as being a good dancer. These findings support the strength
of group attitudes on adolescent values.

Caution must be taken if an adolescent refers to lots of friends but only
in past years, not today, yesterday, or last week. This is a hint that no new
comparisons are under way and that a defensive strategy may be operating. This condition is of special concern in middle school or early junior
high, when adolescents should be in the thick of peer interaction. This
prime period continues into the senior high school grades, with beginning

reductions in senior year.[3] In the senior year and in the early college years or during the first serious job after graduating high school, there is a reduction in the number of peers an adolescent desires and the respective comparative acts that are performed. This reduction signals progression from Stage 1 adolescence, the primary Peer Arena, into Stage 2, the final stage, the secondary Peer Arena period, when it is natural for adolescents to want to reduce the number of friends to those with similar interests, ambitions, and goals. Stage 2 adolescents are closer to adulthood.

8. Lately, do you prefer to spend more time with your friends or your family members?
Friends _____ Your age _____ Older _____ Younger _____
Family _____ Which family members? _____ Age _____
9. What do you think your parents feel about the number of friends you have? Too many _____ OK _____ Too few _____
10. Do your parents like the people who are your friends? Yes _____ No _____ They don't care _____
11. What do they think about the amount of time you spend with your friends? Too much _____ Too little _____ Don't care _____
12. What do you think about the amount of time you spend with your friends? Too much _____ Too little _____ Don't care _____

Parents are a vital part of any adolescent's life, and it is important to know about them and about what adolescents think about them. Questions 8–11 deal with the adolescent's perception of parental opinions, attitudes, and feelings. Question 12 accords respect to the adolescent's opinion by asking what he or she thinks about the amount of time spent with friends; this question helps the professional seem not overly centered on parents. And with question 12 as a backdrop, the next category of questions about siblings can be safely introduced. Here, information can be elicited on the amount of influence of siblings and parents on the adolescent.

For more information on adolescents' influences, consult the Adolescent Reference Group Index (ARGI), which offers illuminating baseline information by disclosing how a large sample of adolescents from various areas of the United States attribute influence. It offers perspective for understanding the responses from PAR-A, but it also may be highly valuable in placing information from PAR-P, PAR-S, and PAR-OS within a context of the relative influence of the various categories of persons.

The ARGI, a question-and-answer protocol, asks adolescents to select from 13 groups whom they would consult on 10 different questions about their practices and preferences and to indicate how much influence each person or group would be accorded. Each group is ranked (from 1 to 13) based on a calculation of the averages of findings from the 10 questions. A conglomerate of five groups of peers ranked first, parents second, and older siblings third. Older adolescent siblings hold a unique two-pronged power position. When they agree with parents on an issue, the sum total of influence raises parents from rank 2 to rank 1. When older siblings' position on an issue agrees with peers, peers remain at rank 1 with an increase in strength of that influence.[4] Thus, crucial information is provided on the issues on which peers or parents become more powerful because of support from older siblings. These findings, which have remained consistent for over 30 years of testing,[5] are highly useful for both diagnosis and therapeutic intervention planning.

13. Are your brothers and sisters older or younger than you? How many of each? Older bros. _____ Younger bros. _____ Older sisters _____ Younger sisters _____

14. Which are you closest to? _____ Why? _____

15a. What do your older brothers think about the types of friends you have? Like them _____ Dislike them _____ Don't say _____

15b. What do your older sisters think about the type of friends you have? Like them _____ Dislike them _____ Don't say _____

Questions 13–15 in PAR-A inquire about the importance of older and younger siblings. Over the same 30-year period, findings from ARGI consistently reveal a very low influence rank accorded younger siblings.[6] Since the findings report a consistently strong influence position of older siblings, if an adolescent reports younger sibling as very important, and the adolescent spends a lot of time with them, an alarm bell should go off. This response from an adolescent would suggest that more information is needed from other sources such as teachers about school performance; obtaining this additional information is particularly prudent prior to hypothesizing about the home and society factors retarding growth. Rule in or out possible problems in the cognitive domain first before exploring the emotional or social domains. If more information is still needed, inquire of parents and teachers about their estimate of the adolescent's level of emotional functioning.[7] Although the domains of growth are interrelated, it is vital to assess them separately first.

16. Do you feel your parents encourage you to participate in activities with friends?
    Mother: Yes _____ No _____
    Father: Yes _____ No _____
17a. Does your mother assist you in getting there? Yes _____ No _____
    Occasionally _____
17b. Does your father assist you in getting there? Yes _____ No _____
    Occasionally _____
    If answer is no or occasionally, How do you get there? _____
    _____

Questions 16 and 17 provide insight into the degree of active parental support for adolescents' efforts to get together with age-mates.

*18. Are you happy with the number of friends you have? No _____ Yes _____ Why?
19a. Is your mother happy with the number of friends you have? Yes _____ No _____ Why?
19b. Is your father happy with the number of friends you have? Yes _____ No _____ Why?
*20. Do the answers to Question 19a and 19b matter to you?
    Mother: No _____ Yes _____ Why?
    Father: No _____ Yes _____ Why?
* Answers of the Yes-No pattern are reversed purposely to catch a spontaneous response, not the more socially acceptable one.

Questions 18–19 are undisguised inquiry into parental attitudes about how many friends their adolescent has, and they indirectly measure parental support for the adolescent's having friends. Question 20—"Does it matter what they think?"—addresses how concerned the adolescent is about parental views on his or her friendship choices. A reply to this question of "not really" or "I want them to like my friends, but as long as they don't severely object I continue to be friends with whomever I wish" might indicate an advanced stage of development or, if a defensive glitch is suspected, may point to a problem area and should be so noted for further attention. A firm response of "no" or shades of "never" requires further inquiry.

PAR-AA (Adolescent Alternative) Protocol

The PAR-AA (Adolescent Alternative) protocol explores the possibility that the adolescent has serious problems, including defensive glitches. As discussed earlier, this protocol is usually used immediately after completing the referral information. It can also be used either in the midst of or just after using the PAR-A if the professional becomes concerned that a defensive glitch may be operating. In that case, PAR-AA should be used immediately or as soon as possible in part or in full, according to need. A very few questions from PAR-A may be interspersed while using the PAR-AA when they are necessary to clarify a hypothesis.

PAR 3: PAR-AA (ADOLESCENT ALTERNATIVE)
ID# _____ Age: _____ yrs. _____ mos. _____ M _____ F _____
You mentioned that you prefer to be with fewer [*or* more] friends than before. I am interested to know why you have this preference.

1. Are they individual friends you see one at a time, or do you see them as a group?
2. Is the person [*or* group members] older [*or* younger] than you are?
3. What is it that you like about an older [*or* younger] friend?
4. When did this preference begin? What was the reason?
5. Are there special activities, pursuits, or conversation topics you enjoy together?
6. Are you happier? Why? *or* Why not? And why do you continue the friendship(s)?

Now, let's go on to some other questions.

7. Do your parents notice that you have changed your preferences to this one person [*or* persons *or* group]?
8. What do you think about that?
9. Do you ever miss being with a larger group?
10. What is it like if you ever need to be in a larger group?
11. How long has this been your attitude? How did it begin?
12. How long do you hope this/these relationship(s) would last?
13. What would you do if the other person(s) in the small groups seem less enthusiastic than in the beginning to have you with them?

14. Would you look for other friend(s)? What type?
15. Would you want the same number of friends? Why?
16. Or would you find more time to be with your mother or father? Neighborhood friends? Siblings? *If either of the latter,* What age are they?
17. How did you feel about answering these questions?

PAR-Aab (Adolescent Abridged) Protocol

PAR-Aab (Adolescent Abridged) protocol is available to switch to seamlessly if the adolescent is showing extreme distress in responding to PAR-A. It is not used often, but it is useful if needed. PAR-Aab serves as a substitute for PAR-A. It is shorter and elicits less information, but it is generally easier on a very anxious or disturbed adolescent. It may also be used if there is some question as to the validity of the adolescent's responses to PAR-A.

The first seven questions of PAR-Aab are the same as those of PAR-A. Thus, when switching to PAR-Aab, one can begin with, "I am not too sure I have gotten all your answers correctly. I am going to repeat some asked earlier." None of the other questions from PAR-A should be inserted. However, if some of the answers in PAR-A were incomplete, you can ask them again between the PAR-Aab questions. But since there may be a reason for an adolescent's lack of completeness, do not insist; just note the incomplete answer and either add a brief analytic note as to why or indicate "no analysis," but do not leave a blank.

PAR 4: PAR-AAB (ADOLESCENT ABRIDGED)

ID# _____ Age: _____ yrs. _____ mos. _____ M _____ F _____

1. Have you begun to prefer to be with a lot of friends rather than just a few? Yes _____ No _____
   If yes, When? _____
   If no, Any special reason? _____
2. Have the types of people you are friendly with changed? Yes _____ No _____
3. If so, how?
4. Are these friends part of a special group? Or are they from different groups? (*If the responses are negative to both of these questions, ask if the subject has any special friends.*)
5. Has the number of friends you have now
   increased? Yes _____ No _____ Why?
   decreased? Yes _____ No _____ Why?

6. Do you have a lot of friends? Yes ____ No ____ Why?
7. Do you prefer to be with fewer friends? Yes ____ No ____ Why?[8]
8. Which brothers and/or sisters are you closest to? ____ Why?
9. What do your brothers and/or sisters think about the type of friends you have?
   Brothers: Like them ____ Dislike them ____ Don't say ____
   Sisters: Like them ____ Dislike them ____ Don't say ____
*10. Has the type of people you are friendly with changed?
* This question is a validity check to see if the answer is the same as the answer to question 2. A different answer can reflect lack of cooperation or an inability to concentrate. Please note.

At the bottom of the PAR-AA or the PAR-Aab, add a note to "see attached information from the Nonverbal Diary" (see chapter 8), which should be automatically filled in after use of each protocol. Professionals should fill in the PAR 5 Behavioral Response to protocols PAR-A or PAR-Aab.

Behavioral Response Protocol

This very brief protocol records both the verbal and nonverbal participation of a very anxious adolescent. It can be contrasted with the activity levels implied or reported directly in the referral materials. It does not record emotional responses, as the Nonverbal Diary does, but the responses on these instruments may be compared or contrasted to provide early clues to an adolescent's cooperative or resistant attitudes or heightened anxiety.

PAR 5: BEHAVIORAL RESPONSE PROTOCOL
ID# ____ Age: ____ yrs. ____ mos. ____ M ____ F ____
Number of questions asked ____
Number of questions responded to ____
Behavioral response to each question _____
    Number of inquiries from adolescent ____

If either the PAR-AA or the PAR-Aab protocol, or both, supports suspicions that functioning or behaviors are far from the norm, it is advisable to proceed directly to the Phase II PAR-DG (Defensive Glitch) protocol offered in chapter 11. Data from the Phase I Nonverbal Diary and the

Behavioral Response protocol should accompany all findings. If the Phase I Circumstance-Specific Auxiliary protocols have not yet been used, it may be an option and prove helpful to administer them to parents, teachers, or important relevant others as appropriate.

Phase I Circumstance-Specific Auxiliary Protocols

The Auxiliary protocols are designed to be used with relevant adults and siblings. The questions complement those to which adolescents have already replied. The exact wording of the questions may differ as appropriate to the person being asked. The information to be obtained includes (1) parents' perspectives on their adolescent, their familiarity with his or her peer relationships and issues, and their level of involvement in their offspring's life, (2) parents' perspectives on the levels to which they are involved with and sensitive to the adolescent, as well as their perspectives on the adolescent's social experience, (3) teachers' perspectives on the adolescent's functioning in school and interactions with classmates and impressions of the adolescent's general problems or unusual behaviors, (4) perspectives of important environmental others. The overall objective is to add this variety of perceptions to the information already obtained.

PAR-P (Parent) Protocol

PAR 6: PAR-P (PARENT)

ID# _____ Age: _____ yrs. _____ mos. _____ M _____ F _____

1. Has your child begun to prefer to be with a lot of friends rather than just a few?

   Yes _____ No _____ *If yes,* When?

2. Have the types of those he/she is friendly with changed? Yes _____ No _____ *If yes,* How?

3. *If no,* What type of friends does he/she seem to continue to like to be with?

4. Are these friends part of a special group? Or are they from different groups? (*If the responses are negative to both of these questions, ask if the adolescent has any special friends.*)

5. Has the number of friends your child has now
   increased? Yes _____ No _____ Why?
   decreased? Yes _____ No _____ Why?

6. Does he/she have a lot of friends? Yes _____ No _____ Why?

7. Does he/she have a preference for fewer friends? Yes _____ No _____
Why?

8. Lately, does he/she prefer to spend more time with friends or family members?
Friends _____ Same age _____ Older _____ Younger _____
Family _____ Which family members? _____ Age
_____

9a. What does he/she think you feel about the number of friends he/she has? Too many _____ OK _____ Too few _____

9b. What does he/she think your mate feels about the number of friends he/she has? Too many _____ OK _____ Too few _____

10a. Do you like the people who are his/her friends? Yes _____ No _____
Don't care _____

10b. Does your mate like them? Yes _____ No _____ Doesn't care _____

11. What do you think about the amount of time he/she spends with his/her friends? Too much _____ Too little _____ Don't care _____

12. What does your mate think about the amount of time he/she spends with his/her friends? Too much _____ Too little _____ Doesn't care _____

13. Does he/she have older siblings? _____ Gender _____
Does he/she have younger siblings? _____ Gender _____

14. What do his/her brothers and sisters think about the types of his/her friends? Like them _____ Dislike them _____ Don't say _____

15. Are there exceptions to this attitude among them? Yes _____ No _____ *If yes,* Who? _____

16a. Do you encourage your adolescent to participate in activities with friends? (Respond for yourself and then for your mate.)
Mother: Yes _____ No _____ Does your mate? Yes _____ No _____

16b. Father: Yes _____ No _____ Does your mate? Yes _____ No _____

17a. Do you (mother) assist your child in getting to activities? Yes _____ No _____ Occasionally _____
If occasionally, How often? _____

17b. Do you (father) assist your child in getting to activities? Yes _____ No _____ Occasionally _____
If occasionally, How often? _____
If no or occasionally, How does he/she get there? _____
_____

*18a. Are you (mother) happy with how many friends he/she has? No _____
Yes _____ Why?

18b. Are you (mother) happy with how many friends you have? Yes ____
No ____ Why?

*19a. Are you (father) happy with how many friends your child has? No
____ Yes ____ Why?

19b. Are you (father) happy with the number of friends you have? Yes ____
No ____ Why?

*20. Do your spouse's answers to questions 18a and b and 19a and b matter
to you?
Mother: No ____ Yes ____ Which? _____
Father: No ____ Yes ____ Which? _____

* No is placed first to receive a spontaneous answer on a sensitive
question.

Parental Response Tracking in a Joint Interview: Analysis of PAR-P

If both parents strongly prefer to be interviewed together in spite of
the request for individual interviews, make a diary of the verbal activity
of each:

PAR 7: JOINT INTERVIEW VERBAL DIARY
Male parent: ¼ ____ ⅓ ____ ½ ____ ⅔ ____ ¾ ____ All ____
Female parent: ¼ ____ ⅓ ____ ½ ____ ⅔ ____ ¾ ____ All ____
Joint responses: ¼ ____ ⅓ ____ ½ ____ ⅔ ____ ¾ ____ All ____

An Example of How Protocols Work for the Professional: Paul

This brief case example shows how an initial analysis of the responses
to three protocols can help professionals move beyond the information
provided in the referral materials. It uses information obtained from PAR-
A, PAR-P, and PAR-OS.

Paul answered yes to the question of whether he has a lot of friends,
but an older sibling responded quite differently: "Not really. He likes to
think he does." The sentence "he likes to think he does" offers a natural
opening to question why the older sibling believes that to be the case. Because the PAR-P and the PAR-OS protocols provided the diagnostic impression that there was positive family interest in Paul, an issue external
to family problems that might be identified for further exploration is the
extent to which fantasy ("he likes to think he does") overshadows reality

for Paul: how serious is it? Or it may be a good idea to look further into Paul's relationship with his siblings.

The next step would be to ascertain from parents, siblings, and importantly from the school if Paul appears to be a daydreamer. If so, does daydreaming affect his family or school functioning? If his schoolwork is affected, academic testing can be useful. In Paul's case, testing revealed his performance to be slightly behind what is expected at his age. Could he possibly be a slow developer? If so, his cognitive development might lag behind that of most of his classmates, in which case there are a number of possible recommendations: (1) just waiting for some more growth, (2) special diagnostically oriented tutoring, or perhaps (3) a drop in one grade level to give Paul a chance to excel compared to age-mates.

It is wise to think twice before rushing into cognitive remediation strategies. For example, if Paul's physical stature and evidence of sexual development contradicts the diagnosis that he is a slow developer, he may be expected to do well in all areas and thus be misunderstood. Advanced physical development often encourages expectations of similarly paced development in all the growth domains, an incorrect assumption with any adolescent. In fact, Paul's cognitive development was slow, but this does not mean that it was insufficient. Just as sometimes shorter adolescents turn out ultimately to be among the tallest adults, cognitive development is dependent to a great extent on the speed with which myelinization of the nervous system occurs. So it may take a longer time for some adolescents to reach full development. Without this perspective, since Paul looks older, he is expected to perform as well as anyone in his classes, or perhaps better. He could even be mistakenly labeled an underachiever.

On the other hand, if there is a general consensus in a case such as Paul's that he is taking defensive flight to daydreaming, further work should be directed toward uncovering the cause. Use the PAR-AA protocol as soon as possible to explore this possibility further. No matter the type of troubling initial indicators, if the adolescent's behavior is distinctly far from the norm, proceed immediately to identify the antecedents of the adolescent's seeking relief through defensive flight. Continue with other Auxiliary protocols that seem appropriate. Sometimes it may be wise to start with the Sibling group.

PAR-S (Sibling) or PAR-OS (Older Sibling) Protocol

PAR 8: PAR-S (SIBLING) OR PAR-OS (OLDER SIBLING)

ID# _____ Age: _____ yrs. _____ mos. _____ M _____ F _____

Precise relationship: Full genetic sibling _____ Half genetic sibling _____

Other _____

1. When did _____ begin to prefer to be with a lot of friends rather than just a few?

2. Have the types of people _____ is friendly with changed? Yes _____ No _____ How?

3. Are these friends part of a special group? Are they from different groups? (*If responses are negative to both of these questions, ask if the subject has any special friends.*)

5. Have the number of friends _____ has now increased? Yes _____ No _____ Why?
   decreased? Yes _____ No _____ Why?

6. Does _____ have a lot of friends? Yes _____ No _____ Why?

7. Does _____ prefer to be with fewer friends? Yes _____ No _____ Why?

8. Lately, does _____ prefer to spend more time with friends your age? _____ Or with family? _____ *If family,* Which family members? _____

9. What do you think your parents feel about the number of friends _____ has? Too many _____ OK _____ Too few _____

10. Do your parents like the people who are _____'s friends? Yes _____ No _____ They don't care _____

11. What do they think about the amount of time _____ spends with friends? Too much _____ Too little _____ Don't care _____

12. What do you think about the amount of time _____ spends with friends? Too much _____ Too little _____ Don't care _____

13. What do you think about the amount of time you spend with your friends?

13a. What do your brothers/sisters think about the type of friends _____ has?
   Brothers: Like them _____ Dislike them _____ Don't say _____

13b. Sisters: Like them _____ Dislike them _____ Don't say _____

**14. Where do you stand in the age order of your family?

15a. Do your parents encourage _____ to participate in activities with friends?

Mother: Yes _____ No _____

15b. Father: Yes _____ No _____

16a. Does your mother assist _____ in getting there? Yes _____ No _____ Occasionally _____

16b. Does your father assist _____ in getting there? Yes _____ No _____ Occasionally _____

17. *If answer is no or occasionally,* How does _____ get there? _____
_____

18. Do you think _____ is happy with how many friends he/she has? Yes _____ No _____ Why?

*19a. Is your mother happy with how many friends _____ has? No _____ Yes _____ Why?

*19b. Is your father happy with the number of friends _____ has? No _____ Yes _____ Why?

20a. Does the answer to question 19a matter to _____? Yes _____ No _____

20b. Does the answer to Question 19b matter to _____? Yes _____ No _____

* Again, whenever "No" appears first, it is to capture a spontaneous response.

** A validity check is inserted to determine truthfulness of response and/ or understanding of the questions.

PAR-T-I (Teachers and School Personnel I) Protocol

As in the case of Paul, it may be important to have information on the adolescent's behaviors at school, such as his academic performance, his classroom relations with peers, or the circumstances that stand out in the minds of teachers or school personnel.

PAR 9: PAR-T-I (TEACHERS AND SCHOOL PERSONNEL I)

ID# _____ Age: _____ yrs. _____ mos. _____ M _____ F _____

1. Does _____ complete homework assignments?

2. Does _____ participate in class? Yes _____ No _____ Frequency
_____

3. Does _____ generally appear comfortable? Yes _____ No _____ Somewhat _____
If no or somewhat, probe.

4. Does _____ appear to have friends?

5. Does _____ appear to be popular?
6. Does _____ appear to be a loner?
7. Does _____ approach you for assistance?
8. Is _____ a behavior problem? Yes ____ No ____ Sometimes ____ How?
9. Is _____ quieter than most students? Yes ____ No ____ Rowdier? Yes ____ No ____
10. Does _____ appear alert most of the time? Yes ____ No ____ Out of it most of the time? Yes ____ No ____
11. What is _____'s level of work?
12. What is _____'s customary mood?
13. Have you had any problems with _____? Any concerns? About what?
14. Have you needed to consult a counselor? About what?
16. Does _____ excel generally? In a special way? At nothing?
17. Does _____ appear happy? Yes ____ No ____ Appear unhappy? Yes ____ No ____
18. Do you have any worries regarding _____?
20. Have you felt the need to contact parents? If so, why? Did you make contact?
21. Problem addressed and outcome: _____

_____

PAR-T-II (Teachers and School Personnel II) Protocol

PAR-T-II follows up on any information from a teacher or school personnel individual about a change in the adolescent's behavior or attitude since the time that parents were last in contact with the school.

PAR 10: PAR-T-II (TEACHERS AND SCHOOL PERSONNEL II)
ID# ____ Age: ____ yrs. ____ mos. ____ M ____ F ____
1. When did the change you noticed in the student's behavior begin?
2. What caused the change?
3. Do you believe the change is connected to the atmosphere at home? Yes ____ No ____
4. Any special person? Yes ____ No ____ At home? Yes ____ No ____ Elsewhere? Yes ____ No ____ Who? _____ Why?

_____

5. What information do you have from parent(s) about the identified person?
6. What is your impression of mother's/father's efforts to assist?
7. What is your impression of the person identified?
8. What is your impression of the impact on _____?
9. Do the parents believe there is a problem in school? If so, what? If not, why?
10. Do both parents approve of how the school treats their child?
    Father: Yes ____ No ____ Why?
    Mother: Yes ____ No ____ Why?
11. Do you believe the parents will continue to be involved? Why? *or* Why not?
12. *If no,* Do you believe the lack of involvement has the potential to change to some level of involvement? Yes ____ No ____
    If yes, How? _____
13. Is any change in school performance due to help from you? Yes ____ No ____ From classmates? Yes ____ No ____
    Whether answer is yes or no, ask for particulars.

PAR-E (Environmental Other) Protocol

PAR 11: PAR-E (ENVIRONMENTAL OTHER)
ID# ____ Age: ____ yrs. ____ mos. ____ M ____ F ____
1. How do you know _____?
2. How long have you known _____?
3. How would you describe _____?
4. Do you feel you are emotionally distant? Yes ____ No ____ Close?
   Yes ____ No ____ Friendly? Yes ____ No ____
   Do you consider yourself a friend? Yes ____ No ____ An adviser?
   Yes ____ No ____
5. Are you critical or do you praise most of the time? Critical ____
   Praise ____
6. What are your hopes for _____?
7. What are your criticisms of _____?
8a. Are _____'s friends (a) Decent ____ (b) Special ____ (c) A
    bad influence? ____ How? _____
         Why do you think _____ has those friends?
8b. Is _____ afraid to meet new people? Yes ____ No ____ Eager
    to meet new people? Yes ____ No ____

8c. Does _____not care one way or the other? Yes _____ No _____

9. Why did you decide to accept this invitation to come in and talk with me?

10. Do you have any concerns about _____?

11. Are there any questions you might like to ask me?

12. Do you have an idea why it is helpful for me to talk to you about _____?

PAR-G (Group Administration) Protocol

An adolescent's behavior in a group setting can be quite different from his or her behavior when alone or with a relative, teacher, or older person. Information gained from brief observation of an adolescent's behavior in a group is important in placing him or her for PAL group therapy and gives the professional a heads-up on that placement during the diagnostic phase. If an adolescent's referral data and early contact with the intake professional raise the possibility that he or she will display atypical types of behavior with a group of peers or will display other, new behaviors, one or two small group sessions of no more than four adolescents can be arranged.

Examining group protocols of four adolescents together for even a very limited time adds useful information about how they may handle themselves within the therapy group. Questions can be generated such as the following: Is their manner the same or different from what is seen in individual session? In which setting do they appear more or less comfortable? How is this comfort level expressed, verbally and nonverbally? Are leadership qualities expressed? Is sarcasm expressed? Is there interpersonal humor or asides to just one other person in the group? Are there smiles or sour expressions? What type of individual may silence them or encourage them to share?

Since adolescent interaction is primarily group related, findings provide important data not only for placement in PAL group therapy but for the therapy itself, as well as sometimes indicating that PAL therapy is not the appropriate therapy. Particularly important is the adolescent's nonverbal relationship with the professional, that is, whether they look to the professional for support and with what frequency. The professional should be alert to messages that the behavior carries, from "Help me" to "Am I watched more than the others?"

All four adolescents in a group may show behavior not apparent in one-to-one consultation. In a diagnostic group, the professional should observe dynamics such as who starts the discussion going, interactions, extent of verbal and nonverbal behavior of each participant, degree of self-control, mannerisms, body posture, expressions of agreement or disagreement, and whether participants are active or withdrawn. It is very important to notice who is watching whom. Special notes should report nuances, observable emotions, and mannerisms and whether behaviors reported in the referral materials are observed and, if so, when.

For each of the adolescents in the group, fill out a PAR Group Process Record:

PAR 12: PAR-G (GROUP PROCESS RECORD)
Adolescent names
A _____
B _____
C _____
D _____
Adolescent A [or B, C, D] name _____
  • Observable affect: Relaxed ____ Moderate stress ____ Troubled ____
    Beginning affect _____ Midway affect
    _____ Ending affect _____
  • Initial question/matter contributed for discussion: Name
    _____ Question/matter _____ Affect
    _____
  • Ending question/comment contributed for discussion: Name
    _____ Question/matter _____ Affect
    _____
  User summary statement _____

In Tandem Analyses

New hypotheses are often stimulated by analyzing responses from two different sources in tandem. Clinicians are especially encouraged to ponder over the significance of agreement between two sources. For example, such an analysis may reveal that siblings have created an alliance against their parents. Questions can then be raised about where the power is in the family, which may provide a whole new set of insights into the family dynamics and their impact on the adolescent. It is also useful to think about what strategies are being used by the adolescent subject and his or her siblings to gain power. Are they also deliberately or unconsciously employed in his or her choice of a defensive glitch? When professionals look beyond the assumption of rebellion against parents to other powerful dynamics such as power, they can entertain new hypotheses.

Now, we move on to protocols that yield information on adolescent relationships proper. The following chapter offers Phase I Supplementary protocols with which to obtain perspectives to add to that elicited by the Basic and Auxiliary protocols. This Supplementary series focuses on the adolescent's experience with school and other peers, his or her attitudes about home life, and his or her perspectives when alone. Among this group are protocols designed to penetrate the essence of the Peer Arena comparison experience.

10

Phase I Continued: Supplementary Protocols for Further Exploration

Many of the questions in the Supplementary protocols focus on peers and friendship, on comparative-act dynamics in the Peer Arena and their results and impact on matters of interest to adolescents in the present and on their future goal setting (issues introduced in parts 1 and 2 of this book). Embedded in the Supplementary protocols are questions that may seem quite neutral but actually elicit the information sought or lead up to eliciting qualitative information such as emotional reactions to comparative acts with age-mates. A few questions may be recognized as having been asked in prior protocols; they are asked again in order to compare the adolescent's consistency, as well as his or her disassociation or just plain avoidance, expressed in nonserious responses. These repeated questions also serve well as ice-breakers to reopen issues involving school and parents. Please note the presence of "trailer" questions interspersed between the numbered questions. These questions ask adolescents for more depth in their response than what they initially volunteer.

A cautionary note: When a professional suspects that an adolescent may have a defensive glitch, there may be an impulse to go directly to Phase II Defensive Glitch protocols (chapter 11). Except in emergencies, when an immediate action is required, a cautionary stance is best. Taking the time for a careful study of all pertinent Phase I Supplementary protocols that may yield additional information before making a definite diagnosis will reassure or give clues to other operative dynamics and thus assure the integrity of a *ruling-in and ruling-out* process, which is essential to accurate diagnosis.

Present-Focused Supplementary Protocols
PAR-Su-SEP (Student Educational Perspective) Protocol

PAR 13: PAR-SU-SEP (STUDENT EDUCATIONAL PERSPECTIVE)

ID# _____ Age: _____ yrs. _____ mos. _____ M _____ F _____

1. Lately, would you rather spend time with friends or family members?
   If family members, Which and why?
2. How do your parents feel about the number of friends you have?
3. About the types of friends?
4. About the amount of time you spend with them?
5. Do your parents try to help you with your friendships, or do they try to change them?
6. Do they make you stay at home a lot?
7. If so, doing what?
8. Is schoolwork included?
9. Is it only schoolwork?
10. Do you think your schoolwork is at the same level this year as it was previously?
    If no or equivocal, ask questions 11–16 and 19. If yes, skip those questions.
11. Has it gotten better or worse?
12. When did the change start?
13. What caused the change?
14. Is the change connected to the atmosphere at home? Yes _____ No _____
15. *If yes,* Why?
16. *If no,* Is the change connected to any special person outside your home?
17. Do you like school? Yes _____ No _____ Why?
18. Would you like to quit? Yes _____ No _____ Why?
19. Is the change in school performance due to teachers? Yes _____ No _____ To classmates? Yes _____ No _____
    If yes, ask for particulars.
20. Are there other out-of-school reasons that might be affecting your schoolwork that have nothing to do with schoolwork? Yes _____ No _____
21. Might it be connected with types of people you run into at school? Yes _____ No _____
22. Are they like you? *If yes,* How? *If no,* How are they different?

PAR-Su-PEP (Parent Educational Perspective) and PAR-Su-TEP (Teacher Educational Perspective) Protocols

These two protocols focus on the impact of home, neighborhood, and school on the adolescent's peer relations and schoolwork. Please note the extreme similarity of these protocols, which is both for informational purposes and for comparison analysis. These protocols are used to elicit additional information on the pressures on adolescents from the home and school environments. Teachers may state or imply that they suspect a home-based reason for an adolescent's maladaptive school behavior, such as overt aggressiveness toward peers or withdrawal from interaction with them. On the other hand, parents may feel that it is the school atmosphere that contributes to the problems.

PAR 14A: PAR-SU-PEP (PARENT EDUCATIONAL PERSPECTIVE)

ID# _____ Age: _____ yrs. _____ mos. _____ M _____ F _____

1. Lately, would your adolescent rather spend time with friends or family members? Friends _____ Family _____ Why? *If friends,* What type?
2. How do you feel about the number of friends your adolescent has?
3. About the types of friends?
4. About the amount of time he/she spends with them?
5. Do you try to help the friendships grow or change them? All _____ Some _____ No _____ Please explain.
6. Do you make your adolescent stay at home a lot? Yes _____ No _____
7. *If yes,* Doing what? Why? *If no,* Why?
8. Is schoolwork included? Why?
9. Is it only schoolwork? Why?
10. Do you think the schoolwork is at the same level this year as previously?
    If no or equivocal, ask questions 11–15 and 18–20. If yes, skip those questions.
11. Has it gotten better or worse?
12. When did the change start?
13. What caused the change?
14. Is the change connected to the atmosphere at home?
15. Is the change connected to any special person at home?
16. Do you like the school? Yes _____ No _____ Why?
17. Would you want _____ to be moved to a different school? Yes _____ No _____ Why?

18. Is the change in school performance due to teachers? To classmates? *If yes, ask for particulars.*

19. Are there other out-of-school reasons that might be affecting your adolescent's schoolwork that have nothing to do with schoolwork?

20a. Is it possibly connected with adolescents your adolescent runs into at school?

20b. Are they like your adolescent? *If yes,* How? *If no,* What is different? *If no reply, cease questions.*

21. Do you see any connection between school subjects and what your adolescent will do or be in the future? Yes _____ No _____ Why?

22. Do you see any connection between people he/she is friendly with now and what he/she will do or be in the future? Yes _____ No _____ Why?

23. Do you see any connection between friends he/she was with in the past and what he/she will do or be in the future? Yes _____ No _____ Why?

24. Can your adolescent manage school and friends? Yes _____ No _____ Why?

25. Is there something totally different that might be in your mind? Please explain.

PAR 14B: PAR-SU-TEP (TEACHER EDUCATIONAL PERSPECTIVE)
ID# _____ Age: _____ yrs. _____ mos. _____ M _____ F _____

1. Lately, is it your impression that _____ would rather spend time with friends or family members? Friends _____ Family _____ Which friends or family members? Why?

2. How do you feel about the number of friends he/she has in school?

3. About the types of friends?

4. About the amount of time he/she spends with them?

5. Do you have an opportunity to try to help the friendships grow or change them? All _____ Some _____ No _____ Please explain.

6. Do you think _____ stays at home a lot? Yes _____ No _____

7. *If yes,* Does _____ tell you what he/she does when at home? Why? *If no,* Why?

8. Is schoolwork included? How do you know? Why does _____ do schoolwork?

9. Is it only schoolwork? *If yes,* Why? *If no,* What else?

10. Do you think his/her schoolwork is at the same level this year as previously?

If no or equivocal, ask questions 11–15 and 18–20. If yes, skip those questions.

11. Has it gotten better or worse?
12. When did the change start?
13. What caused the change?
14. Is the change connected to the atmosphere at home?
15. Is the change connected to any special person at home?
16. Do you think _____ likes the school? Yes ____ No ____ Why?
17. Is the change in school performance due classmates?
    If yes, ask for particulars.
18. *If no,* Would a move to another school be advisable? Yes ____ No ____ Why?
19. Are there other out-of-school reasons that might be affecting _____'s schoolwork that have nothing to do with schoolwork?
20. Do you think it might be connected with types of peers he/she runs into at school?
    Are they like _____? *If yes,* How? *If no,* How are they different?
21. Do you believe _____ can manage school and friends at the same time? Yes ____ No ____ Why?
22. Is there something totally different that might be in your mind? Please explain.

PAR-Su-FP (Friendship Preferences) Protocol

This protocol offers an overview of an adolescent's friendship preferences and any changes from his or her past patterns. It also offers a validity check on information given previously.

PAR 15: PAR-SU-FP (FRIENDSHIP PREFERENCES)
ID# ____ Age: ____ yrs. ____ mos. ____ M ____ F ____
Procedure: unless clinically indicated, ask in consecutive order.

1. Where did you and your friends meet each other?
2. Are they neighborhood friends or school friends or both?
3. Are they from other places? Yes ____ No ____ *If yes,* How did the friendship develop?
4. Did you always meet new friends the same way you do now?
5. Does that help you make all the friends you want?
   If no, How do you think you will get to meet others?
6. How many friends would you like to have?

Get-Togethers

    7. Where do you and your friends generally get together now?
If "lots of places," inquire gently for specifics.

    8. Are there any activities most all of you like to do?
        a. *If yes,* What is the activity? _____ *then*
        b. Is your preference to carry on this activity alone _____ or with friends _____?

    9. Do you have favorite places to go to?
If yes, Where? _____ Do you prefer to go to these places alone _____ or with friends _____?

   10. How do you get there?

   11. Do you go alone or with friends?
If it is at a distance, How do they get there?

   12. Are you personally ever left out because you can't get there? Yes _____ No _____
If yes, How do you deal with that? _____

   13. How do you feel about that outcome?

Appeal of the Usual or the New

   14. Are you interested in being with old friends? Yes _____ No _____ Why? How many? _____

   15. New friends? Yes _____ No _____ Why? How many? _____

   16. How long has it been that way for both categories?

   17. Any special reason?
If choice is only old friends, ask the reason.
If choice is only new friends, ask why the preference for new, not old.
If choice is both, say, "Oh, that's interesting. Please explain."

Past Actions

   18. In the past, did you make friends with most everybody? Yes _____ No _____

   19. Were you fairly selective? Yes _____ No _____ *If yes,* How? *If no,* Why?

   20. What do you do now?

   21. Are you sad or happy about the current situation with friends? Sad _____ Happy _____ Both _____ Don't care _____ Please explain.

   22. Is there anything you might like to change? Yes _____ No _____ Why?

   23. *If yes,* How would it help?

   24. Is this something you need to do? Yes _____ No _____ Maybe _____
Please explain.

25. Would you rather just go off on your own? Yes ____ No ____ Sometimes ____ Please explain.
26. Do you think it would/does make you happier? Yes ____ No ____ Please explain.

Status Summary: The data collected in the questions so far will give the practitioner a very good picture of the gestalt of friendships.

PAR-Su-GU (What Do You Have to Give Up) Protocol

This protocol begins the inquiry into when the adolescent shut off friends, why, and what it has been like. This information begins to relay the point at which findings from comparative acts became too painful and a way out was pursued.

PAR 16: PAR-SU-GU (WHAT DO YOU HAVE TO GIVE UP)
ID# ____ Age: ____ yrs. ____ mos. ____ M ____ F ____

1. When you decided to turn off being with friends, what do you gain? Lose?
2. When you decided to turn off thinking about characteristics, abilities, or opinions that friends hold, what do you gain? Lose?
3. When you decided to turn off thinking about actions that friends take, what do you gain? Lose?
7. What could a substitute for a good friend be? Please explain.
8. How might you feel when others have a crowd and you do not?
9. Has this ever happened to you? Yes ____ No ____ *If yes,* Please tell me about it.
10. Have you ever picked folks to befriend just because you wanted friends and anyone was better than no one? Yes ____ No ____
    If yes, Was it successful? Yes ____ No ____ *If no,* Why not? *In either case,* Please explain.

PAR-Su-FO (What Do Friends Offer You) Protocol

This protocol should be used on the same day that any of the other protocols are used. It is best that it be used directly after another protocol, without interruption, so that the response mode is carried over. Since the protocol asks hard questions, it is best to adopt a quiet and gentle demeanor. Give the adolescent as long as he or she needs to answer each question before asking if he or she is ready to go on to the next question.

PAR 17: PAR-SU-FO (WHAT DO FRIENDS OFFER YOU)

ID# _____ Age: _____ yrs. _____ mos. _____ M _____ F _____

1. Is it better to have friends than not to have friends? Yes _____ No _____
   Noncommittal _____ *Ask an explanation for any answer.*
   If noncommittal, say, "You seem to be noncommittal. Why?"

2. What do they offer you that makes it worth the time spent with them?
   If answer is not responsive, repeat What is it that they offer you?

3. Is what they offer you something you could only get from them?
   Yes _____ No _____ Noncommittal _____ Please explain.

4. Instead of being with friends, would you ever prefer just to watch TV?
   Yes _____ No _____ Not really* _____ Why?

5. Read? Yes _____ No _____ Not really _____ Why?

6. Play with younger siblings? Yes _____ No _____ Not really _____ Why?

7. Talk to older siblings? Yes _____ No _____ Not really _____ Why?

8. Talk to parents? Yes _____ No _____ Not really _____ Why?

9. Drink alcohol or smoke marijuana? Yes _____ No _____ Not really _____
   Why the preference?

10. Some other drug? Yes _____ No _____ Not really _____ Why? Which?

11. Was this always the way you thought? Yes _____ No _____
    If no, When did you change? In recent times? Times in the past? What brought about this change?

13. Would you rather just be with friends your age? Yes _____ No _____ Not sure _____ Maybe _____

* *"Not really" is a response, as is "maybe," that should be explored further, for example, by asking, "Can you tell me what 'not really' means? If "not really" is not defined, probe further with, "Does it mean it is more on the positive side than the negative or the opposite, more on the negative side than the positive?"*

PAR-Su-R (Recuperation) Protocol

This short transitional protocol offers uncomplicated questions to allow adolescents to recuperate from prior questions, which have been stressful. It offers adolescents the opportunity to turn the tables a bit and be something of an expert. It serves two functions: eliciting new information and providing some psychic rest. If the adolescent appears uncomfortable, note the fact and do not raise the matter, but keep this time off as short as possible.

PAR 18: PAR-SU-R (RECUPERATION)

ID# _____ Age: _____ yrs. _____ mos. _____ M _____ F _____

1. What is it about a friend you like to be with a lot that attracts you? How so?
2. Is it the same as a few years ago? Yes _____ No _____ How so?
3. If the reasons have changed, what is different now?
4. Are the characteristics that you like easy or hard to find in others? Easy _____ Hard _____ If finding these characteristics is easier or harder than last year, explain why.
5. Does what you look for now differ from what you looked for in friends two or three years ago? Yes _____ In what way? No _____ Why?

PAR-Su-KF (Keeping Friends) Protocol

This protocol elicits emotional responses regarding situations in which the adolescent is not in agreement with peer positions. The questions may strike tender spots.

PAR 19: PAR-SU-KF (KEEPING FRIENDS)
Finding Friends

1. How does it feel when you can find the kind of friends you want fairly easily?
2. Is it important to you to find friends easily? Please explain.
3. What is it like when you can't easily find the friends you want? Hard _____ OK _____ I manage _____ Other _____
4. Can you describe what it feels like when it is hard?
5. What makes it hard?
6. What do you mean when you say "OK"? Or "I manage"?

Agreeing versus Not Agreeing with Friends

7. What is it like when you don't quite agree with what most friends *say*?
8. What is it like when you don't quite agree with what most friends *believe*?
9. How do you deal with this?
10. What is it like when you don't quite agree with what most friends *want to do*?
11. How do you respond?
12. Is this how you really want to respond? Yes _____ No _____ Sort of _____ Please elaborate.

13. What is it like when you don't quite agree with what most friends actually *do*?
14. What do you do at those times?
15. Is this the way you always handled these situations? Yes _____ No _____
    If no, When did it change? Why the change? *If yes,* Why?

Status Summary: The professional has begun to tap risks and outcomes in the adolescent's interactions with peers.

PAR-Su-AC (Awareness of Comparisons) Protocol

This protocol initiates a probe to determine what level of awareness an adolescent has of engaging in comparative acts. If responses are easily forthcoming, the PAR-Su-CA (Comparative Act) protocol should follow seamlessly. If responses are not easily forthcoming, stop until later, when the adolescent may be more ready, or cease questioning. If you cease questioning, proceed in your diagnostic evaluation with the information that was elicited, noting reasons for stopping at the point you did.

PAR 20: PAR-SU-AC (AWARENESS OF COMPARISONS)
ID# _____ Age: _____ yrs. _____ mos. _____ M _____ F _____
1. How do you know if your friends are like you? If they are unlike you?
   If the subject has difficulty answering, prod by asking, "Do you look at or listen to what friends say?" If no, ask, "Just what do you do when with friends?" If the response is "I don't have any," ask if you can be of help. If there is no answer, or if the answer is that there is nothing you can do, note the response on the record and go on to next question.
2. What are the best places to observe age-mates?
   If the response is withdrawal, note the behavior on the record and say, "It looks like today is not a good day for you. Shall we try another?" Depending on the response, make a future date and time, or just stop.
3. How often do you observe them just to see how they act and/or what they do?
4. Is it just with familiar friends?
5. Others too? Yes _____ No _____ Who are they?
6. How about age-mates that are not close at hand, like in the movies, in magazines, on TV, or on the Internet? Do you observe them often? Which ones?

7. Is it helpful when you are having troubles to watch others?
8. Where do you find same-age friends? Other-age friends?
9. Which are you most interested in, same age or other age? *If other age, ask what age.*
10. Do you observe a few kids? Yes _____ No _____
11. A lot? Yes _____ No _____
12. As many as can be found? Yes _____ No _____
13. Are they actual people you see in your life or people in the media? Actual _____ Media _____ *If media,* Are they real people or cartoons? Real _____ Cartoons _____
14. Does looking at them give you ideas about yourself? *If yes,* What kind? *If no,* I wonder why not. Any idea?
15. Generally speaking, do you get something out of checking others out? *If yes,* What?
16a. Is it encouraging? Yes _____ No _____
16b. Discouraging? Yes _____ No _____ *If no,* I wonder why. Any ideas?

PAR-Su-CA (Comparative Act) Protocol

This protocol goes right to the heart of the issue. Generally, it is used after PAR 20, but it can be skipped if the introductory information has already been sufficiently elicited in some other protocol or verbal exchange.

PAR 21: PAR-SU-CA (COMPARATIVE ACT)

ID# _____ Age: _____ yrs. _____ mos. _____ M _____ F _____

1. Do you think you compare what you are doing to what other people your age are doing? Yes _____ No _____
2. With what they are saying? Yes _____ No _____
3. With how they act? Yes _____ No _____
4. On what do you compare?
   If the answer is "nothing," probe with easy questions to which subject is likely to say yes, e.g., "On what movie they last saw?" or "On who their favorite sports star is?" Then go on to question 5 and add "about me" at the end of the question.
5. What are you trying to find out?
   If answer is "I never thought about it before," suggest he/she thinks about it now and replies to the question. Note response.

6. How do you find answers to questions you have about them? *Replace "them" with "me" and ask again. Note response. Read question 7 as written.*

7. About yourself in comparison to them?

   If subject is quiet and really struggling, suggest you can come back to this question and others at a later time. Ask if this seems reasonable to him/ her. If answer is yes, cease the questions in this protocol from questions 8 through 21 and pick up at question 22. Return at a later session to questions he/she did not feel up to answering. At that time, ask if he/she is up to it now. If answer is no, probe gently as to why and record response but cease questioning. If he/she wishes to continue, return to question 6 or 7 and say, "We were talking about how you might feel about yourself in comparison to others you know." Continue through question 21. Stop at any point he/she wishes to stop, ask why, but meet his/her request.

   Questions 7–21 reach tender zones. Observe subject carefully for signs of real stress, note question numbers and response, but if your clinical judgment dictates, cease questioning and say, "Tomorrow, we will turn to something else," unless this is the last diagnostic contact, in which case advise subject when he/she might hear from you.

8. Which questions do you sometimes ask only about yourself?

9. Do you compare with peers who you think are better than you on the characteristics you usually wonder about in yourself? Yes _____ No _____

10. With peers not as good as you are? Yes _____ No _____
    If yes, About what? *If no,* Why not?

11. With peers about the same as you? Yes _____ No _____

12. When with peers better than you are, what are you trying to find out?
    If necessary, suggest categories such as school, sports, dancing, etc.

13. Did you ever *find out* you are better than you thought?
    Does this happen every now and then _____, frequently _____, or seldom _____?

14. How does it *feel* when you find out you are better than you thought?
    Great _____ Good _____ OK _____ Bad _____

15. Worse than you thought? _____
    Does this happen frequently _____, every now and then _____, or seldom _____?

16. Right around where you would predict? _____
    Does this happen frequently _____, every now and then _____, or seldom _____?

17. Does looking closely at your peers give you ideas about your own self?
    Yes _____ No _____ Sometimes _____ *Whatever the reply, probe gently.*

18. When you are disappointed in yourself, do you consider forgetting
    what age-mates do or say? Yes _____ No _____ Sometimes _____ *What-
    ever the reply, probe gently.*

19. Did this happen before or after you felt you started feeling disappointed
    in yourself? Before _____ After _____ Never happened _____ Other _____

20. Did it affect the number of friends you have? Yes _____ No _____ Why?

21. Did you compare with others around your own age before you joined
    groups you are in now? Yes _____ No _____ At times _____ *If at times,*
    When?

22. Do you compare with others around your own age now? Yes _____ No
    _____ At times _____ *If at times,* When?

23. With whom? Are they members of your old groups? Yes _____ No _____
    New ones? _____ Yes _____ No _____ *If yes,* Which?

24. Does looking closely at them give you ideas about yourself? Yes _____
    No _____ At times _____

25. What are some of those ideas?
    If no reply, Like what you might want to be in the future? Yes _____ No
    _____ Sometimes _____ *If no,* Why?

Future-Focused Supplementary Protocols

After completing the selected protocols up to this point, the professional
should have enough information for a working diagnosis. The protocols
that follow are appropriate for older adolescents who have completed assembling most of their temporary self-elements and are nearing the end
of high school (end of Stage 1 adolescence). At this time, the future becomes prominent in their conversations. For adolescents whose cognitive
development is still slow, however, planning for the future does not have
much importance. It is unnatural for younger adolescents to be as interested in future matters as older peers. If they are, be wary of their using
fantasy and future planning to insulate themselves from the present.

PAR-Su-FFD (Fantasies and Future Dreams) Protocol

This protocol taps the subject's thoughts and ambitions about postadolescent life. It gives clinicians an insight into the extent to which adolescents are able to set aside their present concerns. It also assists clinicians

to find out about adolescents' dreams of their future, including their aspirations and which individuals will assist them in achieving those aspirations.

PAR 22: PAR-SU-FFD (FANTASIES AND FUTURE DREAMS)

ID# _____ Age: _____ yrs. _____ mos. _____ M _____ F _____

1. When looking at others your age, do you see yourself as equal, superior, or inferior to most of them? Equal _____ Superior _____ Inferior _____ Don't know _____ Please explain.

2. Do you ever meet someone who appears to be what you might want to be in the future? Yes _____ No _____ On rare occasions _____ Please explain.

3. How you would like to appear in the eyes of your friends? *If answer is "I don't know," gently probe a bit.*

4. Would you want them to think you are cool? Yes _____ No _____ Please explain.

5. Would you want them to think you are a leader? Yes _____ No _____ Please explain.

6. Would you like to wear expensive clothes and look rich? Yes _____ No _____ Please explain.

7. Or be very smart? Yes _____ No _____ Please explain.

8. Or be very good at sports? Yes _____ No _____ Please explain.

9. Or have a fancy car? Yes _____ No _____ Please explain.

10. What does having a fancy car mean?

11. What is it like if you don't have one? Or if you do have one?

12a. Will being with the group of friends you like to be with get you the things you would like to own? Yes _____ No _____ Maybe _____ Please explain.

12b. *If no,* Why are you in the group?

12c. *If no,* Why don't you join a different group?

13. Will being with the group(s) of friends you like to be with make it easier for you to be what you would like to be? Yes _____ No _____ Maybe _____ How? *Or* Why not?

14. Will they help you to get what you want? Yes _____ No _____ Maybe _____ Please explain. *If no,* Why do you spend time with them?

15. Do you consider yourself a member of their group? Why?

16. Do you feel trapped with the friends you have now? Why?

17. Is there a reason you don't separate off from them? Yes _____ No _____ *If yes,* Would you like to tell me about it?

If no, proceed no further and say, "We have finished all the questions. Do you have any?"

18. Do you see any connection between school subjects and what you will do or be in the future? Yes _____ No _____ *If yes,* Which subjects and why? *If no,* Why?

19. Do you see any connection between school activities and what you will do or be in the future? Yes _____ No _____ *If yes,* Which activities and why? *If no,* Why?

20. Do you see any connection between those you are friends with and what you may do or be in the future? Yes _____ No _____ *If yes,* Which and why? *If no,* Why?

PAR-Su-DA (Defensive Actions Reflection) Protocol

This brief protocol asks the adolescent to reflect on his or her fantasies and dreams and whether they are achievable.

PAR 23: PAR-SU-DA (DEFENSIVE ACTIONS REFLECTION)

ID# _____ Age: _____ yrs. _____ mos. _____ M _____ F _____

1. What made you think that [insert a, b, c, d, or e] would make you happier?
   a.   new friends
   b.   new hobby
   c.   new cause
   d.   staying around older folks
   e.   staying around folks younger than you
   I just did _____ I don't know _____ Reason given _____
   _____

2. Is it turning out the way you thought it would? Yes _____ No _____ Why? *Regardless of answer, probe further.*

PAR-Su-F (Future) Protocol

This protocol offers pragmatic questions about what the adolescent thinks of his or her future. It yields information about who will be at his or her side and probes a relationship between now and then. In essence, the protocol tests the subject's sense of reality.

PAR 24: PAR-SU-F (FUTURE)

ID# _____ Age: _____ yrs. _____ mos. _____ M _____ F _____

1. What do you think or feel about this statement: "Your future is ahead of you"?
2. How old will you be when your "future" begins? _____ Please elaborate.
3. What do you see in your future?
4. Do you have to prepare for it? Yes _____ No _____ Other _____
   If no, Why not?
5. How will you do this?
6. Will any others be there to help you? Yes _____ No _____ Who?
7. How will friends contribute to your future?
8. Will they be there for you? Yes _____ No _____
9. Might they hinder you at times? Yes _____ No _____ Might others hinder you? _____
10. Will any relatives be there for you? Yes _____ No _____ *If yes,* Who?
    If no, Why not? Will others be there for you? _____ *If yes,* Who?
11. How well do you think you will do?
12. Is there anything you can do now to help you prepare?
13. Who is at your side now? _____ Please explain.
14. Do you think you could manage alone? Why? _____
    Why not? _____
15. If you are truly alone, and feel alone too, do you think you can manage? Why? _____ Why not?

_____

Status Summary: Protocols 22 (FFD), 23 (DA), and 24 (F) yield both present reflections and future expectations. They are rich for reality testing of potential as well as for discussing plans to achieve these goals.

PAR-Su-EI (Emotional Income and Deprivation) Protocol

This brief protocol seeks information about the moments of happiness and pride, if any, in an adolescent's life, as well as information about moments of sadness and shame. It introduces questions about parents' regard for the adolescent. The last question can yield information on the level of disappointment felt by the adolescent or the strength of the denial.

PAR 25: PAR-SU-EI (EMOTIONAL INCOME AND DEPRIVATION)

ID# _____ Age: _____ yrs. _____ mos. _____ M _____ F _____

1. When were you the happiest? Please explain.
2. When were you the saddest? Please explain.
3. When was your best time? Please elaborate.
4. When was your worst time? Please elaborate.
5. What was your most embarrassing moment? Any other feelings?
6. What was your proudest moment?
7. When was it?
8. When were your parents most proud of you? Please explain.
9. When were your parents least proud of you? Please explain.
10. Were your parents ever ashamed of you? Please explain.
11. Does it matter to you? Yes _____ No _____ Please explain.

PAR-OD (Observable Demeanor): A Comparative-Act Behavior Protocol

Although the next protocol (#26) may appear almost to duplicate the Nonverbal Diary (#1) or the Behavioral Response protocol (#5), it has been developed not for the intake process but for use directly after the completion of each necessary Supplementary protocol in order to record the subject's stress responses during the comparison experience and thus to tap possible behavioral clues to his or her eventual flight to a defensive glitch.

A summary analysis of all an adolescent's behaviors can be forwarded to the PAL group therapy oversight professional, because such a summary provides clues into the adolescent's experience of stressful topics when *away* from peers and can be valuable in comparing and contrasting the behaviors observed during the course of PAL group therapy.

Ideally, the PAR-OD protocol is filled out by the professional as soon after the session as possible. Doing so promotes accurate memory and thus provides higher validity to the information. A separate record should be filled out for each protocol used. PAR-OD can be used with all PAR protocols. If dictated by clinical judgment, special exception can be made to use it for PAL group therapy or during the intake period.

PAR 26: PAR-OD (OBSERVABLE DEMEANOR)

ID# _____ Age: _____ yrs. _____ mos. _____ M _____ F _____

1. Age appearance relative to actual age:
   Older _____ Younger _____ Appropriate to age _____

Reasons _____

2. Dress appearance relative to customary dress for actual age:
   Older _____ Younger _____ Appropriate to age _____
   Reasons _____

3. Attitude displayed at beginning of session:
   Cooperative——1——2——3——4——5——Uncooperative
   Reasons _____

4. Flexibility–Rigidity Continuum: Does the persona appear flexible? Yes
   _____ No _____ Both _____ If both, explain.

5. The adolescent handled a one-to-one relationship with
   Comfort——1——2——3——4——5——6——7——Discomfort

6. Attitude at midsession:
   Cooperative——1——2——3——4——5——Uncooperative

7. Attitude at end of session:
   Cooperative——1——2——3——4——5——Uncooperative
   Why?

8. Length of first session: _____ minutes. Why?

9. Temporary hypotheses: Appearance and manner suggest subject may
   have adopted a _____ defensive glitch
   Rationale _____
   Or subject may have adopted the following defensive glitches: _____
   _____
   Rationale _____

10. Today's diagnosis of hypothesized glitch, if any: _____
    Rationale _____
    Date _____

The following chapter presents the Phase II protocols used with adolescents who have been determined to have turned off Peer Arena comparative acts, thus aborting their development. These protocols assist in identifying defensive glitches.

11

Phase II: Defensive Glitch Protocols

The Phase II protocols are used with adolescents who have been determined to have psychologically turned off Peer Arena comparative acts, thus aborting or seriously delaying development. Notwithstanding these adolescents' psychological turning off, most of them remain in settings with peers, though some do flee these settings altogether. They engage defensive behaviors that I have been referring to as *defensive glitches*, some serious and some less so. But all these glitches divert energies away from normative tasks of growth. As discussed in chapters 6 and 7 glitches are defenses that adolescents build up to shield themselves from painful and disillusioning findings from their evaluations of comparisons with attachment-others, their peers. Some of these behaviors are open to view; others may have been selected by the adolescent in part because they do not appear problematic and do not raise suspicion. Perhaps these behaviors are perceived as merely "troublesome," not needing attention but noted in referral materials. As analyses of Phase I protocols proceeds, defensive glitches may be suspected.

Phase II protocols are geared to precise detection of which defensive glitch has been adopted. Findings often also offer clues for PAL therapy oversight professionals that help anticipate issues and behaviors that may arise during the course of therapy. Although protocols can be used during the PAL process if necessary, it is best to collect the information necessary for group placement in the intake period.

The Phase II protocols begin with PAR-DG (Defensive Glitch); the protocols that follow it ask subjects questions to elicit special aspects about their interactions with peers in order to fill out gaps from PAR-DG findings. This specialized information fills diagnostic holes and stimulates new ideas. Use of these targeted protocols normally brings the professional to a higher level of confidence about the correctness or incorrectness of the initial diagnosis, ensuring its validity and aiding in the creation of a final treatment plan. All the Phase I and Phase II protocols also constitute a rich source of information for professionals who en-counter special problems with specific adolescents in the course of group therapy and who would benefit from knowing about the adolescent's history.

As compared to the Phase I protocols, which serve many professional tasks including clarifying referral and admission information, searching out missing information, organizing the data and communicating it to oneself and others together with an initial diagnosis, the Phase II proto-cols are very specialized. They serve a specific task: identifying the defen-sive glitch which the adolescent has adopted and making sure the diagno-sis is correct, determining that the adolescent does not have a defensive glitch, or something in between.

Caution must be used in diagnosing a defensive glitch in order to avoid confusing a glitch with nonglitch behaviors that show similar behaviors or attitudes. Since each glitch has a distinct definition and description, chap-ter 7 of this book can be used in two ways:

- As a resource for framing an initial hypothesis that is supported by data from all Phase I protocols used and from all sources of observation of verbal and nonverbal behaviors
- As a manual that lists behaviors that need to be identified

The Design and Approach of the Phase II Protocols

There is only one Basic Phase II protocol, the PAR-DG (Defensive Glitch) protocol. The function of this protocol is to identify the type of defensive glitch an adolescent has adopted and the occasion of its onset. The other three protocols in Phase II are Supplementary protocols.

As mentioned in chapter 10, PAR-DG is *never* a Phase I protocol. It must be preceded by at least two Basic Phase I protocols or one Basic Phase I protocol and one or more from the Circumstance-Specific Auxil-iary or Phase I Supplementary protocols. In addition to the primary ob-jective of identifying the defensive glitch, PAR-DG is used for the follow-ing diagnostic purposes:

- To find out what psychological assaults the adolescent has experienced
- To identify when the adolescent's crippling hurt began
- To determine the extent of the adolescent's insight

Defensive flight can begin soon after puberty or even at a much later time, when the adolescent has successfully entered Stage 2 of adolescence. Thus, take care with older adolescents not to be fooled by an apparent maturity. A defensive glitch cuts short psychological development, no matter when the flight begins. In order to diagnose the type of defense adopted and the causes, it is essential to establish the point in time that the shutdown occurred.

PAR-DG is both an interview question schedule and a diagnostic guide. It is loosely structured as a general guide to uncover clues to the cause and point of onset of adolescent flight from the psychological Peer Arena and to which defensive glitch was adopted. The questions' lack of sequence with regard to topics differs from earlier protocols. PAR-DG is the least structured of all the protocols in order to give professionals freedom for creative interactions, though within limits.

In order to arrive at a preliminary diagnosis of which type of glitch, if any, is active, referral materials and findings from the Phase I Basic protocols and the Phase I Auxiliary and/or Supplementary protocols that were used are examined. Though preliminary, this diagnosis must be based on a thorough examination of the materials. If PAR-AA has also been used, those findings are included. Ultimately, the summary diagnosis also includes responses to the 10 PAR-DG open-ended questions. With all this information, the type of glitch can be identified and a determination can be made which, if any, of the Phase II Supplementary protocols might also be helpful to the final diagnosis.

Beginning Phase II

It is always a challenge to convince an adolescent that the interview experience is not a threat. Adolescents are understandably wary. These are adolescents who have suffered a lot of pain as a result of interactions with peers and have been working hard at masking that pain. They are accustomed to hiding their thoughts and emotions. Adolescents' responses to the questions open avenues to their expressing themselves, but with their aching psychological backgrounds, it is unrealistic to expect instant forthrightness or candor. In fact, expect avoidance or masked openness expressed in hostility, sarcasm, innocence, pity seeking, angry projections onto safe others such as parents and siblings, and similar reactions. At times, adolescents may even totally deny any type of comparisons and evaluations at all. Each type of response provides information about the depth of the adolescent's disappointments and about the type of therapy he or she needs.[1]

It is wise to start off the contact with a highly defended and most likely very nervous adolescent with some recognition of the difference between how you, the professional, feel about beginning contact and how you assume the client feels. For example, "I assume that you and I have very different feelings about getting together this afternoon. I am pleased to see you so that I might be of help to you, but you might not feel that way about being here with me. I suspect you might rather be someplace else." Do not expect to get more than a grumble in response. If the adolescent does respond, either it will be a patronizing response or he or she will claim to be there on someone's orders and not to have much, if anything, to talk about. In the latter case, a good reply would be, "That's OK with me. But I would like to try. So let's get started." *Do not* ask the client to tell you when he or she would like to get started.

Handling Different Responses

If adolescents' responses become increasingly hostile or clearly avoidant, it is usually an indication that the going is getting rough for them. Remember, notwithstanding an adolescent's outside bravado, the professional is dealing with a fragile, frightened individual. If an adolescent responds this way, cease further questions for a while. Resume with discussion of material related to questions in the more benign PAR-A or PAR-AA protocols. If and when there seems to be a change in attitude, return to PAR-DG questions. Spend as long or as short a time as is appropriate to gain vital information without risking the adolescent's psychological retreat. Remain alert to masked cooperation that reveals little. Again, cease questioning in a nonconfrontational manner such as, "Perhaps we have worked enough today. I look forward to meeting again at our next session."

It is highly important always to bear in mind that the adolescents with whom you are working most likely also hide from themselves. For example, they may be experiencing some decline in functioning that they cannot describe or name but of which they are quite aware. Take great care not to alienate or further frighten them by saying such things as "I have an idea that you have a problem with your findings when you compare with peers" or "I know you may not think much of yourself and it hurts when you think of what some of your peers are like." Instead, only convey your understanding that the heart of their difficulties may lie in their interactions with age-mates. It can also work well to pique their interest in continuing the discussion with you by asking questions relevant to them, for example, by asking females, "I was wondering if females around your age would choose to spend money on accessories for clothes or on hair highlights?" Even if adolescents do not answer these questions, when they can get the idea that you have some clue that the real issues lie in their peer relationships and perceptions, you are way ahead of the game. They are accustomed to adults who have only a superficial understanding, if any, of the depth of their peer attachments to one another and who see problems primarily as home or school centered. Try to maintain confidence that they may not want to lose the opportunity to be with an adult who shows signs of really understanding them. Guide your pace to what your adolescent clients can manage, their fears notwithstanding. Drop short hints that reveal you to be different from some adults in their lives and that you do understand what is central to them: growing up and being successful both in the present and in the future. But it is also a good idea to ask them at least one question relevant to them personally during each session, lest they feel that they have you fooled too.

Make certain to allow adolescents the time they need to be relaxed with an adult and at least temporarily let go of a portion of their fears. You have questions to ask and a road to follow, but you have *time* to do it. Adolescents at risk do not generally see this kind of patience in others. Such patience can intrigue them, and they will test it. If they sense that they need to make quick, complete, or perfect responses, you risk their reverting to escape mode. Following this "trust time" model will enhance your chances of arriving at a proper diagnosis, the first step to effective remediation planning.

The Defensive Glitch Protocol

The Defensive Glitch protocol (PAR-DG) is a different type of protocol. Its questions are more open-ended than those of other protocols. The first question begins solution to a mystery. If you begin to form a temporary hypothesis while moving along in PAR-DG, you can augment the listed questions with some of your own. Casually interspersing short commentaries may also help bring to light possible additional hypotheses to be explored. Eventual study of data from the Phase I materials together with the PAR-DG findings may stimulate even more possible hypotheses to consider or may eliminate some. This creative process ends with a beginning diagnosis for assembling a therapeutic plan.

Remember, the adolescent you greet may be a very troubled young person. After a warm greeting, such as the one described in the preceding section, a greeting that may or may not go unanswered, proceed with the first rather direct question of PAR-DG. This question is intended to send a message that defines the spirit of the conversation to follow as one of frankness.

As is the case with the initial protocol of Phase I, the #2 PAR-A (Adolescent) protocol, a commentary is interspersed between some questions of the PAR-DG protocol for explanatory purposes.

PAR 27: PAR-DG (DEFENSIVE GLITCH)

ID# _____ Age: _____ yrs. _____ mos. _____ M _____ F _____

1. Is there anyplace else you would you like to be instead of being here?
   If there is an answer, acknowledge it. If no answer, go on to question 2.
2. What would you like to be doing?
   If the response is "nothing special," then ask, "Is that what you usually do?" If the answer to this question is no, then continue on to question 3.
3. If you have some idea of what you like to do in your spare time, would you usually be with friends or alone?
   If no answer, ask, "Do you prefer one over the other?" If no answer, discontinue this line of questions. A more general exchange might be engaged for a few minutes, and then go on to question 4.
4. I was going to ask you some questions about yourself when you were younger, but instead let's start another way. Let's start with today.
   If the adolescent wishes to know why you first wanted to ask about when he/she was younger, respond, "I thought it might be an easier way for you to start." This response, an honest one, allows you to seem embarrassed about getting caught. The adolescent thus sees that the relationship is open to both honesty and embarrassment, which sends a good beginning message that no one is perfect. This message may serve to relax the adolescent somewhat. Go directly to question 5.
5. How about if we start on matters that you might be thinking about today? Can you tell me what some of them are?
   If there is any type of refusal, open up questions about after-school activities such as sports or hobbies. If there is no response, note (privately) that the question may have hit a sore spot since it involves peers. Move back to the school itself, its structure, its curriculum—fairly neutral ground.

6. What does your school look like? *or* What type of teachers do you have this year? *or* Are any of the subjects interesting to you?
   Go easy and continue only if you have gotten signals that the adolescent feels safe to answer. Then gingerly ask one of the questions in number 7.

7. Do you have any friends in school? *or* Do you have friends to do things with after school?
   Both silence and enthusiasm provide insights. Simple responses of yes or no, unless validated, might reveal that the adolescent has no friends or might be a hostile challenge to you. Ask an additional question such as "Do they work, or do they have chores at their house?" This question implies that peers are busy with responsibilities. Thus, having few or no friends is not necessarily a rejection. It may be possible to segue to an exploration of whether the adolescent has fled the Peer Arena to take on a Veiled Person-Dedicated glitch. For example, it may be possible to take a step further by asking, "Do you have a friend or a teacher whose work you are really interested in?" This question furthers hypothesis testing that may or may not confirm a Veiled Person-Oriented glitch.

8. What kinds of things do you like to do after school?
   If the response remains unclear—whether it refers to a hobby, one or two persons he/she is generally with, or a crowd of others, and if it is fact or fiction—it still affords a passageway for return at a later point or at a later date. Reference to a crowd in an undisclosed activity is particularly useful if there is suspicion of a Parallel Feel-Good Loner glitch. Any reference at all to age-mates or groups of age-mates should be noted carefully and marked for possible importance to the ultimate diagnosis. If resistance continues, it may be wise to ask if he/she has been together with you long enough that day or would like to stay longer. If the response is "enough," suggest a time for a future get-together, giving the adolescent leeway within a two- or three-day span. If he/she expresses the desire for a shorter lapse, inquire if there is something he/she might like to talk about now. This response may be due to a state that was not visible or audible: a reduction of anxiety to the degree that he/she does not find the contact threatening but rather that he/she cannot get the issue out. Or it may be a clever avoidance measure. Question subtly on both counts until you are satisfied with the answers or cease questioning. When the time comes for you to resume questioning, bear in mind that although questions 8 and 9 may be combined, creating a break between them may help the adolescent to focus on when the activities occur—for example, after school or on weekends—which may provide a clue to the glitch.

9. Do you have any after-school activities?
   If yes, ask what they are and if they are alone or with others. If with others, inquire with whom. This same process can be followed if the question is about an interest or a cause. If the adolescent claims no after-school activities, he/she could possibly be a form of Loner, the Isolated Game-Player Loner.

10. *This three-part question is optional and can be asked at any point in the contact, based on your professional discretion. One, two, or all of the parts may arise during the exchange, and they offer a path to take the exchange further. Use those that you think will not be threatening.*
    a. Are there special types of peers you prefer as friends?
    b. Would you rather be alone or with a group of peers? Or with just a friend?
    c. Is there anything you might like to make better?

A Caution about Variations

Varying the questions may appear benign to professionals, but it often is not. For example, with question 7 on PAR-DG, the professional might decide rather than to ask about friends at school to ask, "What time do you usually go to sleep and wake up?" If the answer suggests that the adolescent goes to bed late, it follows naturally to ask how he or she gets to school or gets excused absences and why he or she goes to bed so late. Answers to those questions may or may not seem benign to the adolescent. You must always be ready to ask yourself whether what you are observing suggests that the adolescent has a glitch. For example, if the adolescent replies that he or she works late volunteering on political campaigns or works nights with the homeless, you should explore the possibility that he or she has a Veiled Mission-Dedicated glitch.

Some Notes on Diagnosis

As mentioned in chapter 7, more rarely detected glitches such as the Mission-Dedicated, the False Facade, and the Early Commitment glitches avoid being identified as problematic because they are socially acceptable, even desirable. But if defensive flight is not detected as soon as possible, the delay can strengthen the adolescent's fear and work against his or her psychological growth. An adolescent's delinquency does not necessarily in and of itself indicate a glitch. But be cautious: some delinquencies may be behaviors connected *with* a type of glitch. Also, if you find that the adolescent has shut off on peers and peer groups very soon after puberty, it is a good bet that the adolescent may be a False Facade or a Veiled Loner.[2]

Once you identify a specific defensive glitch as probable, it becomes the guide for a few subtle questions. For example, if you suspect the adolescent of substance abuse, the questioning might go this way: "Do you spend time alone reading or watching TV? Do you enjoy it? Do you occasionally enjoy pretzels or potato chips? And a beverage with them? Perhaps pop or soda?" Ask these final two questions in rapid sequence, since they suggest the consumption of beverages but stay just short of mentioning alcohol, and watch the nonverbal behavior carefully, making special note of the expression of strong denial or withdrawal in barely audible comments or lack of interest in going any further. If the glitch is a Parallel Feel-Good Loner glitch, even a seemingly benign question such as "Are you a chocoholic?" correctly placed in a conversation can produce some giveaway nonverbal behavior. Even with an adolescent's obvious withdrawal from discussion, make every effort to continue talking but proceed on to unconnected areas of conversation. Delay additional pertinent questions until the following session. It is not wise to confront the adolescent with any information from other sources at this time. Instead, privately take time to think about what it was you learned.

Do not expect an adolescent to acknowledge openly a glitch that he or she wants to keep secret and certainly does not want to give up. At such a delicate point in the interaction, consider seriously going on to the Supplementary Phase II protocols that follow or the appropriate Phase I protocols that have not been used before. They offer questions that can add to the store of information. But take caution to make sure that the time is just right to use them in your discussions with the adolescent.

Another consideration regarding diagnosis is if the adolescent has been referred from another source such as school or court, and the adolescent's history appears to meet a glitch-specific category. In that case, instead of the customary procedure of using PAR-A or PAR-AA protocols first, *proceed directly to the PAR-DG protocol.* Whether the reasons for use of a protocol involve the rule or an exception, they should be documented on either the introductory blank section of the protocol or, if lengthy, on a separate attached sheet.

It is a mistake to skip over PAR-A or go directly to the PAR-AA protocol without using PAR-A first in cases in which the adolescent was *not* previously identified as potentially having a glitch or in cases in which the adolescent's record does not contain information that suggests this designation. If the PAR-A protocol was never fully completed, professionals should return to it to finish its questions as soon as possible after sufficient supplementary information is gathered. Try, very gently if necessary, to encourage the adolescent to complete all questions in this protocol. In general, any protocol may be used twice if there is a solid rationale. Indicate the rationale in notes.

Clinical Judgment Issues: The Example of Elizabeth, Age 16

Elizabeth was referred to therapy because she was caught stealing. She socialized in a group of individuals 10–15 years older, was sexually promiscuous, and had two unwanted pregnancies and abortions. The friendships began when she was age 15 and 4 months. The referring materials noted her petty theft and sexual acting out and stated, "at this point, it is clear she may be headed for major delinquency." Elizabeth told her referring therapist, "[My parents] are more interested in what bothers them than if I am happy or not." The parents were experiencing severe economic problems, which caused them to be consumed with paying their bills, with little energy left for their daughter. They had two other daughters, both under 10 years old. Elizabeth saw no option for happiness but to pursue substitute parents and pleasures. She hooked up with young adults to be part of their group. No mention was made by the referring therapist of her history of age-mate relationships.

The PAR-A protocol revealed that Elizabeth had few friends of her own. She had a good number of friends at age 13, but the number reduced starting at 14½. She reported being placed in a lower math class than her best friends, who were in the "Challenge Program." "My IQ is not as high as theirs. . . . They are in the Challenge class, . . . and anyway my scores are usually not as good as theirs." They made other friends, and she began to feel out of place with them.

Her mother in the past had usually been free to take her places, but now she had to work. Elizabeth said she really did not feel self-conscious about that because most of those "girls were snotty and thought they were hot stuff 'cause they had made it into Challenge." She said she no longer cared about what they thought about her parents.

Elizabeth was a really good singer, but nobody seemed to care about that, until she met her new friends at a concert she saved money to go to. It was so expensive that she went alone without inviting someone "who probably would have refused anyway." Her parents wanted her to be happy, so they paid for half the cost of the ticket, though it was more than they could really afford. The people she met at the concert liked to go to concerts and do all sorts of fun things. They liked to get dressed up and have fun and did not talk about much else. They liked her fine, she reported. So she started to steal a little here and there, even from her mother's purse, since she knew her mother would never give her the money. In answer to questions about why she did not seek new non-Challenge friends, who might be happy doing the things she liked that did not cost so much money and who might stand in for those with whom she was no longer friendly, she replied that she did not want to be with all those "losers." Information from the PAR-A protocol revealed that the number of her friends had decreased (question 5), which had begun about one year prior. Part of her reply to question 18 was that she would not go back to her old friends, nor would she want to be with her parents or siblings. Some neighborhood folks might be "OK" since they were older and "more sincere." She replied with a strong "no" to question 9 of the PAR-AA: she never misses being with a large group of friends.

A beginning hypothesis was that Elizabeth was at risk of adopting a veiled Mission-Dedicated glitch, if she had not done so already. In Elizabeth's case, this glitch would not involve the usual self-sacrificing behaviors but delinquencies devoted to serving *group needs*. Comparative-act feedback from her indicated that she evaluated herself as a Downward figure to former peers, very low down. How she perceived her status with her former Challenge peers added fuel to her own low view of herself. These "old friends" had traded her in for other elites. She held on to a fragile self-perception by being unwilling to lower herself even further by making friends with known "losers" (Downward comparison figures). Her new, older friends knew nothing about the limitations of her parents' economic situation: her clothes budget was severely limited, and while her former friends were talking about driving lessons, her family had to sell their car.

Preliminary analyses of the PAR-AA and PAR-A protocols disclosed that the things that Elizabeth bought helped her function. She spared nothing to become one with this older crowd that dressed cool and led a sophisticated life. She liked the status of being accepted by an older crowd, of having such urbane friends. Her delinquencies increased, and she maintained her value to her new friends by paying for treats. Fortunately, there was no substance abuse connected with this crowd, or else she may have succumbed to that too.

Elizabeth's defensive flight away from psychological interactions with age-mates allowed her to avoid the pain of findings of comparisons with age-mates and the public humiliation of having unsuccessful friends. She aborted her psychological development for the emotional comfort these new associations brought. Former Peer Arena peers lost relevance. She still had friends, but their age difference was so great that comparisons were not necessary. Instead, she identified with their maturity and could fantasize that her own maturity was far superior to that of her age-mates. She paid her dues in this group, literally, by footing the bill for miscellaneous types of goodies. Eventually, taking bits of money from the relatively empty pockets of her parents was not enough. She began to steal from the pockets of strangers.

Elizabeth's personal emotional devastation at her Downward status compared to her Challenge peers was in large part due to her slower cognitive growth. She had not yet achieved formal operations, the final stage of cognitive growth, when she would have developed sufficiently to understand that poverty was a state not a trait and that it could be temporary.[3] Still at the level where her judgments were immature, she also remained at the level of "imaginary audience," so that she experienced her family's financial status as visible to everyone, particularly her formerly cherished friends, who could only regard her as below them. It did not help her to comprehend that poverty was only one of many personal and family descriptors, a number of which were admirable. These findings from her comparative acts drove her escape to an ego-enhancing glitch. Connection to these sharp young adults brought her perceived high prestige. She borrowed glamour self-elements from them and made herself worthwhile as she joined the mission of pursuing fun. The positive strokes she got from contributing "pleasure supplies," whether her body or what she could buy with stolen funds, was her preferred defensive glitch. But trouble found her: she was caught stealing.

Supplementary Protocols for Suspected Defensive Glitches   ·

The following Phase II Supplementary protocols can be useful when additional information is needed after reviewing findings from PAR-DG.

PAR-SuII-CC (Continuity and Change) Protocol

This protocol is used when it is suspected that the adolescent has taken flight to older or younger individuals to avoid engaging in age-appropriate comparative acts. Questions are phrased to determine who the individuals are and when the flight began. This protocol would have been useful in Elizabeth's case, in the example in the preceding section.

PAR 28: PAR-SUII-CC (CONTINUITY AND CHANGE)

ID# _____ Age: _____ yrs. _____ mos. _____ M _____ F _____

1a. Do you like to be with the same people you were friends with when you were a lot younger? *If yes,* Why? *If no,* Why not?

1b. Do you like to be with people older or younger than you are?

1c. If older, how much older?

1d. If younger, how much younger?

[*Regardless of whether older or younger is preferred, continue on.*]

2a. Are these people at school? Yes _____ No _____ Other _____ Why?

2b. In the neighborhood? Yes _____ No _____ Other _____ Why?

2c. At church/synagogue/mosque? Yes _____ No _____ Other _____ Why?

2d. On the streets? Yes _____ No _____ Other _____ Why?

2e. Other? Please elaborate on each.

3. Are they old friends or new friends? Old _____ New _____

[*In questions 4–7, insert "older" or "younger" as chosen in question 1.*]

4. Where else do you encounter the new people you meet who you feel are friends?

4a. In the neighborhood? Yes _____ No _____ Other _____ Why?

4b. At church/synagogue/mosque? Yes _____ No _____ Other _____ Why?

4c. On the streets? Yes _____ No _____ Other _____ Why?

4d. Other? Yes _____ No _____ Other _____ Why?

5. How many new friends do you want? _____

6. Have you met enough already? Yes _____ No _____ Why?

7. How do your parents feel about all the effort you are putting into getting new friends?

8. Do they feel you are changing? In a good way? _____ In a bad way? _____ How?

9. Do you agree? Yes _____ No _____ Not sure _____ *Gently probe.*

Problem Identified Protocols

The following two protocols are for use with adolescents who have already been identified as exhibiting problem behaviors whose descriptions qualify as *defensive glitch behavior.*

PAR-SUII-AS (ANTISOCIAL) PROTOCOL

Questions from this protocol probe the adolescent's rationale for his or her behaviors.

PAR 29: PAR-SUII-AS (ANTISOCIAL)

ID# _____ Age: _____ yrs. _____ mos. _____ M _____ F _____

1. It has been mentioned that you have run into some trouble with the law. Is that correct?

   If subject says no, say, "Maybe you don't think of it in quite that way, but that is how it is described. How do you see it?" Ask the adolescent to explain anything that is not clear. Take as extensive notes as possible. Continue on by saying, "Well, let us compromise and agree that something at some level must have gone over the top." Do not wait for agreement before continuing.

2. It seems you may have been committing some petty crimes (*or whatever a benign description of the acts is*). Have I heard correctly? Yes _____ No _____ Don't know _____

   If no, ask how he/she would describe it. If resistance continues, say, "Or was it something a group of you just did together?" Yes _____ No _____ If yes, continue to next question. If no, express concern at possible confused communication, but carry on to next question.

3. Does joining the group's activities help you get friends? Yes _____ No _____ Other _____

4. Do kids like you better when you are in sync with their actions? Yes _____ No _____ Other _____

5. Do you then become part of the group? Yes _____ No _____ Other _____

6. What makes [*select proper social problem such as drinking alcohol, taking drugs, delinquencies, etc.*] attractive?

7. Might it make it easier to be with people your age? Yes _____ No _____ Maybe _____

   Regardless of the response, continue with question 8.

8. In what way?

9. Do you know just why you might feel that way?

10. Was this different from the way you used to feel before you got in with new friends?

11. What was it like then?

12. What is it like now?

13. If you had to choose between being with your old peers or your new friends, which would you choose? Old friends _____ New friends _____ Neither _____ No answer _____ Why?
    Regardless of whether you know for sure whether the adolescent is in legal trouble, continue with question 14.
14. Would you rather not be in trouble? Yes _____ No _____
15. Why?
16. How do you feel about my asking you these questions? OK _____ Not OK _____ Doesn't matter _____ Lousy _____ I hate it _____ Stop it _____
17. Are we talking about the correct subject? Yes _____ No _____
18. Is there something else you might want to talk about? Yes _____ No _____
19. Would you like to talk about it now? Yes _____ No _____
20. *Regardless of answer to question 19, ask a question that as a professional you consider pertinent. Note the reaction, verbal and/or nonverbal.*

PAR-SUII-ASCR
(ANTISOCIAL COGNITIVE RATIONALE) PROTOCOL

This protocol may be used as a follow-up to the preceding PAR-SuII-AS. It is used when additional information is needed to understand the cognitive rationale for an adolescent's glitch affiliations as well as the emotionally based rationale evident in his or her choices and actions that were reported in the referral and possibly in PAR-SUII-AS.

PAR 30: PAR-SUII-ASCR (ANTISOCIAL COGNITIVE RATIONALE)
ID# _____ Age: _____ yrs. _____ mos. _____ M _____ F _____
1. Please explain why you want these friends.
2. What do they do for you?
3. Do you learn from them? How?
4. Do they help you to get happy? Please explain.
5. Do they help you in matters important to you? Yes _____ No _____ Not always _____
6. Is it worth it to you to take such risks? Yes _____ No _____ Why?
7. Is it about:
   a. Clothes? Yes _____ No _____
   b. How to act with the opposite sex? Yes _____ No _____

    c. How to handle your family? Yes _____ No _____ Parents? Yes _____
No _____

    d. How to get by in school? Yes _____ No _____

    *e. How to be popular? Yes _____ No _____ Please explain.

    *f. Or do you just feel better about yourself? Yes _____ No _____ Please
explain.

  8. Are you happier than you were before? Yes _____ No _____
     In either case, probe gently.

  *9. When were you the happiest? Why?

*10. When were you the saddest? Why?

 11. When was your best time? Why?

 12. When was your worst time? Why?

 13. When was your most embarrassing moment? Why?

 14. When was your proudest moment? Why?

 15. Were your parents ever proud of you?

 16. When were they the proudest? Why?

*17. Was there a time when they were not proud of you at all? When?
     Why?
     If no, probe gently about why the adolescent has taken the dangerous and
     serious actions described earlier (and possibly noted in the referral).

* *Hot-button* issues to which other questions lead.

Diagnostic Timetable

Four sessions are generally recommended for completion of the necessary protocols, subject to clinical judgment, which should be entered into the note section of the protocol. There will be minor individual differences, short of an adolescent's refusal to continue. In each session following the initial session with the adolescent, the professional will find it helpful to do the following:

- Use Auxiliary protocols with appropriate persons, as needed.
- Conduct interviews for a length of time occasionally set by the client. Note time spent in each session on protocol for further analysis.
- Note contradictory findings between the adolescent and other persons responding to Auxiliary protocols. Assess the extent to which these contradictions may be typical of misunderstandings between them now and in the past.

- Discuss selected contradictions with respondent(s) in session, raising specific issues.
- Remember that some contradictions are better left to the treatment phase, except those that are essential to diagnosis. Make decisions accordingly.
- Be sure to secure permissions from adolescents and auxiliary figures if disclosures from their contributions are seen as important. Make sure the disclosure is of sufficient importance to warrant the risk of lack of trust. Present your rationale in the summary analysis.

Summary and Final Analysis

- Consult the supervising professional group if the summary analysis appears incomplete after use of appropriate protocols.
- Follow the summary analysis with a final analysis containing diagnosis and detailed treatment recommendations.
- Submit the final analysis to the supervising professional group after all Phase I and Phase II protocol information is integrated. Your diagnosis and treatment recommendation should be included.

The supervising professional group made up of intake and group therapy professionals review the final analyses. They arrive at one of four decisions: (1) admission to PAL group therapy, (2) two to three individual sessions to prepare the applicant for admission to PAL, (3) referral for individual therapy, or (4) a session or two to prepare the applicant for referral to a facility better suited to his or her needs, including inpatient care.

Since the sequence of questions follows a road map of theory to obtain essential diagnostic material, use of the protocols offered in part 3 can assist the professional in arriving at a diagnosis far more quickly and accurately than other methods, thus avoiding a longer intake process or the risk of failing to elicit pertinent information at all. In order to sharpen skill in selecting and using various combinations of the protocols, in-house continuing education or informal regularly scheduled group colleague study is recommended. The chapters in this book can act as your guide. The protocols have construct, face, and predictive validity.

Part 4 presents the particulars of PAL (Peer Arena Lens) group therapy, which is designed exclusively for adolescents.

Peer Arena Lens (PAL)
Group Therapy

12

Working Together

Group therapy with adolescents that simply replicates adult group therapy is not geared to adolescents' particular needs. Nevertheless, such approaches have been dominant, with little recognition that just as children and adolescents are not the same, adolescents and adults are not the same. Adolescents are not little adults, just as they are not big children. They are an independent, different kind of individual. They are persons under development. Thus, the type of group therapy that will be effective must replicate the dynamics of the psychological world in which they live, not the psychological worlds of children or adults. Simply stated, what other therapies have missed is that for adolescents peer groups are the central forum in which developmental dynamics are active. The developmental point where comparative behavior was suspended and where development was detoured is the point where intervention should begin.

Peer Arena Lens (PAL) group therapy is designed not only to assist troubled adolescents work through their need for a defensive glitch but also to ready them to return to the Peer Arena to complete the adolescent psychological task of growing successfully into maturity. Therapy groups are assembled to come close to replicating the adolescent's home Peer Arena. Since PAL group members remind adolescents of those who were their "rejectors," PAL becomes a setting for a second try at staying in the group with them and not psychologically or physically running away. All the group members are troubled adolescents transitioning from child to adult. Together they build attachments and diminish their attachment deprivation.

The overall goal of PAL group therapy is to strengthen adolescents' return to their natural Peer Arena, so that they are ready to deal constructively with peer interaction. To accomplish this goal, they will learn to use comparative acts constructively, cope with the findings, and sustain ups and downs without resorting to defensive glitches. They will identify what it was that stimulated their flight to defensive glitches and will use this growth perspective to master a new set of tools for their interpersonal interactions, and with subtle therapeutic oversight, they will be less likely to falter as they did previously.

Putting PAR Protocols to Use

The 30 Peer Arena Retrospective (PAR) protocols outlined in part 3 are designed for use in PAL group therapy, where they can be used for diagnosis and treatment phases as well as placement in appropriate PAL groups. As we have seen, their interview form offers a concise guide for eliciting important information within the first few sessions that might otherwise be overlooked or collected over a longer time. The information elicited also is useful in the intake period to enrich referral information, and it is particularly useful if the referral was made a long time before.

Although the vast majority of the protocols have been developed for individual use, they can also help determine whether the adolescent should start in a PAL group immediately or whether preparatory individual sessions first might be helpful. For example, an adolescent who gives several contradictory responses may reflect his or her extreme anxiety and confusion or may mask resistance. It is essential to clarify this question before deciding whether he or she is a good candidate for PAL. When PAL group therapy is not available, some of the protocols may be appropriate to other models of adolescent treatment, but only if the treatment is based on the DFI model.

Peer Arena Replication

All adolescents begin frameworkless, seek attachment, individuate, use one another as models, have the same growth task, and witness changes in themselves and in age-mates constantly.[1] The replication of adolescents' original peer groups is the best route to stimulating their reexperience of the dynamics of their original groups that drove them away and to which they need to return. This is a unique and fundamental feature of PAL group therapy and must not be violated if the therapeutic group experience is to be effective. The replicated group is meant to be a living microcosm of the experience from which the adolescent fled. Adolescents become filled with memories in the real setting of the therapeutic group. The difference in the group is that the adolescent's struggle to run away is noted and discussed. Paradoxically, this time those similar figures who threaten emotional comfort also encourage the target adolescent's use of newly developed strengths and abilities to return to real peer groups and take on their challenges.

The common criteria for adolescents' referral to most types of therapy include their history, the type and severity of their problem, their chronological age, gender, race, ethnicity, sexual preference, and social economic class, issues in their family, and their school performance. Two additional criteria are unique to PAL group therapy: developmental age and defensive glitch or suspected defensive glitch. It is crucial to replicate as nearly as possible the size of the group that had the painful impact on the adolescent. When such a group is too large to assemble, it is advisable to elicit from the adolescent an ordering of the figures who were most influential to him or her. It is vital to be alert to the possibility of an adolescent's craftiness in mentioning peers who were not intimidating to him or her in the hope of being placed in the most benign group possible. If you suspect that an adolescent is employing this tactic, take the opportunity to broaden his or her understanding that although the beginning days with the group may be easier, there is a risk that the goals of PAL to drop the glitch and return to full psychological health may not be met.

Participant Goal Structure: Seven Objectives

The objectives of PAL group therapy for the adolescent are the following:

- See the connection between his or her self-destructive behavior and his or her self-selected defensive glitch
- Learn to be able to tell the difference between adaptive and maladaptive behaviors and be determined to eliminate the maladaptive ones
- Put an end to defensive glitch behaviors and habits
- Organize adaptive thoughts and behaviors within a positive goal-related framework
- Learn that the group can be helpful despite not always being complimentary
- Use the group process to gain psychological strength to stay on a difficult road back to normative functioning
- Build strength to take leave of the group and return to his or her normative psychological Peer Arena

The process is a reciprocal experience, and the benefits increase incrementally. Troubled adolescents experience caring, concern, and cooperation, giving as well as taking. For adolescents with a troubled history, taking is harder to learn than is giving. It is important that adolescents learn that what sounds negative may be born of a positive intention. The essential goal of PAL group therapy is met if the adolescent takes what is needed from it to do what is necessary to reach the goal of returning from despair to growth.

Adolescents as Guides

The emphasis of PAL group therapy is twofold: (1) diagnosing why interactions and comparative acts with peers resulted in such intense pain and (2) remediating the result. Together, group members address one another's defensive glitches. Except for the in-group therapist, who is unobtrusively present but very occasionally is active in the group itself, only adolescents work together on one another's problems. Although adolescents' interaction with a group of peers that feels very much like the one they fled produces anxiety, the interactional dynamics of this simulated grouping set an appropriate stage for them to discover the what and why of their pain's reaching such intensity as to stimulate their escape from it. This time, the task in PAL is *not to run away but to stay in*, to work hard to cope with it and continue developing.

Once admitted to PAL by the intake professional, each group member shares accountability for the progress of others. Success or failure depends on one another's insight and generosity. It is a heavy load to bear in addition to one's personal goal. Among the benefits of this accountability are expectation and respect. Perhaps as important is the message of trust sent to youngsters with histories of disappointment, anger, aloneness, and suspicion. As the number of positive comparisons in the PAL group grows, adolescent participants risk feeling optimistic about hopes for success in the present and in the future. This sense is bolstered by increased self-understanding. Shame and doubt decrease. Yet, intuitively, they come to know that before they achieve a true maturity, many more comparative acts will need to be carried out. The one-and-a-half-hour sessions two times per week bring home the message that surviving findings from comparative acts will need to be done without PAL group support. Once this major piece of the task is grasped, they are on the route to recovery.

It can seem astonishing that a model of adolescent group psychotherapy would involve other adolescents also with defensive glitches as agents of cure. But what other grouping would be so intuitively skilled at understanding one another's concerns or what to try next? Of equal merit is that they know one another's developmental challenges and share one another's stake in both present and future success, the tasks yet before them, and the constraints they will face.

Forms and Procedures for Admission to PAL Group Therapy

The PAL group therapy intake process determines whether a referred adolescent is an appropriate candidate for PAL. For some adolescents, PAL is not necessarily the best therapeutic venue, for example, adolescents with problems that are not connected to adolescent development but that have persisted from early childhood, such as enuresis. What follows is an outline of the application process for PAL group therapy, with a sample application form followed by discussion of the admission procedure. Please note that in the application itself, there are spaces to be checked off for acceptance, referral, or decline (rejection).

The Application Process

APPLICATION FOR ACCEPTANCE INTO PAL GROUP THERAPY
Part I: Adolescent Descriptive Information Form
   Name:
   Age:
   Race/ethnicity/sexual preference (if applicant wishes to give it):
   Family composition:
   Grade in school:
   Scholastic achievement level:

Part II: Diagnosis and Group Particulars
   Defensive glitch:
   Type of group needed:
   Number:
   Gender and gender ratio:
   Age:
   Race/ethnicity/sexual preference distribution:

Part III: Background Information
  Family history of quality of relationships, particularly with applicant:
  Adolescent history with family and peer relationships:
  PAR protocols used:
  Findings summary:

Part IV: Referral Request and Information
  Paragraph summary of record and request:
  Recommendation: 1. Advance to Level II admission consideration
  _____ 2. Decline _____ 3. Refer to _____
  (public or private agency/person)
  Rationale for recommendation:
  Urgency level (highest to lowest): 1——2——3——4——5
  Rationale for decline:

Part V: PAL Group Admission Decision Form and Process Data
  Accepted _____ Date: Month _____ Day _____ Year _____ Reason:
  Wait list _____ Date: Month _____ Day _____ Year _____ Reason:
  Decline _____ Date: Month _____ Day _____ Year _____ Reason:

Assignment Date to PAL Group Therapy
Group _____
Pre-PAL individual time-limited therapy
Month _____ Day _____ Year _____

Admission Procedure

Upon receipt of a recommendation for PAL group therapy for a particular adolescent, the intake professional carefully studies an application for entry, the referral history, and the findings from PAR protocols to reaffirm (1) the appropriateness of PAL therapy for the applicant, (2) the applicant's readiness, (3) whether pre-PAL time-limited individual therapy is necessary, (4) the degree of urgency of group placement or individual therapy, (5) specific group placement, (6) length of wait for admission, and (7) assignment to pre-PAL time-limited individual therapist and waiting time. Exceptions to an applicant's full placement status are noted on the application, and the reasons and plan are entered on an accompanying document.

Group Assignment

Once the adolescent is ready for group placement, the next task is to assign him or her to an appropriate group. The applicant's records must be surveyed again, this time to identify a group that replicates the one in which the painful findings occurred. Since there is not always such a group immediately available, the adolescent may have to wait, if he or she can.

GROUP INFORMATION

Group number:

Therapist (Name):

This professional is assigned to the ongoing group to which the adolescent is therapist

Diagnosis:

    Beginning date: Month _____ Day _____ Year _____

There is no stated goal in PAL other than to prepare the adolescent for eventual discharge upon "finishing" with the group, as decided by the group. The group itself works with the new member to set ultimate and intermediate objectives. It is a dynamic, evolving process, not one of strict adherence to a schedule of objectives. Most groups are not newly formed; they are ongoing and thus are joined by newly assigned adolescents and left by others who qualify to leave and return to their own Peer Arena.

Pre-PAL Individual Therapy Information

A very few adolescents may require a short period of individual therapy before beginning PAL. For these adolescents, individual therapy can be arranged for insight work for a short a period. Since the admission of these adolescents is "pre-PAL," three or four therapy sessions are usually sufficient to prepare them for PAL group work. If individual therapy seems necessary for a substantial period of time, referral to a different in-house division or to another clinic or practice is recommended.

Permission Criteria for Entry

Permission to enter a specific PAL group depends on the group's appropriateness for the adolescent and the space and readiness of the group.

Descriptions in the referral package of what appears to be a defensive glitch must concur with the diagnosis of the PAL intake professional. When a nonmatch is evident, records should be checked for accuracy of information, and a telephone or face-to-face conference should be scheduled with the referring person for additional information. A session or two with the adolescent may be needed. If nonagreement is not resolved, consultation should be sought with an in-house professional.

Behaviorally unmanageable defensive glitches such as serious criminal behavior are inappropriate for acceptance into PAL group therapy. Behaviors that are not criminal but are identified as troublesome should be followed up with a review of the PAR-P and PAR-T protocols or even another interview. New information may take on new significance. The issue may be clarified in a very short period or may indicate a problem. Depending on the problem, three options should ordinarily be considered by the intake professional: the adolescent (1) requires individual sessions for a limited period of time in addition to group sessions, (2) requires individual sessions for a short period of time, after which a decision will be made about joining a PAL group, or (3) PAL group therapy is not the therapy of choice at this time. The possibility of individual or family sessions or both might be investigated.

Gender Issues

In some cases, gender-specific groups are appropriate because of the types of issues being worked out by the adolescent. An example is the case of Thomas, an early adolescent, age 13, who attended an all-male school and was not perceived as "one of the boys" because he had no interest in sports. Since sports were the center around which most male socialization took place at the school, this lack of interest was considered "weird." Thomas immersed himself in mathematics, which became for him a defensive glitch (Isolated Game-Player Loner). Professional assessment determined that PAL group therapy was appropriate, and Thomas was placed in an all-male group in which athletics was often a central topic.[2] On the other hand, in a case such as that of Charlene, age 14, who was having problems being at ease in heterosexual environments, PAL professionals generally would place her in a heterosexual group immediately and work from there. An alternative plan that illustrates an experimental science orientation would place Charlene in a group of females first and then one of all males; if no problems occurred in either of these two groups, it might be reasoned that the problem arose when genders were mixed. Although this approach may be valid in other situations, it would be difficult to make such a determination in the PAL intake process. It is a far better decision to respect the guidance of the referral materials, which are reinforced by findings of the protocols used in the intake process. Thomas's and Charlene's situations exemplify the complexity of intake decisions: a variety of variables need consideration, including referral recommendations and where a group spot is available.

Preparing New PAL Members

Once an adolescent has been placed in a group, the job of the intake professional ends, and the in-group professional takes over. Care must be taken in "entering" an adolescent into a group. All adolescents need some "readying for entry," some more than others. This process involves arriving at a beginning focus on what the adolescent intends to work on fixing. Initial meta-analyses are best carried out in private sessions with the intake professional. Generally the adolescent and professional should look back together on the causes for the adolescent's defensive flight and try to get an idea of what provoked it. Afterward, the in-group therapist and adolescent can together assemble goals for therapy. This back and forth may be the adolescent's first venture into self-responsibility. It is not important that most of the conclusions arrived at in this early process are reworked in the group.

If in-group professionals and adolescents spend some time working on uncovering the factors that contributed to adoption of the defensive glitch, adolescents will have some idea of what group members will ask about their joining their group. Adolescents new to PAL will find PAL members skilled at evaluating the correctness of one another's assumptions, assessing their validity, reviewing outcomes, and drawing one another into the discussion. Presenting a sequence of questions is the first step in engaging the adolescent in a careful review of his or her analysis and decision-making process, which is part and parcel of group meetings.

As the preparation process continues, short and simple trial questions should encompass matters such as "When did the discomfort with peers begin? Was it the result of comparing with them? Did the findings upset you? When? How? With anyone in particular?" These questions will not be unfamiliar because some may have already been asked in the intake process. The inquiry then moves to the sensitive topic of evaluating the findings from comparative acts: "When did the evaluations take place? Where? Why? Did you seek out others to consult regarding the evaluations? Who? Why? When? Privately? Why? Why not? What was the result? What do/did you make of that?" All of these questions combine to shock adolescents but also to prepare them for the hard work ahead.

The Group Process

The process of PAL group therapy is not structured, just as interactions in peer groups of the Peer Arena are not structured. The interactions sometimes occur easily and sometimes with more difficulty. The dynamic is similar to that of a small dinner or cocktail party where most of the individuals do not know one another; conversations begin somehow. In corollary fashion, each PAL group takes on a unique character. It evolves over time through group members' interacting together. Each group is unique in its composition, its exchanges, and its process. For example, one PAL group may be easy to join and participate in right from the outset; another group may get more difficult as the questions become more penetrating.

The conversation in a PAL group gets started spontaneously, if not immediately, then eventually. Generally it does not take long since everyone is not new at the same time. No topic is set unless the group itself sets the topic before, during, or at the close of the previous session. Some sessions may spontaneously focus on a particular member, or a member may ask for special attention time to bring up an issue. This special attention may or may not be granted, depending on the group's decision. In other words, everything is up to the group, except that the in-group therapist corrects serious misinformation and ensures safety by controlling verbal aggression, acting quickly to quell a disturbance, or calling in help from in or outside the group. Physical aggression is rare, but if it occurs, emergency resources are contacted by the in-group therapist. At times, if disturbances recur and are caused by the same member, it may be necessary to arrange for referral or transfer of the unruly adolescent.

Fritz Redl's representation of "the group under the couch phenomenon" describes the milieu of the Peer Arena and its replication in PAL.[3] It is in this replication, devoid of elders, structure, or direction, that remediation of troubled behavior does in fact take place.

Entering a New Group Member—Therapist Activity

Introduction of a new member to the group may be handled with an opening such as the following:

Let's welcome [name]. He/she is new today and you all must remember how that felt. Let's identify ourselves by name. [Group does so.]

Perhaps it might be well to take a look at what may have gone wrong for [name], our new member. [Therapist turns to face the new member.] The reason we are here together is to help one another get out of troubles, not to bring you more. Our conversations are always confidential. Some questions may seem strange to you. Try not to spend a lot of time figuring them out. There is nothing secret about them, so you may feel free to ask why they were asked. Try as best you can to overcome your discomfort or any fear, and do your best to answer as truthfully as you can. If as we talk you find you made an error in your answer to a previous question, just interrupt and explain. That can happen . . . sometimes even a lot. So let's get started. Any questions?

When introducing the new member to the group, professionals should encourage questions from group peers, even if the new adolescent appears uncomfortable. It is natural for prior members to want additional information. New members are generally fearful that what they say will not sound right. Some fudge a bit and worry that lies or exaggerations will be transparent and try awkwardly to control them. They worry that once more they will be rejected. A therapeutic benefit is that the new member will not want to risk being disliked by the group and will usually choose to answer the group's questions.

The therapist should not feel uncomfortable with group critiques of the new member's conclusions and actions. Discomfort is exactly what the new member has been escaping, and learning to tolerate discomfort is a therapeutic goal. Adolescents' discomfort must not influence how questions are asked. However, since PAL exchanges can be rough, prior group members can be urged to alert the new member that the group is a protected place.

The pressure of a group of peers can carry great force. While each is struggling to "understand and undo," to "make better" his or her own issues, the group as a whole, a phenomenon more than the sum of its parts, serves as a force as members raise questions and ask for responses. PAL members eventually understand that insights that help them back to health are strengthened by helping one another. The case of Bobby, age 16, offers an example. Bobby was silent and hardly, if ever, joined in group conversation. At first, Bobby was surprised at the way he felt in the group, since it seemed the same there as it had been in other peer groups. The same subjects of conversation came up a lot of the time, as did the same looks and the same pain of feeling different. Bobby did not have a clue as to the impression he made on others in the group. But from this group there was no escape: in PAL sessions other members of the group do not hesitate very long to bring up difficult questions or observations. Bobby had to struggle to change his silence to response because the group de-manded it. What he did not expect was that PAL members would not let him get away with his detachment: they *wanted* him to stay in. For all the group's similarity to other peer groups outside therapy, this is what makes PAL different.

The In-Group Professional/Therapist Role

The role of in-group therapists in PAL therapy is also unique. It is a *subtle* role, not an overtly active one. Therapists' support is implicit in their presence, though they maintain silence through most of the session. This silence is designed to reinforce the right of all members to the time they need, including new looks at their own physical, emotional, and cog-nitive capabilities. On the rare occasions when therapists do intervene, their comments or suggestions for adjustments are usually taken with ut-most seriousness.

This sense that one's clinician is right there at one's side is crucial. As the in-group professional succeeds in getting this supportive stance across through body language and subtle affirmations such as occasional nods, eye-to-eye contact, a smile, or a grimace, adolescents are empowered to move through the process of working with their group peers to discover which internal and external forces stimulated their flight to a defensive glitch, to recognize the perceptual distortion involved in such flight, and to reevaluate the consequences of retaining the glitch. This type of unseen therapeutic oversight is a unique approach, and it is consonant with PAL therapy's principle of maintaining the group setting as a protected place for group members to try again and ensuring that the group operates as a safe place for them to plan for the future.

The in-group professional rarely is involved in individual work. The primary functions of the professional are careful tracking and analysis of each adolescent's group process and intervention, privately and outside the group meeting, when called for. In the group, the therapist's function is interpretation, support, protection, and prodding when absolutely necessary. The professional does not act as group leader, though he or she starts off the session with a reference to where the last session ended and also summarizes each meeting at the end of it. The group's lack of formal structure does not mean that it is uncontrolled.

The therapeutic process does require keen observation on a professional's part, as well as skill to discreetly strengthen the group's responsibility to interpret members' behaviors and support their change. Furthermore, in spite of the importance of remaining largely unseen, the professional needs to assure civil exchange and to make educational interpretations at crucial moments, such as suggesting that group members think about desisting from mocking the attempts of a new member to try to make him- or herself valuable to the group, for example, by showing off a skill. Longer-time members of the group might understand that this same behavior could have been misinterpreted by school peers too. The in-group therapist must know when and how to warn a group member with a subtle gesture that it is too early to make an interpretation.

The in-group professional is also responsible for keeping records, for making a brief monthly contact on an individual basis with each member, very occasionally for altering a course of therapy for unanticipated reasons and conferring with colleagues about appropriate temporary alternatives, and for arranging a referral within the clinic or to another source if necessary.

In-group professionals also take great care to prepare members for "finishing" when members appear to be nearly ready to leave PAL. They carry major responsibility for assisting with special needs during this ending point of PAL therapy. In-group professionals are alert at all times to each member's process and progress, or lack thereof, and immediately after the session, they enter into the group record group process and individual participation notes on each adolescent.

Intake Professionals, In-Group Professionals, and the Oversight Group

At any time, highly trained professionals in the practice or clinic may occupy any of three positions: intake professional, in-group professional, or director or member of the oversight group, depending on need and availability. Some professionals prefer one role over the others, but all three positions should draw on both new and more experienced PAL professionals. The roles taken should rotate, with some room for personal preference. Top-level professionals make assignments and discuss them with the assignees. Consultation between professionals of all three divisions should be the rule, not the exception. Thus, there should be little difference in the level of authority. On occasion, as is illustrated in a case example in chapter 14, an adolescent needs a period of individual therapy. A professional other than the current in-group professional fills this function, unless the number of therapy sessions needed is less than four. A short in-service training period is in most cases sufficient if role responsibilities are traded, for example, from individual to group therapy or vice versa.

Since the PAL group therapy structure and process is exclusive to use with adolescents, professionals who are new to PAL should receive some in-service specialized training. Normally a few days with supervision will suffice. This special three-pronged structural model is conducive to optimal use of the PAL group therapy model by clinics and private practices. It should be uncomplicated for PAL structural needs to coexist alongside traditional individual, group, or family therapy services and for experienced professionals to move between them.

Summary Report and Recommendation

The PAL summary report for each adolescent should be comprehensive. It must address an adolescent's PAL participation from beginning to end. The report is drawn from end-of-session notes and materials from weekly, monthly, and six-month reports by the in-group therapist, in addition to consultation from any other professional included in postadmission therapy. The full report goes to the oversight committee for review when the in-group therapist applies for "finishing" permission for an adolescent.

The reports for each group member should contain the following:

Weekly: opening presentation of self and response to group interaction, verbal and behavioral; notations of exceptional progress or marked increase in problems, including the date of occurrence with an update within one month's time.

Monthly: progress report and recommendations.

Six-month summary report: assessment of changes or lack of change
and information on how the adolescent uses the group; evaluation
of progress and new issues evident, along with reasons, if any.

The six-month summary reports on each adolescent are completed every six months until a recommendation for "finishing" and its rationale is
readied. This recommendation, together with its rationale, is accepted or
rejected by the professional oversight committee. If the committee accepts
the recommendation, the in-group professional submits a proposed Action Plan for discharge, which includes the views and recommendations
of group members. If the group's recommendation agrees with the professional's position, the proposed "finishing" date is entered at the bottom
of the report, pending submission by the in-group therapist of a plan for
discharge. Any final decision at some point includes the in-group therapist's consultation with the adolescent.

Nonprofessional and Educator Participation

Parents, who most likely have been interviewed through an appropriate Phase I PAR Auxiliary protocol, do not ordinarily play an active role
in PAL group therapy. They are occasionally consulted for informational
purposes only. Unless problems arise during the course of the therapy, the
sessions with parents are limited to just one or two, more times than not
in the intake period. These sessions with parents serve the following purposes: (1) gaining information about the nature of the adolescent's typical
style with family members and immediate community, (2) ascertaining
the level of present and past parental support, (3) gaining a sense of the
extent to which parental roles are or are not fulfilled, (4) learning of the
adolescent's supports or pressures within the greater family, and (5) finding out about the nature of parents' emotional connection to the adolescent.[4] There may also be circumstances in which therapists seek parental
input; for example, in order to discover whether an adolescent's tardiness
at therapy is due to the adolescent or to extenuating circumstances at
home, a call to parents might reveal an illness or a family death. This limited use of parents contrasts the approach of the popular family therapy
model in which parents and siblings are active and a parent might even
be used as formal or informal cotherapist. Of course, when work in progress directs that a change is necessary, moving an adolescent from PAL
therapy to another form of therapy does require parents' approval.

There is generally little need to involve educators once they have completed the PAR-T protocol. Sometimes exceptions are made for practical or information reasons, for example, questions about an applicant's overreactions to low marks or questions about a teacher's or adolescent's confusing responses to protocols. Involving *both* educators and parents is occasionally helpful to diagnosis. If an adolescent's behavior is seen as detached in group session, asking teachers if and when such behavior is also present in the school setting may illuminate whether the behavior is specific to the PAL group. Family may be also contacted to inquire if this same behavior is demonstrated at home and, if so, when it started and how frequently, how long, and where it is demonstrated. If any unusual behavior turns out to be exclusive to the PAL sessions, it is handled first in the PAL group. If handling it in the PAL group is insufficient, the in-group professional may choose to deal with it in individual session with the adolescent or in consultation with the professional oversight group.

Sequential Therapists

Therapists who are used to the couples or family therapy model sometimes judge it to be best for two or more therapists to participate in the therapy. Doing so can also be considered with PAL group therapy, with an important difference: the therapists should be active one at a time. For example, intake professionals oversee application and group placement, in-group therapists are involved with the group therapy experience of each adolescent and manage interferences to the group process if they arise, and oversight professionals provide consultation and perform final decision-making tasks. Sometimes it may become advisable for an adolescent to cease PAL therapy, in which case arrangements for an alternative therapeutic modality need to be made, for example, a period of individual therapy with a different therapist. Less often, the in-group professional may recommend that a parent or sibling pursue therapy with an outside professional simultaneous with the adolescent's participation in PAL; the professional would then assist in a proper referral.

PAL Group Discharge

PAL group therapy is unique in another way. Participants declare readiness for discharge themselves. This readiness for reentry to their original Peer Arena as a full, active physical and psychological participant is called "finishing." With the consensus of the group, participants take the matter of their readiness to the next level: professional/administrative. Operating as a whole, PAL members must reach certainty that adolescents' appraisal of their readiness to leave PAL is valid. It is group members' responsibility to be confident that finishing members are truly prepared to be on their own.

A decision that the adolescent is ready can be quite contentious. Having been a member of the deciding body for a prior applicant, the finishing adolescent is familiar with the depth of thought and discussion engaged. After all, the PAL group represents the counterpart of the Peer Arena groups that the adolescent will rejoin. The criteria that the group requires for a member's departure are (1) attaining growth levels necessary to rejoin the original Peer Arena, (2) understanding what went wrong, (3) having the ability to deal with psychological disappointment, even assault, (4) having a clear route in mind toward reaching a sense of identity and achieving adulthood. The need for group consensus for a member's departure as the first step in finishing, rather than a decision by the adolescent and the therapist, dramatically brings home that upon leaving PAL, once again important judgments will be made by peers in groups.

Admission to a PAL group is closed, except when one member leaves and there is an opening. No others are allowed to visit or be involved in any way within the group. Each group may also enact group-specific rules, such as limiting contact among group members outside sessions. Once PAL group members leave, they are not permitted to call others in the group, so as not to interfere with the PAL group process by developing a dependency that is not open to the view of all members.

The Interactional Process of Leaving the Group

Members learn one another's strengths and weaknesses and learn the positive and negative aspects of one another's persona, and they recognize special talents. And at a basic level, they learn how similar they are, despite readily discernible variation. Most important, they learn by their own trial and error, by seeing the errors of others, and by interpretations that group members return to one another on the correctness or error of their behaviors and the suggestions they make to one another about strategies to handle relationships with other group members better. Emotional support is part of the work of the group. Each member learns that critique can be constructive and even can come from the heart. This realization is quite a turnaround from their perceptions upon arrival. Paradoxically, as hard as it was to start in the PAL group, it may be even harder to *leave* it. It is difficult to depart from a group that is run by the group, with content and process exclusively handled by members.

The adolescent's decision to leave PAL therapy is presented to the group for feedback. If group perceptions confirm that the applicant is nearly ready to return to his or her own Peer Arena, the next step is for the group to role-play potential future situations and critique how the applicant handles them, for example, coming face to face with persons who in the past the applicant regarded as far superior and again fearing rejection. Help from the group may turn to examining if the applicant is reliving the past rather than focusing on the strengths he or she has demonstrated in the PAL group. "This is what you were then, and this is what you are now" represents one of many wise cautions contributed by members of the group. Yet, if even one group member is hesitant about granting an adolescent's application to leave, the entire group deals with the objection and its rationale, as does the applicant. If the issues reach resolution, the application process can move forward. If not, more specific work between the adolescent and the group on the designated difficulty proceeds.

The applicant's anticipation of separation from the group becomes the next project in the process of readiness. The applicant's actual departure is cleared only when all members agree that he or she is prepared to handle the psychological dynamics of the Peer Arena, the many different groups of peers to which he or she will return physically and psychologically. Leaving can occur at any stage in the adolescent period, Stage 1 or Stage 2. When leave-taking of the replicated PAL group takes place, the adolescent has been readied by PAL group peers to rejoin former peers.

Once members depart, they are allowed up to two short return visits in order to touch base again. But most times members who have left do not return more than once. The PAL group that they left is now constituted differently and feels strange to them, which itself brings forth a familiar challenge: be "flexible," recognize changes, and deal with new realities.

Remaining in the Group

Members who remain in the PAL group are prepared to begin again when a new member joins; it will feel like a new group. Each time a new member joins, group process begins anew because each change brings a new set of interpersonal dynamics and a new group dynamic; the whole as more than the sum of its parts is a fundamental premise of group therapy.[5] The sense of closeness between two members may remain stable or it may be interrupted by attraction to the new member. The gender differential may alter, as may the power dynamics. It is important to be aware that the new member is not necessarily behind in development, in maturity, or in the severity of his or her issues. The design of the therapy not only replicates the players in the Peer Arena but replicates life more generally: the task is always to meet new, unexpected challenges. Adjustment is part of all periods in adolescence. PAL group therapy serves to strengthen adolescents' recognition that this process of adjustment is a part of life.

13

PAL Group Therapy in Action
Two Case Studies

Two case examples in this chapter and a somewhat longer one in chapter 14 illustrate the structure and process of PAL group therapy. The first case, that of Sally, concentrates primarily on Sally's experience. The precise role of the professional is mentioned little, except for noting the diagnoses and protocols used. The second case, that of Abigail, presents information on an unusual home environment, impact of scarcity of peers for comparative acts, impact of puberty, developing a defensive glitch, use of protocols, and PAL therapy interactional dynamics. The case example in chapter 14 presents a different type of professional challenge.

Case 1: Sally, Age 15

Sally was from a middle-class Latino family residing in a midsize city in the South. She was the third child of a couple considered "old to have a baby": at the time of her birth, her mother was 42 and her father was 48. She had two older sisters: Louise was 16 and Marcia was 8 when Sally was born. Sally was a welcome addition to the family, but she believed she "cramped her parents' new style." They watched over her physical health but did not spend a lot of time teaching her skills. Instead Sally was showered with material possessions. There were lots of adoring relatives, all older than Sally. So Sally grew up with lots of love, and she was a happy little girl with lovely manners and was affectionate and generous. These attributes became increasingly important as Sally moved into her teenage years. She was easy to travel with when the family would go to see Louise, who was married and living 2,000 miles away, while Eloise was living away at college.

The arrival of Sally's menses seemed like a big change for her. Thus, at age 13 she began to mope a bit. She did not complain; rather, she went upstairs to her comfortable bedroom to surf the Web. She liked eBay and Asian websites because they were artistic, but her favorite website was MySpace or Facebook. She did not befriend anyone on the site but looked in on others' private lives. So although Sally was a bit frivolous in her tastes and took on few responsibilities at home or in school clubs, she did not appear unhappy and was no trouble to her parents. Her parents' friends found her "so mature," especially compared to other adolescents. Sally said she preferred older folks to people her own age. "Kids are so frenetic—busy, busy, busy. Chatting it up with whoever they see. One couldn't have a conversation about anything serious."

Down deep, Sally was not really happy. She had no friends. There were just a few people she spoke to at school. She was rarely available for friends because her family always had something scheduled. She told herself that she did not need friends anyway: she had sisters and parents who adored her and relatives who heaped affection on her. Everyone thought she would be a wonderful lawyer since she expressed herself so well, but she told them that she wanted to be a doctor and save lives or a paleontologist piecing together evidence that shed light on the world hundreds of millions of years ago. Family and older friends thought that these were fascinating choices and ambitious aspirations.

Every now and then, Sally sneaked hard looks at the kids at school. She sized up the leaders and the followers and wondered where they ranked her. She knew they thought she was very nice, but they never invited her along. She tried hard not to long to be invited. She told herself that if she really tried to get invited, she would be.

Sally's sisters wondered why she hardly ever had anyone over when they saw her, but she told them that since they visited so infrequently, she just wanted to be with them. Her parents were pleased at her maturity and kindness and desire to prioritize family.

Sally's Mask

Sally was reinforced in her choice to wear a mask. As we have learned in this book, she had adopted a False Facade defensive glitch and donned a mask of maturity. This mask let no one see the deprived little girl who wanted to be with her peers but felt they were too out of reach to value her or her friendship. Instead, she would say to herself, "I am much more grown up then they are anyway." *She believed her own cover*, which was the beginning of her desperate use of psychological defenses.

Saying to oneself "I am much more grown up than they are anyway" reveals that comparative work is being done. Sally's PAR-A and Supplementary protocols later revealed that she had indeed been comparing but abruptly ceased when nearly 15 years old, when she decided that her peers did not interest her anymore. For a while, she continued to compare with actresses on television and in movies and made constant use of the Web. These virtual comparisons yielded unhappy results since she was attracted to others who were beautiful and had personality but most of all to those who were popular. The findings from these comparisons were very distressing to her, so she mentally rearranged her priorities and her identifications. Real older friends became her psychological attachment others.

Sally set about adopting as her own the self-elements of her elders. In an attempt to be her own person and not a satellite of her family, she identified with those who were not her parents or her sisters and friends. But instead of borrowing cognitive self-elements from peers to replace those discarded from family, she identified with cognitive elements of older people. The outcome was unfortunate: before long, there was nothing kidlike to how Sally acted or what she said; she seemed very different to her peers—older but boring.

A Lucky Misfortune

Ironically, perhaps one the best things that ever happened to Sally was her parents' discovery of marijuana in her room. They never did find out that she had experimented several times with cocaine. The experimentation occurred as she allowed herself to notice that while she had been on a par with her peers in academic subjects, a great many of them had made leaps ahead of her in extracurricular activities and popularity.

Essentially Sally was half aware that she was play acting, and she had become increasingly unhappy. Acting mature protected her from excessive parental disappointment about her grades and from taking on responsibilities she did not want. But the act did not work in the schoolroom and in other activities with peers. She was in a quandary; she was content and self-satisfied on the outside but unhappy on the inside. Sally found older adolescents and age-mates who would befriend her if she would smoke marijuana with them. They then began to expect her to supply some of the goods, which she did. She partook only enough to be considered a loyal group member. Fortunately, when she experimented with cocaine, it scared her.

Sally's sorrowful mood at home, frequent lateness, and new remoteness began to worry her parents. Marcia, the closest Sally came to a peer, was assigned to find out what was going on. Sally poured out to Marcia the whole sad tale of her new friends and the marijuana. But even this revelation to Marcia was made in a mature way, since that posture received praise and was her cover, by now even to herself. What she could not bring herself to share was the heartache about having few age peers and about what she did not recognize as attachment deprivation.

Diagnostic Procedure

The marijuana found in Sally's room was the first crack in her defensive glitch. She was referred to a clinic. The PAR protocols selected for use during the intake process were #2 PAR-A (Adolescent), #3 PAR-AA (Adolescent Alternate)—used when a defensive glitch is suspected from the outset—#6 PAR-P (Parent), #9 PAR-T (Teachers and School Personnel), and #11 PAR-E (Environmental Other). The information gleaned from the protocols was of a personable young woman who was socially adept in mature company but who had few peer relationships. Her schoolwork was acceptable, but it was declining of late. Teachers reported that she appeared increasingly remote. Grandparents and a friend of the family described her as "wonderfully mature" and dependable. The information gathered was sufficient to suspect that Sally had a defensive glitch. Protocol #27 PAR-DG (Defensive Glitch) was used for diagnosis, and admission to PAL group therapy was subsequently recommended. Also recommended was use of Supplementary protocols prior to Sally's admission in order to obtain more information on her comparative acts and their outcomes. The diagnosis was that Sally had a False Facade defensive glitch, with drug use being a secondary factor (note that it was drug use and not abuse), and her developmental age was determined to be Stage 1 adolescence.

Sally took flight into a maturity far beyond her years to avoid comparative acts with peers. She remained physically in groups, but psychologically she turned off the dynamics. Underneath Sally's serious cover, she remained sorrowful.

Referral: PAL Group Therapy

Sally was referred for PAL group therapy for Stage 1 adolescents. It was somewhat difficult to find an immediate place for her in a proper group of peers that would replicate the peer groups in her Peer Arena, and she needed to wait two months for placement in a proper group. During this time, she kept medical appointments for her marijuana use but was embarrassed in the company of parents and extended family. She spent as much time as she could on the computer and watching movies.

PAL Group Therapy

Group therapy was not an easy road for Sally. She had not gotten too far in friendships, and now she was with a group that looked very much like the kids at school. Each member of the group had issues, but were they like her issue? Were they all "losers" like she was? Although she was 15 years old, she had spent a long time copying others, so she had a lot of work to do to catch up to the maturity level of others of her chronological age. Developmentally, Sally was no more than just postpuberty.

Since the group represented potential friends, Sally was awkward in relating to them. Her uncertainty was compounded by news that they also had issues. She said very little other than introducing herself for the first sessions. Most of the members had been in PAL for a while and knew one another, which made it harder for Sally. Several sessions later, when she still had not said very much, members of the group asked her how she felt about most of the others having been in the group from before. She said she felt "out of it." But a real step forward occurred when she shared with them that they were actually her first group of peers. With that admission, shame overwhelmed her, and she could not stop the tears. The group quietly encouraged her to go on. Tears continued to flow as she slowly revealed her aloneness. She waited a few sessions to talk about how overcrowded her life was with older individuals who fawned over her. Some members of the group were sympathetic; others expressed mixed feelings. They saw a lot of benefits to her situation and expressed that "that ain't bad" if it is not overdone. This bit of genuine response reinforced Sally's view of herself as weird and a failure. She said nothing and pulled back into herself. A member of the group spoke of how brave she was to share information that so devastated her. It was the first time that Sally had heard anyone cue into what she was really feeling, and she would never forget it. Another adolescent commented on his own desperation when he first bought his way to friendship through alcohol. He knew how false it felt and wondered if she felt any self-loathing. She said she did.

The intake professional had taken care to recommend that Sally not be placed in a group with a majority of relatively new members. Sally's placement in this group of 10 who had been in the group for a while was a brilliant stroke since Sally was comfortable with the mature input of many of the group members. Yet she cringed at what she was prodded to reveal.

Sally was forced to interact, change, grow, and make it with those of her own age. She both triumphed and stumbled. When she triumphed, she needed to look within herself for praise because it was not always forthcoming from the group. When she stumbled, however, they were right there to insist that she not overemphasize the scope of her slip. She heard from them that nobody avoids slipping and that doing so is OK if you take responsibility for it. "Easier said than done" is what she did not express out loud.

During the process, some members left the group and others joined. Thus, Sally had to talk about her "misdeeds" over and over. The first few times, it was tough, but it became easier as she stopped concentrating on herself and became more of a giver, offering caring support to others. She saw part of herself in them as they doubted whether her offers of support were sincere. As some in the group received her gestures as important and true, Sally's sense of self-worth moved far beyond where it was when she began in the group.

Reciprocal Helping

Sally thought it was just plain remarkable that she was finding she had less in common with older friends and family. In one session, she surprised the group by bragging that she had dared to smile at others in her classes. The group urged her to do more: ask them to have lunch together. She recoiled, but she did find helpful the group's suggestions about strategies of just how to join in—such as volunteering to work on a project or bringing cupcakes for the homeroom class when it was a special holiday or event. But positive results were not automatic, and it hit Sally hard. Classmates did not respond in kind, which she read as rejection. The group thought her classmates' reaction might just be surprise and encouraged her to try again, requiring that she report back. This requirement acted to forestall Sally's customary denial of success even when something seemed to her to have succeeded. One group member shared that denying success is a strategy to tell yourself that something is not worth trying again. This exchange is an example of how members of the PAL group, with little professional intervention, help one another.

Over time, Sally seemed to become happier with herself. She tried to help herself, and she listened to group critique. She learned to be aggressive in offering help and support to new members. She began to wonder aloud whether she was getting ready to think about leaving the group. It would be hard to go out without being able to come back to what she called "my cocoon." But she had models who had been in her group, had ended PAL, and had not come back.

Making Progress or Moving Forward

As is standard operating procedure in most PAL groups, before Sally could leave the group, a very important task remained: she needed to explain to her group peers her understanding of what she experienced in the PAL group and what she thought about when she was alone. That seemed really hard to do, and she did not want to fail at it. Now she could better accept that when she put her mind to a task, chances were that she would succeed. She was trying to conquer her denial, which she knew was just plain destructive. So with group support *at least to try,* she expressed an understanding that signified she was catching up developmentally to her chronological peers who thought about thoughts and not just their past acts and who were self-reflective. She arrived at the notion that this ending part of her experience as a member of the group relates directly to the beginnings, middles, and endings of relationships in real life.[1]

Eventually, Sally did wean herself from her group attachment figures. Separation was not easy, but a new inner awareness instructed her that she had to do it, that it was immature not to. In the past, avoiding challenges had set her back. What really was hard for Sally to take hold of was that she was *afraid of people her own age.* She wanted very much to feel within herself how immature that kind of thinking is, and she tried hard and worked with the group on it. Her leaving the group was delayed until she acknowledged out loud that her downfall was her immaturity, which she had covered by acting older than her age, more sophisticated and mature. Some people fell for the act, but she suspected that others did not— especially members of the PAL group. Along her PAL path, Sally claimed an impressive strength in acknowledging her immaturity. She would need to summon the strength of self-honesty again and again as she proceeded in adolescence.

Sally advanced out of the beginning of Stage 1 and was well on her way to Stage 2. She had a way to go, but now she had tools to use, if she so chose.

Impact of PAL Group Therapy for Sally

In the PAL group therapy process, Sally worked on a number of key strategies for positive functioning. She learned to acknowledge her problem, accept help, appreciate support, accept challenges, and do all these things in tandem to achieve success. In addition, she challenged others in a sensitive manner, allowed differences of view or perspective, and supported others' success. To do this, she worked hard within the group to incorporate new emotional learning and to translate it into an intellectual understanding that she could apply with her real-world peers.

Case 2: Abigail, Age 16

Abigail was an attractive White female from a middle-class family living in a country hamlet adjacent to a sophisticated city in New England. She was very quiet, shy, and frightened. She was brought to the clinic by her parents, who were very kind and highly educated. Abigail's father was an expert in his field of biology despite having had no formal education, and her mother was 25 years his junior, a former student. Abigail had two older brothers. Since Abigail was the youngest, her father was old enough to have been her grandfather. The family lived in a rural setting surrounded by acres of beautiful trees and plants. From early childhood, all three children played together most of the time, since it was difficult for others to come to visit them because there was no public transportation near their home.

The students in Abigail's all-female private school mostly lived near the school. There was no need for arranged after-school friendship visits because they all could get together easily to have good times together right in their own neighborhood. Besides, Abigail's fellow students appeared "upper crust" to her, and she concluded that they probably did not want her for a friend. Consequently, books became her friends, as did hobbies with which her mother helped her. And she enjoyed her natural surroundings. Since her brothers were considerably older, they were kind but busy. Abigail's father was also kind, but he was an uninvolved parent busy with his research. Yet Abigail knew he loved her very much and was very proud of all the books she read.

Prepuberty, notwithstanding the aloneness of her life, Abigail was pretty happy. She had solo time with her mother, for whom Abigail was good company, since her husband was usually busy in his small lab on the property. No television was allowed in the house; neither were there computers for family use.

Puberty arrived for Abigail when she was just short of 13 years old. Her mother had alerted her as to what to expect, so she was not surprised, just a little frightened. Since she had no peer confidants, there was no one with whom to compare experiences. She had no idea whether most or none of her classmates had reached menarche, so she kept her own secret.

Abigail also did not compare with peers much on other matters. She did not wear fashionable clothes like others did, nor was she allowed to wear makeup. She often dressed in second-hand clothes purchased at the thrift shop by her mother, who also made some of her clothes and was always more interested in quality materials than style. So Abigail did not appear similar to many of her peers and did not attract friends.

Abigail deeply felt the need to be with others her age. Much as she had come to love nature, she ached to live in a crowded neighborhood where she would have tons of built-in neighborhood friends. She thought others lucky: always laughing and telling secrets and hugging one another. She really hurt from her aloneness. Of course, neither she nor her parents knew she suffered from peer deprivation, deprived in satisfying the adolescent need to attach to peers.

Since all Abigail's "in-person" peers were those in school, she became more and more nervous about what her classmates thought about her. Physically, she did not feel as good about herself as she had when she was younger. Her breasts had become obvious, and she was ill at ease with her brothers, even though they were older and always kindly toward her, as was her father. The only person who would understand her might be her friend Frankie, but Frankie was a character in a book and not *real*.[2] It was sheer torture to go to school, and sometimes her parents sent her even though she did not feel well: no fever, then off to school no matter what. Academics were very important to her household.

When Abigail and her parents went into the city together, she would steal glances not only at girls but at boys her age. There was a boy a bit older than she who used to come and hang around her brothers. She was really nervous around him and almost afraid of him. It was "her secret" because once again she had no peers to share it with. She wanted friends her own age so badly that it physically hurt to think about it. Of course, she did not know just how developmentally justified her desperation was.[3]

Abigail's anxiety spilled over and interrupted her studies at the academic private school where she was enrolled. Her grades dropped, and for her the worst of it was that she was embarrassed in front of her classmates. She had actually started comparing with schoolmates and with those she occasionally saw to and from school. She was not really looking at academic talent, or at talent of any kind. She was looking at physical features, attractiveness, and popularity. Abigail saw herself as a lesser person and as highly inadequate for the girls she would have liked as friends. She was comparing upward all the time and never compared downward, and achievement was the name of the game in her family. She felt devastated, helpless, and very much alone, so she became more involved with books and characters in them with whom she identified as friends. Abigail felt close to these fantasy friends: she knew they would be just the ones to worship her. She read and reread *Member of the Wedding* over and over again because Frankie, the main character, was the only person, albeit fictional, who really would understand her. They both suffered from not being a "member."[4]

Abigail was allowed to go to six movies a year. These movies, carefully selected by her parents, were generally historical stories or science fiction. This avenue for Peer Arena models was thus blocked too, as the characters in these films were generally adults. Her loving parents did not have a clue that their good intentions had helped to deprive Abigail of the food for developmental growth that she desperately needed: looking and listening to kids her age. Neither of Abigail's parents were churchgoers, another frustrated avenue for possible peers. Thankfully, the schoolrooms and hallways were full of adolescent females.

Since Abigail was not exposed to the supermarket of models with whom she needed to compare and contrast, she did not move through and out of Stage 1 psychological development but was stuck in it even as she got older. Notwithstanding how much information her good brain took in, only sufficient comparative acts would bring her to the end of Stage 1. At this point, normally around age 16 or 17, adolescents have assembled a temporary cognitive self structure, reducing the need to be surrounded by so many peers. Abigail had no way to understand the negative impact connected to denial of these growth opportunities, but she did feel the sting of being unlike others in her age group, and she felt the confusion. At age 16, Abigail did not comprehend why her age peers were happy with fewer friends and why they usually chose friends with similar interests. She did not know that they had narrowed down the options for what they wanted to be like and who they wanted to be. Of course, Abigail would have been happy with any friends at all, but she still wanted many of them. She was stuck in Stage 1 adolescence.

A Misguided Solution

Abigail began to be a "garden fiend," outside whenever possible. The outdoors felt stimulating. She attached to greenery: She read books about plants, flowers, trees, and all sorts of insects. She made reports in school and gained prestige as an expert on the outside (as an Upward comparison figure or even a Positive Instance). Her parents were proud, and her teachers reassured them that she was not wasting her brain. Still, these interests were unlike those of most of the girls, now 16 and interested in clothes and boys in addition to their studies. Abigail did not excel in other studies, and her classmates, though nicer now, were disinterested in her. Abigail extended her reading to small garden animals such as worms, crickets, ticks, and some larger rodents such as gophers, rabbits, and muskrats. She was immersed in writing a book entitled *Friends in the Meadow*, which took all her time and energy; nothing was left for anything else. The book's scope grew and grew and became more and more precise at the same time. She wanted to transform all animals and varieties of natural growth into her friends in the meadow. All were being renamed and given an intricate history.

Abigail's defenses expanded. Although book writing remained her primary goal, a socially positive purpose was added: saving the environment would be accomplished through the animal characters' acts of kindness to their natural environment. Here, her writing, her research, and her wanting to be a model citizen (all of which gained her additional Upward comparison points) all fell together. Even at school, she was talked about as being some kind of genius but as being far too bright to spend time with.

Abigail's mother was not happy about what she saw. She began to worry that Abigail was far from a sweet 16. Abigail expressed little interest in the opposite gender and no concern about having no boyfriends. The positive purpose behind Abigail's activities did not remove her mother's worry, so she brought Abigail to a mental health clinic. She was concerned about two things: Abigail's sad demeanor except when she was outside in the fields and the high anxiety Abigail displayed about any social outings. While responding to protocol #6 PAR-P (Parent), Abigail's mother, an obviously very bright woman, admitted to a third concern: she was alarmed that her daughter's hobbies seemed too serious for a girl her age. She delayed ending the session with questions, until she revealed her chief concern: did this almost obsessive devotion portend serious mental illness? This very worried mother had no clue that lack of peers might be contributing a great deal to her daughter's desperate choices. She was advised to contact the PAL group therapy intake division.

Revelations from PAR Protocols

Once Abigail was referred for application to PAL group therapy, protocol #9 PAR-T was used immediately to obtain education-based background information. Information from the school revealed that she was an unusual student, ahead in interests of her own but behind in traditional courses. She was not considered a behavior problem. School personnel who were interviewed observed that she had some friends but then questioned their own perception since she actually sat alone at lunch. But they said she was "a nice girl, well mannered, no trouble, quiet." No one at this elite private school had paid much more attention. Perhaps Abigail's assessment that she was not "upper crust" enough had some merit.

These observations and the data elicited from use of protocol #2 PAR-A (Adolescent) revealed that Abigail did look and listen and, hence, compared. Ironically, her parents' insistence on her attending school functions, notwithstanding how painful these were for her, did keep her with age-mates. She was sure others did not invite her to eat lunch at their table because it would get in the way of their making fun of her.

It was a difficult for the intake therapist to decide whether PAL was the best type of therapy for Abigail. This dilemma is not uncommon: in many situations, the decision is between separate individual therapy for the adolescent and for parents or PAL. In Abigail's case, the professionals agreed unanimously that it was not likely that therapy with Abigail's mother would loosen her up enough to understand the reason for the ache for peers that her daughter felt. In fact, Abigail's mother had been delighted by Abigail's excitement with nature and did not realize that nature had become her daughter's only tangible friend. She did not realize that the intense activity was a haven from the sting of disappointment and failures.

PAR Protocols

PAR Supplementary protocols were helpful in assessing whether Abigail was firmly in Stage 1 or whether she showed greater maturity. A lag in Abigail's cognitive progress was uncovered when the intake therapists used Supplementary protocol #22 PAR-Su-FFD (Fantasies and Future Dreams), which is ordinarily used at a later point. The therapists were intrigued. Abigail was so creative but also was so immature in her thinking. She confided that perhaps if she took her family nickname of "Gaila," she would seem more exotic. This response, sad and hopeful as it was, displayed a small speck of Stage 2 fantasy, but not enough to be any real indication of higher cognitive levels beyond Stage 1 status.

PAR Supplementary protocols are used to find out more about an adolescent's comparisons and affective responses and cognitive processing, as well as for diagnosis and for therapeutic planning and intervention. In addition to the protocols mentioned earlier, other PAR Supplementary protocols were helpful in Abigail's case, particularly #25 PAR-Su-EI (Emotional Income and Deprivation) on moments, if any, of happiness and pride in her life. In addition, protocol #26 PAR-OD (Observable Demeanor), which is normally filled out by the professional after each PAL meeting, can also be used in intake to analyze nonverbal impressions.

Diagnosis

Diagnosis of the problem is always time consuming since the professional must feel very confident of a proper analysis. Abigail was diagnosed as having a Veiled Mission-Dedicated defensive glitch, which as we have seen, involves obsessive behavior regarding an interest or cause and takes the adolescent away from painful comparative acts. The time and attention Abigail devoted to this glitch interfered markedly with all domains of her psychological development. As all glitches do, it aborted Abigail's growing up.

PAL Group Therapy

Abigail did not require any preparatory sessions before joining a group, beyond the usual initial introductory sessions. She was not hostile and responded to questions from the professional about her favorite activities. She was assigned to a group with a majority of developmentally early-adolescent females. One-third of the group was 15 or 16 years old, with the rest being somewhat younger. The assembled group that Abigail joined replicated the school classmates that had rejected Abigail. Thus, the group instantly brought back her emotional response to the original hurtful experiences.

Abigail was very shy for a considerable time and sensitive about "being quizzed" on her all-consuming interest in the environment. It is up to group members, who are told nothing about the new member before he or she arrives, to establish communication and relationships. And it was clear from the abruptness Abigail felt in their inquiries that her interest in the outdoors appeared odd to them. To Abigail, that interest was the only thing that brought praise from peers, so the reaction of the group shocked her. Abigail was forced to look further into herself to see what else she had to offer, but she saw nothing. She wondered why she ever let her mother take her to therapy. But she figured that she had committed to stay the course, and besides, it was only twice a week.

Abigail received frank responses from group members that supplied her with important feedback to consider. She had never seen herself as pretty, but the females in the group expressed that they thought she was. Some commented that they thought she must be talented in something. She did not say anything in response, but she did respond through her behavior: one day she wore a sweater she had made, and another day, when it was quite cold, she brought in a small quilt cover she had made for her parents as a Christmas present, which she offered to anyone in the group who was feeling cold. But more risky was bringing in some of her nature work, such as turtles she had carved from wood: the girls looked at them but asked no questions. But what was really successful was a winter pullover hat in red and orange that she had just completed. She asked if others would like to try it on, and some did.

The group challenged Abigail to search for qualities beyond handicrafts and being good with animals and trees. Some talked about how her insightful remarks helped them to dig further and how kind her natural character was. This praise was meaningful to her because it was from her attachment others, not from parents, relatives, friends of parents, or even her brothers but from peers.

Suddenly, Abigail found that she could risk making comments and observations about others, whether praise or correction. The latter was a lot harder, but gradually she felt she made progress. She really did want to think about others and not just about herself or about how she could get out to the meadow and take care of her animals and plants. She recognized that something different was stirring that felt good.

It is important to note that from the first day in the group, Abigail related more easily to two males in the group than to any of the females. When a new male member joined the group, she was also able to relate to him more easily, and she sincerely tried to be helpful to him. But the girls did not let this apparent preference go unnoticed; they confronted her and asked her why. Abigail surprised herself with her answer. Slowly and carefully she shared a huge insight: she had never been hurt by males, either actually or in comparisons. Indeed, there were no males in her school with whom she could compare. She felt safer with them than with females. Later she shared that the number of females in the therapy group was a lot for her to deal with. It made her feel she was at school again. Much later, it occurred to her that the composition of the group was a deliberate part of the therapeutic plan.

Abigail identified something very deep and hidden: she was really afraid of girls. Their rejection had wounded her identification with them, and it made her wonder about just how female she was. This question is not unusual at this early stage of development, but it was especially hard for Abigail because she had no female friends to ask whether they were ever concerned in the same way. With her animal friends, she was spared the pain of making comparisons. When she opened up and shared this with the group, a female member asked, "Is that why you like to spend so much time in the meadow?" The questioner herself did not realize that her question, in its innocent way, exposed Abigail. It really poked at the "humanitarian" distortion attached to Abigail's love of animals and plants. Abigail felt the impact but could not yet understand the issue underneath the question. She just said that she just felt good when she was with them.

But several weeks later, she understood. With animals and trees and plants, she felt superior: they needed her to help them grow through feeding and caring for them. What was very important in this insight was that it indicated a cognitive advance: she could think in abstracts. Thus, Abigail came to two very important pieces of self-understanding. The first was that the love that was denied to her (by peers) was something she could give others. The second insight, which represented her new more mature understanding even more, was that the rationale behind PAL group therapy was reciprocal support, the food of growth—the very thing she did with pets and green plantings.

Private Consultation

Abigail asked for a private session with Mr. Lawrence, the in-group professional for her group. Since it was common knowledge that this request for special time is rarely granted, she was afraid. But she had to share her insight with someone. Mr. Lawrence did grant her request in this case, and Abigail presented her two insights to him. She could tell he was impressed. He encouraged her and offered a recommendation: "Wait until you are ready to share your insights with the group to see what they think." Thus, he passed her right back to the group and thwarted her subtle attempt to exclude them and bond with the male therapist. But she did get some recognition from him, and that was a plus.

Back to the PAL Group

More and more Abigail was feeling that girls at school could be kind to her too, but it was hard to take the first step toward being their real friends. In what she figured might be a good beginning, she asked the group to call her Gaila instead of Abigail. When they asked why, she told them that the name had always felt more like her; it was not so formal as Abigail, and it sounded more like a kid than a grown-up. The PAL group helped her understand that she was sharing from the heart and that once she could express the extreme difficulty of sharing from the heart, she could get down to working on her issues for real. She realized that Gaila was a name her mother loved and told the group so. Then she said that her father preferred the more formal Abigail, but she was challenged by members of the group: was this true or not? Actually it was not true: her father liked Gaila too. It was she herself who liked the sophistication of Abigail, but she felt more comfortable with a shorter name. She liked being like everyone else in some respects, and she thought she would like having a name as close to one syllable as possible. When she said her brothers liked the shorter name too, the group observed that she was back with the boys again. They told her she had to work on why she has such a tough time with females.

Over time, Gaila realized how deep the deprivation of female peers was and how hungry she had been to share secrets with her female peers and to have good times together. She was shy and waited for the girls to come to her. She expected the same praise and love from them that she was accustomed to getting from her own family. She needed it, and so, perhaps unconsciously, she did what she was used to doing: she requested private attention. So she asked for another private session with the professional. But this time she was refused and was told to work out whatever her issue was with the group. Her manipulation did not work—not at PAL.

The group also helped Gaila to understand that she was running away from school again; weeks later, she remembered an incident in the eighth grade, three long years before, when she had been publicly ridiculed in class for making a clumsy correction to a popular female schoolmate's answer to a science question. She had not meant to offend the girl, but even the teacher did not understand Gaila's correction and criticized its tone. Gaila remembered her exact words: "It was not constructive. In fact, it was destructive." It was sheer torture to face any classmate after that for a long, long time. It strengthened her pullback. Working out this revived memory with the group effectively relieved the pressure of an old but very deep rejection that was complicated by shame.

Finding Contentment

The remainder of Gaila's course of PAL group therapy had its natural ups and downs, but it was successful. She moved along eventually to become psychologically ready to rejoin her school peer group. She was now in 12th grade, having reached age 17. She was intellectually competent, but because of the slowdown in her developmental progress, she was not as far along in her social development skills as were a good number of her peers. She needed to practice how to get along. She did not want to be always "the smarter one," something the group rebuked her about when she shared her eighth-grade trauma. Being ready to return to the Peer Arena required practice.

Gaila worked on how to invite some less sophisticated members of her school class to her home for some kind of special event. The PAL therapy group all agreed that the plan had to be her own. She decided that she would ask her parents to pick up invited guests and deliver them back home. Her parents, who were a great support throughout PAL, cooperated in planting treats in special places, and the guests could learn from Gaila how to track small animals such as rabbits and squirrels. The PAL group urged Gaila to tell guests to dress casually. The group also supported her plan to seek her parents' permission to see an occasional movie of her choice, and to invite some peers. Although these attempts at friendship were not with the popular sophisticated crowd (the top crowd, in her assessment), she would be happy for almost anyone to join her at home or at the movies. Gaila was successful in channeling her social anxiety away from "everyone" toward a limited group of others. By choosing which friends to invite, Gaila could take on little bits of what she feared. She learned from the group that most adolescents at one time or another have had this same social shyness, though perhaps not so much at age 17.

Gaila was not ready to leave PAL group therapy as early as she had hoped. What she came to realize was that her head was way ahead of her heart: her heart needed to stay in the group. Her attachment deprivation was still not satisfied. What she wound up doing was interesting: she worked on finding contentment from group meetings without being center stage. She could take this role because part of her cup was being filled with being sought after by some of her new girlfriends. Gaila found that she could turn her skill in thinking up strategies into making suggestions to give to others. Surprisingly, she became someone whom others looked up to in the PAL group, something she never thought would happen. That made her not want to leave.

Impact of PAL Group Therapy on Gaila

Gaila worked out the proper balance of giving and taking, and she had learned this balance for herself. She risked sharing unfavorable insights about herself, and once she let go of stiff defenses against being hurt, she relished interaction with PAL members. Her attachment need was fed in the group, and she began to look to her school friends for the rest. She was then able to begin thinking about leaving the group. School was so much better: she felt stronger and far less fearful about returning to her own Peer Arena. Even though after graduation from PAL, members are free for a period of three months to go back to the group for two brief consultations, Gaila did not need to return.

14

PAL and the Professional
Davey's Story

In this chapter, a third case example, that of Davey, is presented in greater detail than the case examples in chapter 13 in order to provide a look at the ever-present potential for complexity in PAL group therapy. Several examples of complexity are evident in this case, including the decision-making process that must take place to meet an adolescent's altered "next-step" needs. Sometimes such adjustments are minor, but at other times the plan might require a radical change of course. Davey's case also demonstrates how PAL procedures can be mixed and matched and how and when PAR protocols can be used even after the adolescent is enrolled in PAL.

Gathering Information
Referral Information

Davey was a 14-year-old Black male of Caribbean descent in the ninth grade who lived in a lower-middle-class neighborhood near a large New Jersey city. A school counselor referred Davey to a private psychologist for psychotherapy, with the permission of his mother, Olivia Barnes, age 34. The referral sheet supplied only the following information: Davey, who is of Caribbean ancestry, was born in New Jersey, where he lives together with his mother and younger brother Philippo, age 7. Two older siblings do not live at home. Davey's father had recently died of cancer. Shortly before his father's passing, Davey's behavior changed. Although he was well liked and progressing well in his studies, teachers reported that he could abruptly become obstreperous or appear withdrawn. Furthermore, he befriended only two others in his class, two boys a bit younger than he. The counselor was concerned about such extreme change in Davey's behavior. Davey now rarely completed homework and was failing several subjects. The counselor recommended individual therapy for Davey regarding his poor academic performance and erratic conduct. In addition, the counselor recommended family therapy, to include Davey, Philippo, and their mother, Olivia, regarding their adjustment to the death of Mr. Barnes. But something vital was missing in the referral information. No information was provided on Davey's past or present peer relationships, other than Davey's having only two friends.

Davey was brought by his sister to the clinic and was directed to Dr. Devlin, an intake professional. Dr. Devlin had sent a letter of appointment for Davey and a letter to Mrs. Barnes with a separate appointment. Mrs. Barnes did not respond to several such requests to come in for an informational interview. Davey said she was too busy to come in because she had to work a lot, came home after 10:00 p.m., needed to sleep late in the morning, and then had a lot to do before she went to work again. Davey was now responsible for the care and feeding of his 7-year-old brother Philippo. He gave Philippo his after-school snack and his dinner (prepared by his mother) and put him to bed after supervising his bath. Little additional information was available about Davey's family home life, past and present.

Family History

If parents are unavailable, the first step the professional takes is to interview siblings regarding family patterns, past and present. Thus, after being consistently unsuccessful in reaching Mrs. Barnes, who was either asleep or working, the professional made attempts to solicit information from the older siblings. (Mrs. Barnes did, however, stay involved with Davey's therapy in one way. She insisted on contributing a small amount of money for therapy costs.) Fortunately, Davey's sister Maritza, age 21, arranged to change shifts with a co-worker at the restaurant where she worked. She did not live at the family home but picked up Philippo so he would not be home alone when Davey had an appointment. Davey's brother Albert, age 19, was a helper on several construction jobs and could not get off work during the day. And he did not accept an evening appointment either, because he wanted to be with his girlfriend. Neither Maritza nor Albert had visited the family home often in the days after their stepfather's death.

The family history was eventually elicited from one or the other of the two older siblings, Maritza and Albert. Many years before, Mrs. Barnes had been an unmarried single mother of Maritza and Albert. Their father's last name was unknown, but he visited the children in their very young years and on occasion gave Mrs. Barnes money for their support. They did not remember much about him except that he was White and that his first name was Matthew. Mrs. Barnes married August Barnes a few years later, when Maritza was 6 and Albert almost 4. One year later, she gave birth to Davey, and Philippo was born seven years after that. Philippo had a different father, a Caribbean man whom he saw from time to time but who had no lasting relationship with Mrs. Barnes or her other children and who contributed no support. After Davey's father died, his only full relative was his mother. All the others were his half siblings, children of his mother and different fathers. But they all were welcome in the Barnes household.

Information from the basic protocols used with Davey, Maritza, and Philippo were consistent in reporting that Mr. Barnes had been kind and loving to his wife, his one natural-born child, his one adopted stepchild son, and his older two stepchildren. The three stepchildren had liked him, but the older two had mixed feelings toward their mother. At that time, Mrs. Barnes worked during the day but was home when the children came home from school. The family had enough money because of Mrs. Barnes's part-time job.

August Barnes had been diagnosed with stomach cancer two years before his death, and he had kept working in spite of his illness. Thus, his death was sudden but not unanticipated. August left almost no insurance or health care coverage, only what was left of his last monthly paycheck. The Barneses owned a small house with a large mortgage. In summary, the referral and findings from the interviews using protocols #2 PAR-A (Adolescent) and #8 PAR-S (Sibling) and PAR-OS (Older Sibling) disclosed a well-functioning family until August Barnes's death almost one year before. Then, everything changed, or so it seemed.

Missing Information

There was little emphasis in the referral history on peers in Davey's life. Who were they? How many were there? What they were like? The only information provided was of a neighborhood friend and one or two slightly younger friends with whom he walked home from school. PAR-A disclosed that Davey enjoyed the days prior to his father's death when he had a good number of friends. Both parents supported these friendships in any way they could. Dr. Devlin took the prerogative to add a few questions to the protocols, such as "Did the number of friends you used to hang out with change after your father's death?" Davey nodded his head, but he did not answer the question of why.

Protocol #9 PAR-T (Teachers and School Personnel) supported Davey's claim of good scholastic performance prior to the last stages of his father's illness and subsequent death. The protocol was instructive on peer-related details of Davey's class participation and friendships but not too much on his after-school activities. But it did confirm a dramatic drop in Davey's participation in such activities as well as in his scholastics following August's death. The teachers saw the change as indicative of posttrauma depression. Dr. Devlin was far more conservative about hasty diagnoses: more information from PAR protocols was necessary before he could arrive at a diagnosis. Sometimes intake professionals concur with the diagnosis in the referral, but many times they do not. At times, it may be necessary to confer with the referring party; at other times, the referral diagnosis seems to be in error.

It is wise to engage whatever near relatives or friends may make themselves available, even if only one valuable piece of information is yielded. This piece may be a key to solving the diagnostic puzzle. Protocols from Davey's sister and younger brother revealed important information but no "aha" moments. Most leads came from what they *did not* say rather than what they did say. For example, the protocols revealed Maritza's lack of involvement. Dr. Devlin had to wonder if there was any relationship at all between daughter and mother. He was dismayed at being denied an interview with Mrs. Barnes. He needed material that only protocol #6 PAR-P (Parent) could elicit. He was left to ponder why Maritza did not visit and why Albert would not cooperate. He framed hypotheses to explore: Was Maritza not visiting for a particular reason? Was Maritza angry that her mother had remarried? Had she been jealous of Davey's living with two natural parents? Or was it something else? Two separate tasks lay before Dr. Devlin: finding the answer and not losing sight that Davey was the client, not Maritza. In doing therapeutic work, one risks "getting lost in the field" if the emphasis shifts away from the primary patient to another person.[1] In this case, solving Maritza's behavior would have been a distraction from Davey's problems. What was necessary to know more about was in what way Maritza's distance might be affecting Davey. The probe must bear that goal in mind.

An important general rule of diagnosis is that nonresponses are not to be overlooked; they can open the road to rich information. However, important information can also come from other sources. In this case, important information was obtained from protocol #11 PAR-E (Environmental Other), used with Alice Norton, Mrs. Barnes's lifelong friend. Ms. Norton provided information about what else was going on in Mrs. Barnes's life, though this information had to be verified. Ironically, verification came from the family member who had resisted cooperation: days before Ms. Norton's appointment, Davey's older brother Albert called for an appointment.

If the question arises as to which additional protocol might yield missing data, it is valuable to make sure first that no Basic or Auxiliary protocols have been neglected. Usually, one or the other will do the job. The diagnostic picture becomes more complex, but complexity in the end assists accurate diagnosis and the design of an appropriate treatment plan. In Davey's case, key additional information came from his big brother Albert's interview with Dr. Devlin. Protocol #8 PAR-OS (Older Sibling) was used both for informational purposes and to verify or raise questions about Maritza's information. Albert shed light on why he and his sister Maritza rarely visited but were very protective of Davey and Philippo.

Davey had also been unresponsive to some of the questions of PAR-A, as well as to some of the questions of PAR-AA, which was used after Albert's visit to verify Albert's input. It became clear that some of the matters that Davey was asked about were not accessible to him cognitively, or they were just too upsetting. Patients often need a period of preparation and trust building before a break in that barrier can occur. Not all silences ought to be pursued immediately.

Assessing Cognitive Development

If the back and forth of conversation causes the professional to wonder if the adolescent's cognitive development may be taking place at a slower or more rapid pace than is the norm for the adolescent's age group, it is necessary for the professional to pose a series of different kinds of questions to ascertain whether the adolescent has achieved the stage of formal operations. If an adolescent's development has reached that milestone, he or she should understand an abstract question.[2] Several PAR Supplementary protocols are useful for this purpose. Before using any of them, however, the analysis of all protocols already used needs to be completed and integrated in order to select the most relevant protocols in the Supplementary series.

In Davey's case, questions from protocol #16 PAR-Su-GU (What Do You Have to Give Up) were selected to test whether he had reached the formal operations stage. This protocol asks abstract rather than concrete questions.[3] For example, the first question is, "When you decided to turn off (shut down) being with friends, what did you gain?" As simple as it sounds, a useful response requires the ability to keep the concept of "shutting down being with friends" in mind while struggling with the many-faceted question of what is gained. Some replies would show a lack of conceptual thought, such as "I would lose having fun with a lot of people I like." Although this response can be seen as appropriate, it is at a far less complex level of understanding than is a response such as "I would lose contact with a lot of people I like being with, but I would gain the freedom to decide when and for what reason I wanted to be with friends." This response sets both the loss and the gain within one answer, two abstract concepts within a series of mental operations. At Davey's age, a simple answer could be due to a slower pace of development toward formal operations, but it could also indicate an unwillingness to cooperate. More seriously, but not likely, a simple answer could indicate a level of injury to the brain, ranging from relatively small to large.

Diagnosing the Defensive Glitch: Supplementary Protocols

The selection of what protocols to use should directly serve the purpose of testing a clinical hypothesis. Thus, in Davey's case, in order to determine if a defensive glitch was operating, Dr. Devlin chose to use protocol #17 PAR-Su-FO (What Do Friends Offer You), a protocol that poses penetrating questions that require a gentle delivery. Since Davey had earlier denied that not having peers was of any special bother to him, question 4 of the protocol was the proper place to start. "Instead of being with peers, would you ever prefer just to watch TV?" "Yes." Then Dr. Devlin asked, "Would you prefer to play with younger siblings?" "No." "Would you prefer to talk to older siblings?" "No." "Would you prefer to drink some alcohol?" "No." "Would you prefer to smoke some marijuana?" "Yes." "Some other drug?" "No." "Was this always the way you thought?" "No." "Would you rather just be with some friends your age?" "Maybe." At that point, Dr. Devlin stopped asking questions, though it should be noted that because Davey was responding, Dr. Devlin continued to ask a few questions even after discovering that drugs were a factor.

Dr. Devlin needed to decide whether it was best to forgo other Supplementary protocols and go immediately to the Phase II protocols. He did not want to risk losing the power of the moment, and he was certain that the marijuana issue was ripe for immediate further exploration. He could have decided to choose some qualitative questions such as "Is it better not to have friends than to have friends?" (#16 PAR-Su-GU) or others that deal with fantasies about friends (#22 PAR-Su-FFD) or their part in the future (#24 PAR-Su-F). He could have spent some sessions having Davey respond to such protocols as #15 PAR-Su-FP (Friendship Preferences), which asks about the meeting place of peers, who they are, and whether or not one is content with old friends or must try to find new ones, a line of questioning that goes on to ask whether one is happy with the friends one has or would like to change. The mention of "your peers" or "your friends" in this line of questioning would not alarm some clients, but Davey appeared more fragile. Therefore, this approach seemed wrong to Dr. Devlin, because Davey had selected how he would deal with *not* having the friends he used to have: marijuana. Thus, Dr. Devlin decided to use Phase II protocol #27 PAR-DG (Defensive Glitch) at the next session to test whether marijuana was connected to a defensive glitch that Davey might have adopted to flee the pain of comparisons. A follow-up session was arranged within a few days so that Davey could face questioning from PAR-DG. Dr. Devlin was able to arrive at a functional diagnosis after that session. It is important to note that at no point in use of the protocols is any specific glitch questioned or identified, unless it is volunteered by the adolescent. The purpose of PAR-DG is to diagnose, not to treat.

The intake group concluded that Davey was a good candidate for PAL group therapy. Fortunately, there was an opening almost immediately. Davey was assigned to a group of four males and six females of his chronological and developmental age. The in-group professional was Dr. Robert Delandy.

PAL Group Therapy

Davey was diagnosed as having an Isolated Game-Player Loner glitch, manifested in marijuana drug use. Other members of Davey's group also had some drug history, although none of them were identified as drug abusers. Developmentally, all were in the middle or ending periods of Stage 1 adolescence. A group of mixed-gender peers was selected for

Davey to replicate both his school and neighborhood Peer Arena, including the 'hood kids. During the course of PAL group therapy, Davey's history slowly and painfully unraveled.

Davey's Story

In the year prior to August's death, the Barnes household changed. Although communication did not break down completely, there was little of it. Thus, Davey was unaware of his parents' feelings and fears or the real condition of his father's health. He still saw his father often and did not ask questions. Davey's life was spent primarily with his peers, and he enjoyed it. A curious reciprocity took shape. Davey's father never stood in the way of Davey's friendships and encouraged his wife not to restrict them. Davey was appreciative and did all he could for his father, willingly, even bedside care. The sicker August got, the greater was his need to ingratiate himself with Davey. When August's cancer became painful, August assigned Davey to procure marijuana to enable him to work, because the family needed that money to live. He had sworn Davey to secrecy, and every now and then, for a treat when Mrs. Barnes was not at home, August allowed Davey to smoke a joint with him. Davey was careful to open all the windows to clear the air before his mother's return.

His mother demanded perfection. She felt that her potential had been cut short and did not want that to be the children's fate, particularly Davey. Mrs. Barnes had little time for street kids, who could lead Davey down a dangerous path.[4] She wanted him to stick to his books. She approved of his school friends. There was conflict between the two parents because Davey's father defended his desire to be with all kinds of kids. He argued that Mrs. Barnes alienated her two older children by imposing strict standards and that Davey needed freedom to try to be a man. As long as August lived, especially when he was sick, Mrs. Barnes did not have the will to counter her husband, and she was grateful to Davey for helping and spending a lot of time with him. Davey's presence brought August so much joy, and she was busy so much of the time doing both their chores.

The more time Davey spent with his father, the less time he had for friends. Then, when his father died, Davey's life changed again. His mother put him in charge of his younger brother after school until she got home, after the boys' bedtime. Davey had to leave her a report on what they had eaten for dinner and whether Philippo had been good or bad. She insisted on good schoolwork, but Davey had neither the time alone to work on it when he was awake nor the will. He missed having time with peers and wanted to go out with all the others. Soon, invitations stopped because he did not have money to join the guys in the 'hood, even for a soda and some mild gambling. He was embarrassed to drag his little brother along: Davey had already been kidded for being a "Mama." And there was no longer any money for marijuana, which had helped his father so much.

PAR-A disclosed that Davey's close examination of kids at school revealed most of them forging ahead with no problems, doing well in studies and in sports, and having fun with girls now too. Davey's analyses of comparisons with them showed that he was less and less on a level with those he respected. He retreated to comparisons with street kids, but he did not do too well there either. They appeared far more savvy than he. Ironically, the only points he could claim would be in babysitting, and he sure hoped nobody knew he was doing that. So he did not invite anyone over to catch him warming food, serving dinner, and bathing his little brother. He was, of course, unaware that his developmental stage contributed to his deep worry: adolescence is the period when gender identification is finalized.

Davey was drawn more and more to getting high but had no money for it. His mother's purse was with her all the time. He sold a few things she would never miss at the pawn shop. Marijuana made him feel better, but he knew getting high would be short-lived. He could not manage to get it too often since he had to take Philippo with him, and he was angry about that. The lust for marijuana drove him crazy. He had to figure out how to block his mind to his deprivations and tend to his babysitter duties all at the same time. So he went to what was available to him.

Mr. Barnes had left a computer that was in pretty good shape. Philippo and Davey played games on the computer, which kept his brother quiet until his bedtime. Then Davey usually watched television a little until his mother came home, when he gave her his report. She was too tired to chat, so it was the perfect time to go to the computer, fake doing schoolwork, and surf the Web. He could find out about really cool places, see clips of movies, even hear music if he kept the volume low. Soon, he did little else: he turned the television on for his brother after school, and he was on the computer playing solitaire instead of games with Philippo. Except for preparing and serving dinner, writing the note to his mother about what they ate, bathing Philippo before bedtime, and cleaning up, he was on the computer. Davey stopped going to the street from time to time, as he used to do. He did not have the money to do stuff there anyway. So the older guys would taunt him in school. It seemed that *no one was like him*. It hurt.

Davey had no knowledge that his stage of adolescence was one in which similar others serve two functions: (1) they offer certainty about oneself during a changeable period of life, and (2) they place themselves in front of you and automatically offer choices connected with who and what you might like to be. He was among peers, but he was not *with* them. Davey had no way of knowing that his distress was due to frustrated attachment needs.

As the weeks passed, disappointing results of comparisons became very hard for Davey to bear. The findings at school were becoming inescapable. The very worst was that it seemed like no one else had a dad who was dead. Maybe some of their parents were divorced or something, but not dead. And hardly anyone's mother worked the early night shift like his did. And school was not the end of it. It was in the neighborhood too: no one else there was sissy enough to be nursemaid and house cleaner.

So Davey kept to himself and kept quiet. The last thing he wanted to do was study books. He wanted to study his peers. He sneaked looks at school kids and street kids, but it was too risky to have friends. They would discover his secrets. He grew frightened and turned these feelings inward in sadness and anxiety, but not depression. The imperative to be with peers still raged, and he looked for a way to get out and to get friends. He thought marijuana would get him friends, but he did not have the money and did not want to steal from his mother. He could not risk her anger and rejection.

Davey was desperate for peers, and eventually he did find a way to get to them. Having tired of challenging himself with games on the computer, he went to sites on the Internet where nobody knew he was a "housewife and mom to his brother" and got himself lots of friends. He had heard about MySpace and Facebook, and he lost himself in learning about all sorts of age-mates, writing descriptions about who he wanted to be, and making Internet friends he liked. He learned a lot about them: the people they like and what they do, eat, buy, and aspire to be. He now had peers to compare with, virtual peers. And he could make all sorts of claims that they would believe, so his comparison findings came out really well. Best of all, it was private: he had hundreds of peers his mother could not see and could not dislike. And they would never know that his father was dead and that he was a cook and nursemaid.

Access to the Web reduced Davey's desire for marijuana, substituting an almost obsessive drive to "get to the Web." It occupied all his time, to the exclusion of everything but home duties for Philippo. It made him feel like he belonged. He could forget his sadness about the low esteem in which he was certain peers held him. He was on his way to an Isolated Game-Player Loner defensive glitch.

The Silent Story

Davey wondered to himself why it was OK with his mother that he was doing so badly in school. Even that fact did not get her away from her focus on working. "I have to make sure there is enough money for us to live on." But what Davey did not know was that his mother was having an affair with her boss, which had started six months before her husband died. Maritza knew but refused her mother's request to quit her job to take care of the boys. Maritza truly wanted to help Davey but needed to ensure that her life would not become the one that her mother had been living. She had her own life "not to ruin" just because her mother sought the attention of men. Out of disgust, Albert told Davey, "You are old enough to know what our mother is." Davey knew he was not going to tell anybody, and he grieved about the past days of his life, when his father was well. He remembered when he played school sports several days a week and could have friends over.

PAL Group Therapy Process

Davey often said, "Becoming a member of my PAL group is the luckiest thing that ever happened to me." In fact, it took only six or seven group sessions of looking and listening for him to share how close he and his father had been and how his father's death had brought great sadness to him. In subsequent sessions, he admitted that he was a drug user, having purchased marijuana to ease August's pain and occasionally enjoyed a joint with him. Some group members understood the depth of Davey's loss and comforted him. Others challenged him about why he shared the marijuana. He replied that it made his father happy, about which some group members expressed skepticism. They did not think that was the only reason, but the discussion went no further. Davey offered no answer.

For some time, Davey's kept his mother's affair secret. When he did finally reveal it, he was questioned about why it took so long for him to share. He responded that he kept quiet out of allegiance to Maritza, Albert, and

Philippo but most of all to honor the memory of his father. Once more, the reason did not sound authentic to the group: two female members probed what the real reason was. Again, Davey did not respond. This time, it was not because he was withholding but because he did not know the reason either. When no one insisted on pursuing the matter, it struck him that although comparisons with each group member revealed most of them to be similar to himself (in part because each had a troubled history), this group was different from the similarity he once felt toward the kids in the 'hood. This realization freed him to unload about himself somewhat. But the group was not always kind: a small minority tolerated his frequenting the Web much more readily than they tolerated his marijuana use. Others, who were drug users on the road to reform, did not consider him to be a true user, and they regarded his Web peers as "gross": "You are insulting 'friendship' just because you are plain afraid!" Those were penetrating words.

Davey was not going to talk about why he shied away from real contact and why he used marijuana to soothe his real hurt. Instead, he talked about the Web and its delights. The group called it "weird," though luckily for him, they did not call *him* weird. Group rules helped, too: group members could not be in touch by telephone or e-mail between sessions. Davey used this time to think about this rule and realized that with no telephone calls or e-mail everyone had to think on his or her own. They expected him to start sharing the tough stuff. In the following session, the group made an exception to the rule: telephone contact would be allowed for Davey two times between biweekly sessions. They felt that his loneliness for peers would be relieved by telephone contact with real people with real voices. To earn this exception to a rule, Davey was required to report on how the contact went and whether it cut down the time he focused on his Web friends. Because it was peers who came up with this strategy, it did not feel to Davey like it was imposed on him or like somebody older was telling him what to do.

Sessions focusing on other members' issues were beneficial to Davey. He privately compared himself with them to measure if he could be good at some of the things they were good at. He also had some surprises. Group members confessed to their imperfections as well as to their traumatic comparative acts with peers. Even how they coped with these findings—successfully or not—was surprising to him. The comfort of this similarity chipped away at his supposition that he was *the only one*. It helped him finally to share that he was not totally free from marijuana's grip, even though it was reduced. At last, he felt free of any deception. Some group members acknowledged the courage displayed by his confession. What a relief from the aloneness that had plagued his past few years. This combination of forces diminished how often he sought escape.[5]

Davey also helped others—it was not a one-way street at all. Together, the group discussed how drugs blocked pain by a numbing, almost dissociated experience. Davey shared his past ironic good fortune that often his father did not have money to buy marijuana. Davey was proud that his father would never steal to pay for drugs, nor would he even borrow money. Users in the group thus heard firsthand that even physical pain could be endured. This was a story of control over a drug, not of a drug in control. It was possible to possess it without being possessed by it.

Davey was not aware that his story was inspiring. Nor did others necessarily know when their stories inspired Davey. These moments capture the dynamic of PAL group therapy. Adolescent peers relate experiences as the subject comes up. They intuitively move into the rhythm of spontaneous sharing. Quite unexpectedly, Davey's status in the group changed. He became an Upward comparison figure, even a model for a much-discussed goal of achieving a drugfree existence. He could not believe that others saw him as a model of courage. How opposite to the Downward figure he was accustomed to believe he had been.[6]

Reminders of Davey's helpfulness came intermittently from group members, yet he still did not feel like a real member. Group members observed Davey's continuing remoteness, broken only by periods of active, almost overactive participation. Group members were not the only ones to notice.

Professional Clinical Intervention

Professionals occasionally decide to interrupt the group process. Such a step is always deliberated carefully because the overarching philosophy of PAL is to leave group process to the group.

Dynamics of PAL Group Therapy Interpreted

Dr. Delandy was uncomfortable about the nature of Davey's rather abrupt active participation in the group. It seemed inauthentic, if not false. Being quiet, if not remote, had been his demeanor when he entered the group. Not very long afterward, his style transformed into very active participation. At that time, Dr. Delandy (referred to most often by the group as Dr. D.) pondered whether Davey's behavior was an avoidance strategy. In a very tentative way, Dr. Delandy shared his confusion about Davey's style with the group, Davey included. The group picked up on his extremes of participation; they called it inconsistent. Dr. D. asked the group to consider selecting a small subgroup to reply to questions about Davey listed on the PAL Behavioral Style form and to return some conclusions to the larger group.[7]

THE PAL BEHAVIORAL STYLE FORM: AN ADVISORY MEASURE

This form, used exclusively during PAL group therapy in special circumstances, documents impressions of an adolescent's customary style within group meetings. One rule is that new members of the group are never targets because the others do not yet know them well enough. To use the form within the group, not more than four individuals selected at random pick one of eight personality styles from the form's list that they believe best describes the specified adolescent.[8] The adolescent in question also fills out the form and may request a period of up to four sessions of time to reflect on the findings before a general group discussion about them.

PAL 1: PAL-BSF (BEHAVIORAL STYLE FORM)

Person Observed _____ ID# _____ Age: _____ yrs. _____ mos. _____ M _____
F _____

Circle the style from those listed below which you believe best describes _____.

aggressive   passive   passive-aggressive   avoidant
controlling   impulsive   laissez-faire   rigid

FINDINGS

Findings from use of the PAL Behavioral Style form supported Dr. Delandy's hypothesis that Davey was exhibiting an avoidant style. Davey was judged to be holding back, though no conclusion was drawn as to whether it was deliberate or nondeliberate. Since a group rule existed that no discussions could take place without the adolescent in question being present, Davey was included in the discussion. The group pondered the puzzle together in the hope of helping Davey identify what he was keeping back. Davey himself was silent. Thus, what had seemed like Davey's prior seamless use of the group to make good strides was evolving into quite the opposite. Group members challenged Davey to make a turnaround.

OPENING UP

Dr. Delandy knew that the success of the group's challenge to Davey depended on how much the group pressure would assist Davey in breaking his own barrier. The risk was that it would instead strengthen his resistance. In fact, Davey rationalized his deception as serving two positive purposes. The first was that his full engagement would establish him as true member and bring up his popularity comparison scores, while he could keep real secrets private. The second was that his full engagement would protect him against pressure to expose secrets. Ultimately, when Davey took responsibility for the disingenuous stories he related from time to time to show his courage, the result was a drop in his reputation. But he scored some points with the group by owning up to the deception.

Davey's anxiety grew as he observed the facial expressions of PAL group members when three sessions later he finally described the chores he took on for his mother, including feeding and bathing his brother. He was nervous that he would let slip that the reason she got home late was that she had a boyfriend and spent the night with him. But ultimately, he did expose this shameful secret. The group supported him to continue. Some females counseled that doing so would help them all, including Davey, to understand better his avoidant front. He shared that his brother Albert, the source of the shocking information, thought his mother was a "tramp." Although he was proud to have Albert's trust, he was heartbroken to feel so deceived by his own mother. He did not blame Albert for being angry but could not bring himself to hate his mother. She and Philippo were all he had.

Davey was savvy enough to figure out that sharing the details of his mother's affair would have some good effects for him. His sincerity was bound to increase his popularity, or so he thought. It did in fact afford him points for the high degree of suffering it cost him. Few others had such a sorrowful tale to tell, and he was quite certain that he was given full credit for his courage and strength.

But the manner in which Davey elaborated how troubled he felt about his mother's actions and character made Dr. Delandy uneasy again. He hypothesized that this manner was a second front that Davey wore, which might be connected to a different issue. Dr. Delandy did not know what this other issue might be but felt certain there was a connection to some major uncertainty, possibly a fear or dread.

A Deviation from the Norm

Dr. Delandy shared his suspicions with others in the oversight group. His unusual recommendation was individual therapy for Davey. Usually individual therapy is most effective in readying the adolescent for PAL group therapy, not in removing him or her, even for a short time. Dr. Delandy's argument set forth two goals for Davey that needed solo time: (1) ferreting out the motivation for his duplicitous sharing and (2) increasing insight into what he was afraid to disclose. Another goal of this strategy would benefit the group: protection of the group from Davey's further manipulations in the service of maintaining his defensive glitch. Dr. D. won support from colleagues for Davey's transfer to individual therapy.

With Davey present, Dr. D. discussed his recommendation that Davey leave the group for a special type of therapy that would best serve his continued progress and that would best avoid the potential negative impact on the group process. Group members wanted some idea when Davey would resume group therapy. Dr. D. assured them that hopefully Davey would return to PAL group therapy but that he could not predict the exact date. Seeing what happened to Davey of course raised doubts for the other group members about their own future destiny. Dr. D. handled this uncertainty by sharing that transfer out was not common and that in this case it did not mean Davey was not working hard. That helped. Dr. D continued to say that Davey's transfer served both Davey's and the group's best interests, and that made them feel even better. Dr. D. told them that a new member would replace Davey.

Group members expressed concerns about the nature of the forthcoming new group. Part of bidding goodbye to Davey was saying goodbye to the structure and dynamics of the current group, in which most of them felt safe. Some expressed that they would miss Davey; others were silent. Davey remarked that it actually might be a relief to be away from the group for a while.

PAL Group Therapy: Individual Time

Davey was transferred to the care of Dr. Rowena Jackson, a Black middle-aged female therapist, who suggested to Davey that they consult PAR protocols, even relooking at some he had already responded to, for hints about factors that were not yet fully understood—below-the-surface reasons why his behavior revealed him to be a troubled adolescent. This was why he had come to the clinic in the first place, was it not? He agreed. Dr. Jackson, not Davey, mentioned his defensive glitch. She hoped use of the selected protocols might help them both understand the how and why of his interactions with peers. But she also took care to remind him of the strides he had made in PAL therapy: as his folder revealed, he was looked up to by the group (Upward comparison) because of how he was handling his home situation. To that, he offered a self-conscious smile. She asked if things were harder for him than what his schoolmates knew. His expression saddened, and he said nothing. Dr. Jackson asked if he was willing to begin with some PAR protocols that deal with peers. Davey appeared apprehensive about the focus but agreed.

Before they began, Dr. Jackson expressed regret over the loss of his father. The folder contained notes about Davey's loving care for him. He nodded, said nothing, and remained expressionless. Dr. Jackson noted that the subjects of family and peers suggested tender points for him. Since these responses were the same as those when Davey entered PAL therapy, they testified to the correctness of Dr. D's request to change therapy venues. Maybe nothing much had really been touched so far, although the group had loosened Davey up to speak out with peers, albeit not on matters he was fearful about.

Using the Supplementary Series of Protocols

The decision to use the Supplementary protocols was a risk. Dr. Jackson knew she was dealing with a very troubled adolescent, and he could close down completely. She decided to include only selected questions from the protocols at that time and return to the rest later. Davey knew there might be some questions asked that he had answered before, but he did not realize that the impact of his PAL experience might bring forth a different answer this time, which is what Dr. Jackson was betting on.

The Supplementary series of protocols covers a potpourri of issues about peer relations. The aim is to elicit not just facts but a range of feelings. The opening protocols (15–19) focus on how, when, and where peers are contacted and what one must do to keep them. Several of Davey's responses indicated that he was still an early adolescent, a stage in which adolescents seek an unlimited number of peers since they have just emptied out identification with parents and elders. They look for new agemates, any kind, from whom to copy self-elements for a while, try them out for size, and judge group reactions. Dr. Jackson knew from notes in the record that Davey had pulled back away from peers, and he was not ready to bring up his Web surfing, which brought him positive comparisons with virtual peers, nor did he bring up his use of marijuana.

Davey rather skillfully avoided answering a number of questions again in protocol #15 PAR-Su-FP (Friendship Preferences) by changing the subject and asking for definitions of words and then arguing a bit about them. But in the midst of this avoidance, he did answer one question. The issue for discussion generally was on what one needs to do to acquire friends. His response was, "to learn to be *masculine*." Dr. Jackson was taken aback at this most unusual reply from a 14-year-old, and it put her on the alert. A second question offered a different insight: his *distortion*. When asked who takes him where he needs to go to access friends, he responded "no one" (questions 9 and 10). Then he quickly added, "But there could be kids on the street I could be with even if my mother didn't like them." The "could be" contradicted his former statement that he wanted "to be with as many kids as he could regardless of *who they were*."[9] The first answer that Davey had let slip out seemed genuine, albeit surprising. But the contradiction inherent in his second response revealed the difference between what he wanted and what he had the ability to cope with. Street kids' delinquencies marked their masculinity for Davey, and Dr. Jackson wondered about the connection between Davey's avoidance and his professed quest to be masculine.

Protocol #16 PAR-Su-GU (What Do You Have to Give Up) yielded another very direct cue. Davey was remarkably candid in answering the questions of this protocol, especially given his shrugs and silence to more personal questions about the potential of friendships. For example, the way he handled "What could a substitute for a good friend be?" was by replying, "the computer." Did that response slip out? Or was there an aspect of deliberateness to it? This type of response can mean either that the adolescent is tiring or that he wanted Dr. Jackson to know that he was not all that unaware. Dr. Jackson decided to push just one more. Protocol #17 PAR-Su-FO (What Do Friends Offer You) delves into matters connected to what being with peers offers and into the specifics about efforts that can be made. Davey hunched his shoulders almost all the way up to his head, indicating "I don't know." Davey had shut down again.

In sum, aspects of Supplementary protocols 15–19 yielded several pieces of information. Davey had masculinity issues, a desire to have as many peers as he could, and a fear of accessing them. He also was resistant to expressing aloud what their importance was. So he pulled back and projected blame. Dr. Jackson knew it was important to find out how he experienced all of these things and what emotions he was carrying around. Behaviorally, she saw enormous self-control on Davey's part.

Dr. Jackson indicated that they would continue with the rest of the protocols at another meeting. Davey replied, "That's fine." He tried to keep private and still appear cooperative. In later sessions, Dr. Jackson hoped to introduce other Supplementary protocols: #20 PAR-Su-AC (Awareness of Comparisons), #21 PAR-Su-CA (Comparative Act), #22 PAR-Su-FFD (Fantasies and Future Dreams), and #23 PAR-Su-DA (Defensive Actions Reflection). Clustered together, an analysis of his responses could reveal if Davey was aware that he was comparing, if he took responsibility for his low comparison rankings, and if he had any confidence that he could improve and pursue his dreams—or if he had allowed himself to have future dreams at all. Finally, it could help determine if he understood at all why he had taken flight to defenses. What Dr. Jackson gleaned from these additional protocols was the *agony* of Davey's aloneness as well as some indications of his fear of being with male peers. She reasoned that these issues would be addressed again, perhaps later, upon return to PAL therapy.

A Second Untold Story

A second untold story unraveled for Davey after a number of individual sessions. First, Davey gained insight into how defenses operated to put a firewall between him and his fear. He also saw how his shame was so devastating that he developed a behavioral style to fend off having to relate to others. He talked, but he did not relate. He was slow to come to any insight into why he was drawn to the Isolated Loner Game-Player defensive glitch. He did discern that he may have exaggerated his anguish over his mother's actions in order to get sympathy and positive regard from the group. Acknowledging that to Dr. Jackson required trust, which was especially hard for him with a female. He had lost trust in the major female in his life, his mother, and he had not trusted most of the females in the PAL group.

During another session, he took a big risk. Davey confessed that as he compared himself to females in the PAL group and that he found himself to be like them in so many ways that it alarmed him. And the fright had grown with each PAL meeting. It took almost two months for him to share more with Dr. Jackson. She waited.

One day, Davey volunteered that he wondered if his mother always wanted him to be a girl. Is that why she gave him female chores to do instead of leaning harder on Maritza to come home and do them? The nagging question was whether keeping him from rough and tough boys in the 'hood served her purpose. Were 'hood boys right when they said he was a Mama?

Davey had only recently experienced puberty and was small in stature. He did not understand why strange feelings stirred within him when he saw females in school, in class, and in the neighborhood. There was no one to ask. His father would have answered him. In school, they learned about sexual preference, but he did not think he was interested in girls in that way. But he was not interested in boys in that way either. A light went on for Dr. Jackson. Davey had no clue that he had begun an important aspect of adolescence: working out one's sexual identification. Davey had taken first steps at feeling a sense of his gender. His beginning identification with his brother was cut short by Albert's exposure of their mother's affair. That exposure had hurt Davey, so he shut Albert out. Duties at home now, and even while his father was still alive, required him to be home after school and not to play after-school baseball, basketball, or track. Thus, school did not offer him opportunities for masculine-type contact either. So he had no opportunity to overhear young male locker-room conversations. Mrs. Barnes's exposed sexuality and infidelity in addition to his new housekeeping and maternal parenting duties could not have occurred at a worse time. He did not understand his own emotions, and he certainly was confused about his own body.

The intake professionals had not been privy to this information and instead concentrated on school and family issues, as had the referring documents, but Dr. Jackson felt she had a lead to explore. She was sure that when Davey replied that masculinity was what he wanted most, it was directly related to a fear that he was female on the inside and just looked male. Was this why the females in the PAL group upset him when he compared with them and felt similar? Dr. Jackson concluded that she felt she now knew where to go with his individual therapy.

For Davey, the progress being made in individual therapy had a very uncomfortable impact. He was sensing self-distrust and loathing. He felt close to hopeless about the fantasy he was having, a fantasy about *now*: returning to PAL, making progress, and actually graduating from it to rejoin school and neighborhood peer groups, his own Peer Arena. His own fantasy scared him. He was getting pretty good at understanding matters about himself, but it was not turning out well. His fears were deepening. So, of course, he avoided bringing them up. So far, Davey had not mentioned his marijuana use to Dr. Jackson, who had not yet opened up the "Game-Player" part of his defensive glitch.

Although Dr. Jackson knew the glitch might be getting worse because Davey really resisted talking about marijuana and his use of the Web, she did not push the discussion. She doggedly pursued further uncovering. Eventually, Davey confessed to engaging in comparisons from time to time that revealed how he could not keep up with the boys in the 'hood when he saw how masculine they were and how he fell short.[10] And he felt deep shame about being so small that people must think he is a girl. Dr. Jackson worked with Davey on whether small stature in a 14-year-old adolescent really meant nonmasculinity. She presented him with statistics on growth patterns in physical height and musculature in males. This information brought reality to bear on his fantasies, but his fear of internal femininity was deep and he was too immature to understand abstract concepts such as development. He needed visual proof. Davey's unexpressed question remained: how could a skinny, short kid be masculine? Since Davey's cognitive growth was at a point where he still did not think much beyond what he saw, giving logical answers was not helping. Dr. Jackson went as far as she could with it, offering information and hoping before the course of therapy ended that his cognitive development would take steps forward.[11] Having a good grasp of the process of adolescent cognitive development is crucial to effective therapy, and Dr. Jackson understood why Davey could not comprehend how he could be a male and look so different from others, to himself anyway. Furthermore, postpuberty preformal thought is a particularly hard state since it is active during a period when youth are particularly self-conscious. Thus, Davey believed that everyone was looking at him and that his "femininity" was noted by *everyone*.[12] At other stages of life, this belief could be considered narcissism, but not in adolescence, when it is characteristic of the period. It is natural, but it passes.

Dr. Jackson's intervention helped Davey take an important forward leap. He connected his uncharacteristic and sudden past disruptive behavior and lack of studiousness in school to being obsessed with how to be masculine. When he compared with street kids, he found he could learn to be masculine by hanging around with them. He learned to act tough and how to stir up trouble. They liked what they saw, and Davey sensed it. That was the route of his unexpected "troublesome behavior," as related in his original referral. He reported hearing from a neighbor kid that even some of the jocks in the class gave him "respect." He also remembered exactly what the school personnel reported: "when not causing problems, he is just quiet." When he resumed PAL, he would learn from his peers that his unique combination of silence and intermittent behavior problems was his strategy to control his world.

Back to Findings from the PAR Protocols

Dr. Jackson just happened to say one day that maybe one of the reasons Davey liked MySpace and Facebook so much was that he could try out *playing male*. That made Davey wonder if she knew the "secret." Nevertheless, when he thought about it, it did feel good to *play the male*. And he could compare with all the other males. Some of the time the comparisons did not come out too badly. Dr. Jackson said that that was something for him to think about.

Davey and Dr. Jackson worked out some of it together. The peer protocols helped him to find out that his rotten findings from comparisons with guys were because he was comparing on skill in and knowledge about sports. Most guys love sports, but sports really did not really turn him on. He liked them, but only a little bit. What he had always liked was art, dancing, and novels. But that is the kind of stuff girls like. He even liked to cook. He knew some guys who cook pizza and hamburgers, even pasta, but he did not know any guy who liked art and novels.

From Dr. Jackson's perspective, Davey was beginning to trust her. This change in Davey began about eight months into individual therapy. Davey talked about comparing and how he always felt that he was considered "a minus." He could not understand why boys always have to compare what they know about sports—all kinds of sports.[13] He was stunned when even Philippo started doing it.

Protocols #18 PAR-Su-R (Recuperation) and #19 PAR-Su-KF (Keeping Friends) gave Davey lots of opportunities to describe what he liked or disliked about peers. He brought up sports again with Dr. Jackson to show how crucial sports were in the lives of his male peers and to highlight two penalties that he pays for his lack of interest in sports. First, it makes him feel different from other males about a lot of things. Second, it shows him how much more he enjoys feminine interests, adding further fuel to his fears.

The Heart of the Matter

During their sessions, Dr. Jackson was not caught by Davey's frequent attempts to spin the topic onto members of his family. She stayed with peers. Davey was not used to being confronted so directly. Dr. Jackson went back a second time to the issues of protocols #20 PAR-Su-AC (Awareness of Comparisons) and #21 PAR-Su-CA (Comparative Act), again opening up discussion of what friends offer. This time, words were on the tip of Davey's tongue. "They are kids just like me." "I can look them over real good and get good ideas about what I like and what I don't. Then I could go right out and try it and see how I make out. I bet sometimes I could be just as good as they are. Maybe even better."

The next session, Dr. Jackson decided to return to protocol #21 PAR-Su-CA (Comparative Act) and also to use protocol #22 PAR-Su-FFD (Fantasies and Future Dreams), which focus on who Davey would choose for friends and open opportunities for comparisons between him and them. He talked about how empty he felt: "If I could only just stand and look at people instead of hiding from them." Dr. Jackson fell silent. She sensed that he was talking to himself as he continued in quieter tones. "So, everyone here at the clinic knows what I did. I went to the Web." It was the first time Davey took responsibility for his actions and his well-kept secrets. He said it was not a good idea, perhaps, but for him it was better than nothing and did not make him so desperate for "the drug." Davey looked up as if to remember that Dr. Jackson was in the room and said that he sort of remembered from when he first went into therapy some kinds of questions like this on what you chose instead of friends. He said he was not telling anybody anything really important at that time, but he knew what he was doing was not good. Then he laughed slightly as he said, "You guys found out anyway."

The growth that Dr. Jackson was waiting for peeked its head out. These latter sessions had been very important. Davey integrated information from his past and related it to his present activities. In PAL group therapy, he had played it safe. He justified his occasional use of marijuana. He blamed others for what he was doing. He claimed little, if any, insight into why he was so intrigued with the Web. Nor did he take it up with the group. Instead, he chose to share his sadnesses, his self-satisfying siblings, and, ultimately, his immoral mother. The only sympathetic figure he described was his father, whose loss he still mourned. Davey did not mention Philippo much, except that he had to spend a lot of time with him and that he loved him. Now, with Dr. Jackson, he finally began to deal with what went wrong in *himself.*

Davey still had a way to go. With the therapeutic advance he had made, he was getting closer to facing out loud to himself the anguish connected with the basic deception he was using to shield himself from a secret so devastating that he could share it with no one. He had been determined never to reveal his dreaded secret, which became conscious to him in the course of PAL group sessions. It was hard to see and even harder to admit: *he identified with girls.* Davey saw himself as *deviant* and did not want to accept it because it would be too hard. He was conflicted and scared: he wanted to be a boy, but he felt he had failed at it. His libidinous feelings toward females were so uninformed that he mistook those feelings for identification with females.

Davey was living with this fear when he parted from the group and began with Dr. Jackson. He finally decided to mention his drug-taking in an offhand way, but as it turned out she already knew. He thought she was pretty cool the way she kept it to herself. Because of this growing trust in Dr. Jackson, he finally told her his secret. Once Davey had shared, he and Dr. Jackson could look at his fear that he was feminine and not masculine. Identifying with the opposite gender is not uncommon at Davey's stage of development; rather, it is generally a fleeting identification. Whether this identification would be ongoing for Davey remained to be seen, and they dealt with this possibility in several sessions. Davey got to express his deepest fears. Most important, he trusted Dr. Jackson, a female, to explore these fears with him. He came to understand why his referral for individual therapy had included a request for a female psychotherapist.

A Final Matter Needing Resolution

Something else also needed attending to. Dr. Jackson reasoned that it would also be helpful to Davey to concentrate on important matters in his life other than his fear of being feminine. She raised with Davey the possibility of arranging a joint meeting with his mother to discuss her current relationship with Tyrone, her boss. Davey agreed that it was important for secrets to be worked out, and Mrs. Barnes agreed to come in out of concern that Davey's transfer back to a PAL group would be delayed until this contact was completed. Mrs. Barnes saw Dr. Jackson alone first and then followed with a joint appointment with Davey. In that joint session, Davey learned that his father knew Tyrone and sanctioned the affair since he had been impotent for a number of years, due to the removal of his prostate gland. When he was diagnosed with stomach cancer, he was aware that the end was near. Mrs. Barnes was still a young woman and devoted to him, but he wanted to see her secure before he died. He encouraged her to reverse her prior resistance to Tyrone's affections. Mrs. Barnes's affair was difficult for Mr. Barnes, but he knew he had no chance to regain normal sexual relations. It was his way of taking care of his young wife. The three adults agreed that after his death, when Mrs. Barnes felt the time was right, she and Tyrone would marry.

Neither Mrs. Barnes nor her husband had shared this information with Davey. The older two children knew, but once again Maritza and Albert felt that they had been replaced by a man and were angry. Albert had shared only his anger, not the whole story. Mrs. Barnes had not responded to calls from the clinic because she feared her story would eventually be revealed to Davey. She was in shock when the professional told her that Davey knew. When she and Davey met together with Dr. Jackson, Mrs. Barnes wept in front of her son. Davey stood back and showed little emotion. Dr. Jackson met two additional times with Davey to help him deal with the effects of the shared disclosures. Although these disclosures reestablished his mother as a moral person, the content was still a bit much for him. He needed more time with Dr. Jackson before returning to PAL, and he asked to postpone the return. Both he and Dr. Jackson agreed that they would work together on a strategy to bring this material to PAL.[14] And he did not want to talk to his mother about it—not yet, anyway.

Reentry into PAL Group Therapy

Within three months, Davey was ready to move on from individual therapy and separate from Dr. Jackson, just as he had from Dr. Delandy. But this separation would be more difficult because the contact had been long and intense. Davey had matured considerably. He recognized that the therapeutic work he now needed was with peers in PAL group therapy. Dr. Jackson and Davey had discussed together the advisability of working on protocol #24 PAR-Su-F (Future) with the new group. With its focus on future matters, there would inevitably be discussions of occupational choice, which would involve conversation about gender and sexuality. It seemed to Davey that it would be good to discuss this subject first with an all-male group and then later with a mixed group. Dr. Jackson agreed, if this was what he was most comfortable with. Getting input from both genders was important, but timing the "when" of each was important too.

Dr. Jackson and Davey scheduled two sessions before the date when final closure between them would take place. Davey needed to fill out an application form requesting admission to return to PAL. The PAL group would be all male initially, and then he would transfer to a mixed-gender group. He also was required to provide details of the request in an essay that would be independently written, with comments from Dr. Jackson after it was finished. The essay needed to include the presenting problem, his progress, and what he planned to focus on in the new group and the rationale for that focus.

As with his initial application for PAL, intake professionals reviewed the application and conferred together on acceptance or rejection. Once again, assignment to the proper group passed to a placement professional who factored in the individual therapist's recommendation. Upon acceptance, Davey resumed PAL group therapy in a new group but at a psychological place very different from where he entered his first PAL group. The new in-group professional was Dr. Melvin Lukasy.

Facing Fears: Davey's PAL Groups 2 and 3

Davey's new PAL therapy group had a mix of members that replicated all-male peer groups in Davey's Peer Arena, as had been requested by Dr. Jackson. This time, Dr. Jackson and Davey set distinct tasks, which were reviewed with Dr. Lukasy. Davey was expected to work through his disappointing comparison issues with males. It was inevitable that his Web overactivity and marijuana use would be subjected to examination and that he would be required to find workable strategies to dispense with them. These strategies might include Davey's preparing aggressively to join groups in school and in the 'hood. First, he was to work hard on carrying out as many comparative acts with group members as possible, dealing with both uplifting and disappointing outcomes and not running away psychologically or physically.

Thus, in Davey's case, return to PAL was more than an opportunity to be with peers once again; it presented a challenge to work hard and succeed. In his head, Davey agreed with Dr. Jackson that it would be an important period in his life. In his heart, he was scared, but this time he also knew in his heart that there would be support from peers, from some at least.

The purpose of an all-male group was twofold: (1) to prevent external female stimuli from luring Davey's focus away from comparative acts with males and interpretations of those comparisons and (2) to get Davey involved in "male topics" and in extending comparative acts beyond those he had previously executed. Once these objectives were achieved, Davey would be ready to transfer to a mixed group. There, he would compare males and females with one another and then compare himself with each gender.

In the second month after Davey's transfer from the all-male group to the mixed one, a particularly intuitive girl in the group asked about Davey's pattern of quiet acting out. Did he think it was related to his "avoidant" style, which he had talked about, or the passive aggressiveness that could be connected to it? Dr. Lukasy told the group that sometime passive aggressiveness is not always directed toward others. It could be a pattern turned inward. Sometimes, it could turn into a variation of self-punitiveness. In the group discussion, the potential of passive aggressiveness turning inward into self-punitiveness scared Davey.

Weeks later, Davey learned that for many years part of his self-loathing might very well have been *shame* over stealing from his own mother, even though she never publicly attributed it to him. He concluded that she knew and, like him, had avoided discussing it—just never said anything about it. Group members then inquired if the quietness he still displayed in school had anything to do with his passive aggression. As he thought about the matter, he guessed that in a way it did. Although he was definitely quiet in school, he irritated both his teacher and his mother by not doing homework and not being the least concerned about it himself. "I withdraw in my head but remain in school in my body so Mama can't get after me for being truant." The group asked him why he passive-aggressively frustrated her attempts to make a student of him. He did not know. Davey admitted to turning off all types of learning by day, schoolwork included. The group wondered if he was still angry at his mother.

Once more, weeks later he realized something very important. As hard as it was for him to say, he felt that his peers, even though they were fairly new peers, were quite mature and would understand the anger he felt toward his mother over two matters: her affair with her boss and her making him a "Mama." He had not progressed very far in working through this anger. So it seemed that his attitude toward the situation at home had not changed from earlier years, except that Philippo could do a bit more for himself. But there was even more: he suffered from findings of comparison with others who he just knew had parents who would never do what his mother had done. He felt he really had a lot to deal with already, and now, more and more was coming out. He was getting overloaded.

Davey remembered that Dr. Jackson always suggested that he replace feeling sorry for himself with facing his fears, which terrified him, especially since he needed to begin looking at issues of the future. He was fearful of finding out who he was down deep, with regard to his interests and his gender. Questions that group members asked brought him to a stunning, complex realization: he kept deflecting his self-loathing into passive aggression. Maybe it was time to face reality and find out about himself one way or the other. By this time, Davey knew that the only way he could do this was with group support. So even though he was relatively new, he needed to try. He wondered if they could help him; there were so many deceptions to disclose. He asked himself if he could manage it.

The group was kind. They suggested going slowly: one thing at a time so as to build up to the hardest to share. Group members assured their newest member that they would work together with him. They reminded him that each of them had a story to tell. Within only a few sessions, Davey was kind of surprised that he preferred being public to being private. He thought that maybe he had come a long way and wondered how long a way it would still be for him to be in pain. His mother had started to pay him a few dollars a week in addition to his allowance for school meals, so he now had money to buy marijuana if he wanted to. Should he share with the group that he could buy it? He decided not to. If he felt really weak, maybe he would buy it. Davey believed that not sharing this information would test his strength.

Taking a Risk

Davey made a rare request for a special time-out session with Dr. Lukasy. He knew he had to have a good reason for Dr. Lukasy to make this exception. In the private session that Dr. Lukasy did grant, Davey shared his secret that he identified with females. Dr. Lukasy supported his plan to bring his shame to the group, which would not be easy for him, especially since the quest for an answer was tearing him apart inside. This was the first time he faced a group of peers with his dilemma over his sexual identity, and his fear was intense. The group response overwhelmed him. Even though he was a fairly new member, he was not looked on as bizarre. Rather, one male and one female shared the pain of a related struggle: deciding on sexual preference. In fact, and of great surprise to Davey, they were more concerned that he give up any intention of buying marijuana; doing so would pave a clear path to facing the troubling issues with which he was struggling.

The group also cautioned Davey against overdoing comparisons between himself and males and females to the point where it became near obsessive, but that was not easy for him. The supply of age-group models on the various Web sites is never ending, and Davey requested help to handle his problem. Ideas were brought forth, old and new, over a period of weeks and months as he worked to master it. It seemed as if each person had a different kind of struggle with the Web because it was such an easy private escape.

Issues other than physical gender also rose to the surface, such as social interpretations of physical strength and power in males with whom short, skinny Davey could not identify and of other characteristics such as artistic dress and performing-arts talent in females with whom he could identify. The group helped him to recall that his father was also not a large man, but his wisdom and character had made him seem broad and tall. This realistic picture of his father helped Davey to identify similarities to himself. He recalled that August had a beautiful voice and enjoyed both rock music and tango dancing. Group surveillance also assisted Davey in better handling the difficult task of avoiding overdoing the Web and the comparisons it provided: he had to turn in time sheets indicating non-school activities and length of time spent on them until he met the parameters set by the group, and only during the first few weeks was he permitted two phone calls two times a week to a group member for support.

Impact of PAL Group Therapy

Davey graduated from high school not too long after he finished PAL therapy. He had met all the requirements to graduate from PAL group therapy more than 18 months after his admission to PAL group 2. He was comfortable being more active with school peers and felt accepted. He mixed with neighborhood peers more easily, but comparative acts revealed that most of them did not seem to be going in the same future direction that he was. He did not have spare cash for drugs since going to college someday was first on his agenda.

Davey did not return to the PAL group for follow-up; he chose not to. He felt he was managing fine. As luck would have it, high school brought Davey impressive physical growth, which caught up with his cognitive growth, and Davey became a handsome middle-height male of five foot eight. His emotional growth took a leap forward too, and his gentle nature was appealing to many females. As Davey grew, he looked more like his father, a feature both Mrs. Barnes and her new husband liked very much. Philippo, a junior high school student was coming along well. Philippo adored his older brother, and that was a role Davey liked filling. Maritza and Albert remained cool, but both Davey and Philippo saw them every few months.

Davey was 18 years old now. His social growth was still lagging, but now that the other domains were fully mature, social growth would follow in turn. Davey planned to work for a few years, both to earn the funds to go to college and as an outcome of discussions in PAL in which all his attachment others, who were also a bit behind in full development, agreed that he still needed time to grow up. In the meantime, Davey was getting educated in art without money: he was going to museums on his free days and taking out art books from the public library. In fact, he found that he loved 16th-century Dutch paintings. That most of the really famous painters were males really pleased him. However, he had to know for sure that he wanted to be an artist. First, Davey felt it would be important to try out some hard physical-labor jobs, and Albert was trying to get him one in construction. He and the PAL group had thought that was a great idea. A side result of this plan would be getting closer to Albert, who after all was his brother. Albert was married now, and Davey liked the couple's apartment. They all figured it could give him a place to get away from the 'hood when he needed to. He was not much like the guys he knew there, who were not interested in art.

Retrospective on PAL Group Therapy Structure and Objectives

No matter the topic, input from peer attachment figures is far more powerful than that from elders or professionals. Each adolescent possesses the internal strength to survive demands of a very complex period of life. Going through the stage with familiar, relatively congenial peers at school and in the neighborhood is optimal. But even then, difficulties do arise. The aim of PAL therapy is to reverse a negative, self-destructive course of action and put the emphasis back where it belongs.

The Use of Individual Therapy

It must be well understood that, Davey's example notwithstanding, prescribing transfer to individual therapy is not common. When it is essential, as in Davey's case, it is done in order to move forward, and the length of this temporary move is closely watched. Throughout, the purpose of the individual therapy must always be to return the adolescent to PAL therapy. The adolescent knows it, and the professionals know it. Thus, only the most experienced therapists should be assigned to provide individual therapy. In addition, intermittent meetings with the adolescent and the family should be scheduled to check on the adolescent's health. The professional team must be available to make any emergency decision.

The Matter of Trust: Curative Dynamics

The ability to trust is a problem for almost every member of PAL therapy groups. Proper help from group colleagues and from skilled professionals assist most members in eventually sharing their deepest secrets in the group. Among the curative dynamics that the group brings are the encouragement of truth-telling, challenge, acceptance, interpretation, and support at low moments. Support includes true caring and deep concern as well as sharing views and information frankly at the risk of one's own reputation. Adolescents in the group become inspired to do this for one another. Most powerful of all is the acquisition of a sense of freedom to redo one's own erroneous interpretations of one's rank compared to others. In group meetings, members are expected to discuss their conclusions out loud and are expected by one another to reform their faulty rationales and methods.

It may appear astonishing that a professional would pay heed to a group of adolescents for their diagnoses of very serious behavioral problems and recommendations for treatment. Yet peer group members intuitively understand one another. They understand one another's task in developing, and they have a sense of where each is and where each needs to grow. They understand one another's concern with the present and with the future and what effect tasks and constraints have on themselves and on their peers. And they are very generous in how they accept one another, notwithstanding their own scars and pimples. They are "one" as at no other period of life. No other group of contemporaries could be so skilled at intuitively understanding what might be going wrong and at suggesting what might be a successful strategy to try next.

Conclusion

In this book we have seen how useful a Peer Arena lens can be in illuminating confusing adolescent behavior. By understanding such behavior as stemming largely from psychological interactions and comparison with peers, we gain the ability to trace adolescents' endeavors to see themselves through the stressful period of individuation and of becoming their own person. With this lens, the professional comes to understand the adolescent imperative to be together with other adolescents. Working skillfully with adolescents requires a grasp of this phenomenon. What has traditionally been perceived as a "conflict of the generations" and "rebellion" misses the essence of adolescence and the core importance of the Peer Arena for adolescent development.

Hopefully this book has provided key insights into the theory and practice of working with adolescents, as well as a road map for teasing out and working to repair glitches in their peer interactions and psychological development. By drawing on the protocols provided here and the PAL group therapy model, you will be well equipped to help your adolescent clients to move back onto the path of healthy development and maturation into adulthood.

Notes

NOTES TO THE INTRODUCTION

1. These days, additional information about the brain is provided through the use of the PET Scan, which allows soft tissue of the brain to light up when stimulated. This technological breakthrough offers exciting potential for application to psychological hypotheses. See Zink 2008.

2. Piaget 1972.

3. Piaget 1932.

4. Erikson 1959.

5. Festinger 1954.

6. Schachter 1959.

7. Bowlby 1969.

8. Lorenz 1965.

9. Mahler 1968.

10. A. Freud 1958.

11. Radloff 1966.

12. DFI takes no position regarding psychoanalytic notions about peer usefulness as substitutes onto whom libidinous feelings are redirected away from the parent of the opposite gender.

13. Seltzer 2002.

14. S. Freud 1953; Bandura and Walters 1963; Minuchin 1974.

15. Muuss 1986.

16. Coleman 1961.

17. A. Beck 1976.

18. Minuchin 1974.

19. Seltzer 1989.

20. Seltzer 1982.

NOTES TO CHAPTER 1

1. These two types of comparison among others are stimulated by another adolescent phenomenon, the adolescent imperative to compare with peers. All are discussed in more depth in chapter 2.

2. Muuss 1982: 2.

3. Aristotle, in Sebald 1984: 1, 19, 180.

4. Ausubel and Sullivan 1970.

5. Ibid.

6. Ibid.

7. Watson 1930.

8. Skinner 1938.

9. Hall 1904.

10. S. Freud 1953.

11. Rank 1952.

12. Sullivan 1953.

13. Erikson 1968.

14. Josselson 1987.

15. Archibald, Graber, and Brooks-Gunn 2004: 24–47.

16. Piaget and Inhelder 1969.

17. Rubin et al. 2005.

18. Bandura and Walters 1963.

19. An interesting and pertinent emphasis is supplied by observing children's group behaviors in natural settings, such as a study on the relationships in groups of children playing in the snow (Strayer and Santos 1996).

20. Asher and Coie 1990.

21. Rubin et al. 2005: 475.

22. Davies 2004: 385.

23. Flavell 1963.

24. Laursen, Hartup, and Koplas 1996.

25. It is quite interesting that direct physical aggression diminishes greatly during preadolescence. Even when particularly angry, most females do not strike out but use words. Crick, Casas, and Nelson 2002.

26. Seltzer 1982.

27. Marshall and Tanner 1974.

28. Brooks-Gunn and Reiter 1990.

29. Ibid.

30. Katchadourian 1977.

31. Tanner 1971: 37.

32. Brooks-Gunn et al. 1994.

33. Jones and Bayley 1950; Jones and Mussen 1958.

34. Brooks-Gunn, Peterson, and Eichorn 1985.

35. Gaddis and Brooks-Gunn 1985.

36. Trebay 2000.

37. Archibald, Graber, and Brooks-Gunn 2004.

38. Allen and Hauser 1996.

39. For a wonderful portrayal of the concerns of a 12-year-old over her potential height, see McCullers 1946: 16.

40. Dusek 1996.

41. Byrnes 2004.

42. See pp. 5–6.

43. Piaget 1972.

44. Ainsworth 1972.

45. Turiel 1974.

46. Elkind and Weiner 1978.

47. Byrnes 2004.

48. Sullivan 1953.

49. Ibid., 245.

50. See the introduction.

51. See Esman 1975 on development and psychopathology; Atwater 1992 for an easy-to-read overview; Schlegel and Barry 1991 for an anthropological perspective.

52. Sears, Rau, and Alpert 1965.

53. Skinner 1972.

54. Carskadon 2007.

55. Zink 2008.

NOTES TO CHAPTER 2

1. See Seltzer 1982 for the entire theory of DFI.

2. Erikson 1956.

3. Seltzer 1982.

4. S. Freud 1953.

5. Shakespeare 1986.

6. S. Freud 1953.

7. A. Freud 1948.

8. Seltzer 1989. See pp. 200–202 for Group Socialization Inventory. This protocol was utilized in a study whose findings revealed 24 peer groups as the mean number of groups to constitute a Peer Arena for 732 adolescents studied.

9. The concept *comparative act* refers to a sequence of comparisons and evaluations of findings in relation to selected persons in any of the peer groups of the Peer Arena, including a virtual one.

10. Defensive flight is addressed in chapters 6 and 7, on glitches.

11. For findings on 4,000 adolescents in four countries, see Seltzer and Waterman 1996. Seltzer's findings on 6,000 adolescents in six countries are unpublished. Both sets of findings support the high level of interest that adolescents around the globe show in their peers' plans for the future. See Seltzer and Waterman 1996; Seltzer 2008.

12. For other comparison types not addressed here, see Seltzer 1982 and 1989.

13. Seltzer 1982.

14. Wertheimer 1944. Gestalt psychology was vital to development of group therapy theory.

15. For a complete discussion of social comparison in adolescents, see Seltzer 1982.

16. Five of the eight comparison types were developed by Festinger. Adolescent definitions and functions were developed by Seltzer. See Festinger 1954; Seltzer 1982.

17. More extensive information on glitches is provided in chapters 6 and 7.

18. See the protocols in part 3.

19. See chapter 7 on glitches.

20. For a fuller discussion of these types of adolescent comparison, see Seltzer 1982: 124–36.

21. See chapter 7.

22. Seltzer, University of Pennsylvania continuing education classes 1996–2007.

23. The same need for self-validation appeared in a study of high school youth in which over 85 percent of the 66 youth tested replied that knowing how a variety of other youth are progressing helps one assess one's own progress (see Seltzer 1982). The 12-year-old in the example in the text expressed a similar sentiment.

NOTES TO CHAPTER 3

1. Some of the literature often consulted includes Myrdal 1944; Rose and Rose 1948, 1965; Takaki, 1993.

2. Fuligni 1998: 124–27.

3. See chapters 4 and 5 for more discussion of this concern and other related ones.

4. For review of adolescent pressures at this time, see chapter 2.

5. Seltzer 2008; Seltzer and Waterman 1996.

6. See Hraba 1994: pt. 2, pp. 27–198.

7. E. Anderson 1978.

8. Sánchez-Ayéndez 1988.

9. Sue 2006.

10. Mindel, Habenstein, and Wright 1988.

11. Hraba 1994.

12. See chapter 1.

13. Mead 1963.

14. Although this phenomenon often occurs in a new environment, adolescents usually catch up quickly. See Seltzer 1982: chaps. 10–13.

15. Having a family status as newcomers and a lack of knowledge of American social customs and mores presents youth with challenges not faced by other minority adolescents. Thus, the primary route to success for these adolescents is excelling in their studies. See Caplan, Choy, and Whitmore 1991; Suarez-Orozco 1989. Because of this emphasis on education as the way up, children of immigrant families who have a lot of motivation generally show a far lesser degree of problem behaviors than do their nonimmigrant peers. See Steinberg 1996.

16. This interpretation borrows from the sociological concept of the researcher's getting lost in the field studies he or she is undertaking. See Orenstein and Phillips 1978.

17. To do such research, books are easily accessed in the public libraries, and university libraries can be used to access peer-reviewed articles. It can be difficult to ascertain the validity of some materials accessed via the Web. Professional continuing education courses can also be taken.

18. Wu 2002: 228.

NOTES TO CHAPTER 4

1. Savin-Williams 1990, 1998.

2. APA 2000.

3. D'Augelli and Patterson 2001.

4. Purkey 1970.

5. Thomas, Chess, and Birch 1970.

6. Elkind 1967.

7. In 1995, the Massachusetts Department of Education reported that youth who reported having had lesbian, bisexual, or gay experiences were four times more likely than heterosexual youth to have attempted suicide in the past year.

8. See chapters 6 and 7 for information on glitches.

9. Herek 1992: 149.

10. Krouse and Krouse 1998.

11. Schoenberg, Goldberg, and Shore 1984.

12. Hunter and Mallon 2000.

13. Festinger 1957.

14. D'Augelli, Hershberger, and Pilkington 1998.

15. Herdt and Boxer 1993.

16. Rosario et al. 1996; Savin-Williams 1998.

17. Morales 1989.

18. Gloria Gay, Women's Center of the University of Pennsylvania, conversation with the author, April 14, 2008.

19. Herdt and Boxer 1993; Hunter and Mallon 2000: 229.

20. See the discussion of substituting elements in the cognitive structure in chapter 2.

21. Blos 1979.

NOTES TO CHAPTER 5

1. See the introduction, as well as research in other chapters.

2. See Seltzer 1982, 1989.

3. DFI neither accepts nor disputes the unconscious model of adolescent storm and stress. Rather, it sees it as one of a number of models.

4. See the introduction.

5. For a detailed explanation of this phenomenon, see Seltzer 1982: chap. 9.

6. Benedek 1959.

7. Seltzer 1982: 219.

NOTES TO CHAPTER 6

1. Seltzer 1982: 131–32.

2. Elkind 1967.

3. For example, there is evidence in the medical literature that marijuana use causes damage to brain tissue (Kolansky and Moore 1971).

4. Offer and Offer 1975.

5. Seltzer 1982.

6. Research conducted by the author, University of Pennsylvania, April 2008.

7. APA 2000.

8. Elkind 1983.

9. Piaget 1952, 1972.

10. Bruner 1973.

11. No statistical differences were found in studies with female students or in a follow-up study 15 years later that included both genders (Seltzer 1982, 1989).

12. Seltzer and Cosner 2006.

13. Seltzer 1982.

14. See chapter 1 for fuller explanation of the pace of development. Corresponding endnotes in chapter 2 offer pertinent literature references.

15. Part 3 offers 30 noncomplex protocols for professionals to use as a guide in sequencing their questions while they interview adolescents so that they can gather important information early.

16. Seltzer 1982.

17. Seltzer 1989: chap. 8.

18. For more detail, see chapter 3.

19. See False Facade and Kid Copier defensive glitches in the next chapter.

NOTES TO CHAPTER 7

1. For the initial depictions of pseudoadults, see Seltzer 1982: 189–93.

2. Ausubel 1954 suggested a category of adolescents he termed "non-satellizer." In other words, he or she did not resatellize to the peer group or groups.

3. The PBS documentary *Power of Choice* (1988) offers a segment devoted to changing friendships as adolescents develop.

4. Elkind 1967; Redl 1974.

5. Dunphy 1980; Brown and Klute 2003.

6. Blos 1970; Josselyn 1952.

7. Seltzer 1982: 89–91.

8. Rokeach 1973.

NOTES TO CHAPTER 8

1. For findings on issues that are significant to adolescents, see Seltzer 1989; Seltzer and Waterman 1996.

2. Protocols may be used as-is or as a guide for back-and-forth exchange.

3. Seltzer 1982, 1989; Seltzer and Waterman 1996.

4. Seltzer 1989; Seltzer and Cosner 2006.

5. PAR supplementary education-related protocols are found in chapter 10.

NOTES TO CHAPTER 9

1. Seltzer 1982.

2. Seltzer 1989.

3. For elaboration on this trend, see Seltzer 1982; for empirical evidence for it, see Seltzer 1989 and Seltzer and Waterman 1996.

4. Seltzer 1989.

5. Seltzer and Cosner 2006.

6. Ibid.

7. PAR-T and PAR-P protocols can be utilized.

8. Note that the number of questions in this protocol are very close to the number in the PAR-A protocol for ease of comparison should PAR-A be used at a later time.

NOTES TO CHAPTER 11

1. Chapters 12 and 13 offer the model of adolescent therapy centered on the impact of adolescent comparisons, PAL group therapy.

2. See chapter 7.

3. See chapters 1 and 2.

NOTES TO CHAPTER 12

1. See Seltzer 1980, 1982, 1996.

2. As per Gestalt theory's basic premise that the whole is more than the sum of its parts, who the participants in the group are contributes to the way the group develops. See Wertheimer 1944.

3. Redl 1974.

4. Rustin 2000.

5. See note 2 to this chapter.

NOTES CHAPTER 13

1. Robinson 1930.

2. McCullers 1946.

3. See the introduction.

4. McCullers 1946: 19.

NOTES TO CHAPTER 14

1. Orenstein and Phillips 1978.

2. Inhelder and Piaget 1972.

3. *Concrete* refers to the here and now, that is, what can be seen. *Abstract* refers to what is not seen but is held in the mind.

4. For a powerful and penetrating analysis of street kids, see E. Anderson 1978.

5. For discussion of intermittent reinforcement as the strongest type of conditioning, see Skinner 1938.

6. For more in-depth explanations on this dynamic, see chapter 2 of this volume on DFI and Seltzer 1982.

7. Adolescents' style is not the same as that of adults. Adolescents' style is transitory, not permanent. It is today's snapshot, and it is not unusual for their style to alter a number of times. It normally settles down considerably in early adulthood once all four growth domains are fully developed. From that time forward, it may be polished up from time to time.

8. The categories were extracted from Seltzer observational studies of adolescent discussion groups as well as clinical contacts. Seltzer 1980.

9. See chapter 2 of this volume and Seltzer 1982 for Stage 1 adolescent needs to be with a supermarket of peers.

10. Physical build or figure is listed by both males and females among the top-ten attributes of greatest interest to them. See Seltzer 1989.

11. Inhelder and Piaget 1972 offers detailed information on cognitive growth and abrupt integrations that bring new levels of comprehension.

12. As discussed in earlier chapters, the belief that everyone is looking at you is characteristic of a cognitively immature adolescent. See Elkind 1967.

13. For more precise information on the eight types of comparison, see chapter 2. In this case, Davey would be a Downward comparison figure, and the better athletes would be the Upward comparison figures.

14. Findings from the Attribute Study, which did separate analyses of male and female high school students, revealed that males had a great interest in other people's mothers, which was not the case for females. Seltzer 1989.

References

Adams, Gerald R., and Michael D. Berzonsky, eds. 2005. *Blackwell Handbook of Adolescence.* Oxford, UK: Blackwell.

Adler, Patricia A., and Peter Adler. 1998. *Peer Power: Preadolescent Culture and Identity.* New Brunswick, NJ: Rutgers University Press.

Ainsworth, M. 1972. "Variables Influencing the Development of Attachment." In *Readings in Child Behavior and Development,* edited by C. Lavatelli and F. Stendler. New York: Harcourt, Brace, Jovanovich. 193–201.

Allen, J., and Stuart Hauser. 1996. "Autonomy and Relatedness in Adolescent-Family Interactions and Predictors of Young Adult States of Mind Regarding Attachment." *Development and Psychopathology* 8: 793–809.

American Psychiatric Association. 2000. *Diagnostic and Statistical Manual of Mental Disorders,* 4th ed. Washington, DC: American Psychiatric Association.

Anderson, Dennis. 1990. "Homosexuality in Adolescence." In *Atypical Adolescence and Sexuality,* edited by M. Sugar. New York: Norton.

Anderson, Elijah. 1978. *A Place on the Corner.* Chicago: University of Chicago Press.

Archibald, Andrea B., Julia A. Graber., and Jeanne Brooks-Gunn. 2004. "Pubertal Processes and Physiological Growth in Adolescence." In *Blackwell Handbook of Adolescence,* edited by G. R. Adams and M. D. Berzonsky. Malden, MA: Blackwell.

Asher, Steven R., and John D. Coie. 1990. *Peer Rejection in Childhood.* Cambridge: Cambridge University Press.

Atwater, Eastwood. 1992. *Adolescence,* 3rd ed. Englewood Cliffs, NJ: Prentice-Hall.

Ausubel, David P. 1954. *Theory and Problems of Adolescent Development,* 2nd ed. New York: Grune and Stratton.

Ausubel, David P., and Edmund V. Sullivan. 1970. *Theory and Problems of Child Development.* New York: Grune and Stratton.

Bandura, Albert. 1964. "The Stormy Decade: Fact or Fiction?" *Psychology in Schools* 1: 224–31.

Bandura, Albert. 1977. *Social Learning Theory.* Englewood Cliffs, NJ: Prentice-Hall.

Bandura, Albert, and Richard Walters. 1963. *Social Learning and Personality Development*. New York: Holt, Rinehart and Winston.

Beck, Aaron. 1976. *Cognitive Therapy and the Emotional Disorders*. New York: New York International Press.

Beck, Judith. 1995. *Cognitive Therapy*. New York: Guilford.

Benedek, T. 1959. "Parenthood as a Developmental Phase: A Contribution to Libido Theory." *Journal of the American Psychoanalytic Association* 7(3): 389–17.

Berry, John W., Jean S. Phinney, David L. Sam, and Paul Vedder. 2006. "Immigrant Youth: Acculturation, Identity, and Adaptation." *Applied Psychology: An International Review* 55(3): 303–33.

Bierman, Karen L. 2004. *Peer Rejection: Developmental Processes and Intervention Strategies*. New York: Guilford.

Bieschke, Kathleen J., and Connie Mathews. 1996. "Career Counselor Attitudes and Behaviors Toward Gay, Lesbian, and Bisexual Clients." *Journal of Vocational Behavior* 48: 243–55.

Blos, Peter. 1970. *The Young Adolescent: Clinical Studies*. New York: Free Press.

Blos, Peter. 1979. *The Adolescent Passage: Developmental Issues*. New York: International Universities Press.

Bowlby, John. 1969. *Attachment and Loss*, vol. 1, *Attachment*. New York: Basic Books.

Boxer, A. M., J. A. Cook, and G. Herdt. 1991. "Double Jeopardy: Identity Transitions and Parent-Child Relations among Gay and Lesbian Youth." In *Parent-Child Relations throughout Life*, edited by K. Pillemer and K. McCartney. Hillsdale, NJ: Lawrence Erlbaum.

Brabender, Virginia, April Fallon, and Andrew I. Smolar. 2004. *Essentials of Group Therapy*. Hoboken, NJ: Wiley.

Brooks-Gunn, Jeanne, Denise L. Newman, Clair Holderness, and Michelle P. Warren. 1994. "The Experience of Breast Development and Girls' Stories about the Purchase of a Bra." *Journal of Youth and Adolescence* 23(5): 539–65.

Brooks-Gunn, Jeanne, Anne C. Peterson, and Dorothy H. Eichorn. 1985. *Time of Maturation and Psychosocial Functioning in Adolescence*. New York: Plenum.

Brooks-Gunn, Jeanne, and Edward O. Reiter. 1990. "The Role of Pubertal Processes." In *At the Threshold: The Developing Adolescent*, edited by S. S. Feldman and G. R. Elliot. Cambridge, MA: Harvard University Press.

Brown, B. Bradford, and Christa Klute. 2003. "Friendships, Cliques, and Crowds." In *Blackwell Handbook of Adolescence*, edited by G. R. Adams and M. D. Berezonsky. Malden, MA: Blackwell. 330–48.

Brown, B. Bradford, N. Mounts, S.D. Lamborn, and L. Steinberg. 1993. "Parenting Practices and Peer Group Affiliation in Adolescence." *Child Development* 64: 467–82.

Bruner, Jerome S. 1973. *Beyond the Information Given: Studies in the Psychology of Knowing*. London: Allen & Unwin.

Byrnes, James P. 2004. "Cognitive Development during Adolescence." In *Blackwell Handbook of Adolescence*, edited by G. Adams and M. Berezonsky. Malden, MA: Blackwell. 227–42.

Caplan, Nathan S., Marcella H. Choy, and John K. Whitmore. 1991. *Children of the Boat People: A Study of Educational Success*. Ann Arbor: University of Michigan Press.

Carskadon, Mary (principal investigator). 2007. *Adolescent Sleep Patterns*. Providence, RI: Bradley Hospital.

Caughlin, John P., and Mary E. Ramey. 2005. "The Demand/Withdraw Pattern of Communication in Parent-Adolescent Dyads." *Personal Relationships* 12: 337–55.

Chan, Connie S. 1989. "Issues of Identity Development among Asian-American Lesbians and Gay Men." *Journal of Counseling and Development* 68: 16–20.

Cho, Hyunsan, Denise Dion Hallfors, and Bonita J. Iritani. 2007 "Early Initiation of Substance Use and Subsequent Risk Factors Related to Suicide among Urban High School Students." *Addictive Behaviors* 32: 1628–39.

Coleman, James Samuel. 1961. *The Adolescent Society: The Social Life of the Teenager and Its Impact on Education*. New York: Free Press.

Coleman, James Samuel. 1980. *Friendship and the Peer Group in Adolescence*. In *Handbook of Adolescent Psychology*, edited by J. Adelson. New York: Wiley.

Coleman, John, Joe Herzberg, and Marcelle Morris. 1977. "Identity in Adolescence: Present and Future Self-Concepts." *Journal of Youth and Adolescence* 6: 63–75.

Collins, W. A. 2003. "More than Myth: The Developmental Significance of Romantic Relationships During Adolescence." *Journal of Research on Adolescence* 13(1): 1–24.

Colsman, Melissa, and Edelgard Wulfert. 2002. "Conflict Resolution Style as an Indicator of Adolescents' Substance Use and Other Problem Behaviors." *Addictive Behaviors* 27: 633–48.

Crick, Nicki R., Juan F. Casas, and David A. Nelson. 2002. "Toward a More Comprehensive Understanding of Peer Maltreatment: Studies of Relational Victimization." *Current Directions in Psychological Science* 11(3): 98–101.

Daly, Maureen. 1942. *Seventeenth Summer*. New York: Pocket Books.

Dana, Richard H. 1998. *Understanding Cultural Identity in Intervention and Assessment*. Thousand Oaks, CA: Sage.

Darley, J., and E. Aronson. 1966. "Self-Evaluation vs. Direct Anxiety Reduction as Determinants of the Peer Affiliation Relationship." *Journal of Experimental Social Psychology*, Supp. 66–79.

D'Augelli, Anthony R. 1991. "Gay Men in College: Identity Processes and Adaptations." *Journal of College Student Development* 32: 140–46.

D'Augelli, Anthony R., Scott L. Hershberger, and N. W. Pilkington. 1998. "Lesbian, Gay, and Bisexual Youth and Their Families: Disclosure of Sexual Orientation and Its Consequences." *American Journal of Orthopsychiatry* 68: 361–71.

D'Augelli, Anthony R., and Charlotte Patterson. 1998. *Lesbian, Gay, and Bisexual Identities in Families: Psychological Perspectives.* New York: Oxford University Press.

D'Augelli, Anthony R., and Charlotte Patterson. 2001. *Lesbian, Gay and Bisexual Identities and Youth: Psychological Perspectives.* New York: Oxford University Press.

Davies, Douglas. 2004. *Child Development: A Practitioner's Guide.* New York: Guilford.

Deshpande, Kamalabai. 1936. *The Child in Ancient India.* London: Arthur Probsthain.

Donnellan, M. Brent, Kali H. Trzesniewski, and Richard W. Robins. 2006. "Personality and Self-Esteem Development in Adolescence." In *Handbook of Personality Development,* edited by D. K. Mroczek and T. D. Little. Mahwah, NJ: Lawrence Erlbaum. 285–309.

Dunphy, D. 1980. "Peer Group Socialization." In *Adolescent Behavior and Society: A Book of Readings,* 3rd ed., edited by R. Muuss. New York: Random House. 196–209.

Dusek, Jerome B. 1996. *Adolescent Development and Behavior.* Upper Saddle River, NJ: Prentice-Hall.

Eccles, Jacquelynne S. 1991. "Control Versus Autonomy during Early Adolescence." *Journal of Social Issues* 47(4): 53–68.

Eccles, Jacquelynne S., and Robert W. Roeser. 2003. "Schools as Developmental Contexts." In *Blackwell Handbook of Adolescence,* edited by G. R. Adams and M. D. Berzonsky. Malden, MA: Blackwell. 129–48.

Elkind, David. 1963. "Children's Discovery of the Conservation of Mass, Weight, and Volume: Piaget Replication Study II." In *Research Readings in Child Psychology,* edited by D. S. Palermo and L. P. Lipsitt. New York: Holt, Rinehart and Winston.

Elkind, David. 1967. "Egocentrism in Adolescence." *Child Development* 38: 1025–34.

Elkind, David. 1983. "Strategic Interactions in Early Adolescence." In *Social and Personality Development: Essays on the Growth of the Child,* edited by W. Damon. New York: Norton. 434–44.

Elkind, David, and Irving Weiner. 1978. *Development of the Child.* New York: Wiley.

Erikson, Erik H. 1956. "The Problem of Ego Identity." *Journal of American Psychoanalytic Association* 4(1): 56–121.

Erikson, Erik H. 1959. *Identity and the Life Cycle: Selected Papers.* New York: International University Press.

Erikson, Erik H. 1963. *Childhood and Society,* 2nd ed.. New York: Norton.

Erikson, Erik H. 1968. *Identity: Youth and Crisis.* New York: Norton.

Erikson, Erik H. 1980. *Identity and the Life Cycle.* New York: Norton.

Esman, Aaron H. 1975. *The Psychology of Adolescence: Essential Readings*. New York: International Universities Press.

Faatz, Anita J. 1953. *The Nature of Choice in Casework Process*. Chapel Hill: University of North Carolina Press.

Fairchild, Betty, and Nancy Hayward. 1979. *Now That You Know: What Every Parent Should Know about Homosexuality*. New York: Harcourt Brace Jovanovich.

Fass, Paula S. 1977. *The Damned and the Beautiful: American Youth in the 1920s*. New York: Oxford University Press.

Festinger, Leon. 1950. "Informal Social Communication." *Psychological Review* 57: 271–82.

Festinger, Leon. 1957. *Theory of Cognitive Dissonance*. New York: Harper and Row.

Festinger, Leon. 1954. "A Theory of Social Comparison Processes." *Human Relations* 5: 117–39.

Flacks, R. 1967. "The Liberated Generation: An Exploration of the Roots of Student Protest." *Journal of Social Issues* 23: 52–75.

Flavell, John H. 1963. *The Developmental Psychology of Jean Piaget*. Princeton, NJ: Van Nostrand.

Flavell, John H. 2000. "Development of Children's Knowledge about the Mental World." *International Journal of Behavioral Development* 24(1): 15–23.

Flores, Phillip J. 2004. *Addiction as an Attachment Disorder*. Lanham, MD: Jason Aronson.

Frank, Otto, and Mirjam Pressler, eds. 1995. *The Diary of a Young Girl, the Definitive Edition: Anne Frank*. New York: Doubleday.

French, J. R. P. and B. Raven. 1970. "The Bases of Social Power." In *Groups Dynamics*, 3rd ed., edited by D. Cartwright. New York: Harper and Row. 259–69.

Freud, Anna. 1948. *The Ego and the Mechanisms of Defense*. New York: International Universities Press.

Freud, Anna. 1958. "Adolescence." In *Psychoanalytic Study of the Child, Vol. 13*. New York: International Universities Press. 255–78.

Freud, Anna. 1966. "Instinctual Anxiety During Puberty." In *The Writings of Anna Freud, Vol. 2*. New York: International Universities Press. 152–73.

Freud, Anna. 1969. "Adolescence as a Developmental Disturbance." In *Adolescence: Psychosocial Perspectives*, edited by G. Caplan and S. Lebovici. New York: Basic Books. 5–10.

Freud, Sigmund. 1936. *The Problem of Anxiety*. New York: Norton.

Freud, Sigmund. 1953. "Three Essays on the Theory of Sexuality." In *The Standard Edition of the Complete Psychological Works of Sigmund Freud, Vol. 7*, ed. James Strachey. London: Hogarth. 145–245.

Freud, Sigmund. 1953. "The Neuro-Psychoses of Defense." In *The Standard Edition of the Complete Psychological Works of Sigmund Freud, Vol. 3*, ed. James Strachey. London: Hogarth. 165–185.

Freud, Sigmund, and James Strachey. 1966. *On the History of the Psycho-Analytic Movement*. New York: Norton.

Frick, Marianne E. 2000. "Parental Therapy, in Therapy and Practice." In *Work with Parents: Psychoanalytic Psychotherapy with Children and Adolescents*, edited by J. Tsiantis. London: Karnac Books.

Friedenberg, Edgar. 1959. *The Vanishing Adolescent*. New York: Dell.

Fuligni, Andrew J. 1998. "Adolescents from Immigrant Families." In *Studying Minority Adolescents: Conceptual, Methodological and Theoretical Issues*, edited by V. C. McLloyd and L. D. Steinberg. Mahwah, NJ: Lawrence Erlbaum. 127–34.

Gaddis, Alan, and Jeanne Brooks-Gunn. 1985. "The Male Experience of Pubertal Change." *Journal of Youth and Adolescence* 14: 61–69.

Ge, X., R. D. Conger, and G. H. Elder, Jr. 2001. "The Relation between Puberty and Psychological Distress in Adolescent Boys." *Journal of Research on Adolescence* 11(1): 49–70.

Goethals, George W., and John M. Darley. 1977. "Social Comparison: An Attributional Approach." In *Social Comparison Processes: Theoretical and Empirical Perspectives*, edited by J. Suls and R. Miller. New York: Halstead.

Goldenberg, Herbert, and Irene Goldenberg. 2008. *Family Therapy: An Overview*, 7th ed. Belmont, CA: Brooks Cole.

Goodman, Paul. 1956. *Growing Up Absurd*. New York: Random House.

Graber, Julia A., Jeanne Brooks-Gunn, and Andrea B. Archibald. 2005. "Links between Girls' Puberty and Externalizing and Internalizing Behaviors: Moving from Demonstrating Effects to Identifying Pathways." In *Developmental Psychobiology of Aggression*, edited by D. M. Stoff and E. J. Susman. Cambridge: Cambridge University Press.

Greenberger, Ellen, and Laurence D. Steinberg. 1986. *When Teenagers Work: The Psychological and Social Costs of Adolescent Employment*. New York: Basic Books.

Greene, Beverly, and Gregory M. Herek. 1994. *Lesbian and Gay Psychology: Theory, Research, and Clinical Applications*. Thousand Oaks, CA: Sage.

Grinder, Robert E. 1975. *Studies in Adolescence*, 3rd ed. New York: Macmillan.

Grinnell, Richard M., Jr. 1997. *Social Work Research and Evaluation*, 4th ed. Itasca, IL: F. E. Peacock.

Hakmiller, Karl. 1966. Need for Self-Evaluation, Perceived Similarity, and Comparison Choice. *Journal of experimental social Psychology*, Supp. 1: 49–55.

Hall, Calvin S., and Gardner Lindzey. 1978. *Theories of Personality*, 3rd ed. New York: Wiley.

Hall, G. Stanley. 1904. *Adolescence*, Vols. 1–2. New York: Appleton.

Har, D., and G. Carlo. 2005. "Moral Development in Adolescence." *Journal of Research on Adolescence* 15(3): 223–34.

Harris, Judith Rich. 1995. "Where Is the Child's Environment? A Group Socialization Theory of Development." *Psychological Review* 102(3): 458–89.

Harris, Judith Rich. 1999. "Social and Personality Development. How to Succeed in Childhood." In *The Nature-Nurture Debate: The Essential Readings,* edited by S. J. Ceci and W. M. Williams. Oxford, UK: Blackwell.

Herdt, Gilbert H., and Andrew Boxer. 1993. *Children of Horizons: How Gay and Lesbian Teens Are Leading a New Way Out of the Closet.* Boston: Beacon.

Herek, Gregory M. 1992. "Psychological Heterosexism and Anti-Gay Violence: The Social Psychology of Bigotry and Bashing." In *Hate Crimes: Confronting Violence against Lesbians and Gay Men,* edited by G. M. Herek and K. T. Berrill. Thousand Oaks, CA: Sage. 149–69.

Herek, Gregory M. 2000. "The Psychology of Sexual Prejudice." *Current Directions in Psychological Science* 9(1): 19–22.

Hershberger, Scott L., Neil W. Pilkington, and Anthony R. D'Augelli. 1997. "Predictors of Suicide Attempts among Gay, Lesbian, and Bisexual youths." *Journal of Adolescent Research* 12: 477–97.

Hetrick, E. S. and A. D. Martin. 1987. "Developmental Issues and Their Resolution for Gay and Lesbian Adolescents." *Journal of Homosexuality* 13: 25–43.

Hillard, P. J. Adams. 2002. "Menstruation in Young Girls: A Clinical Perspective." *Obstetrics and Gynecology* 99(4): 655–62.

Hoag, M. J., and G. M Burlingame. 1997. "Evaluating the Effectiveness of Child and Adolescent Group Treatment: A Meta-Analytic Review." *Journal of Clinical Child Psychology* 26: 234–46.

Hollingshead, August B. 1949. *Elmtown's Youth: The Impact of Social Classes on Adolescents.* New York: Wiley.

Hollingworth, Leta. 1928. *The Psychology of the Adolescent.* New York: Appleton-Century.

Horowitz, Donald L. 1985. *Ethnic Groups in Conflict.* Berkeley: University of California Press.

Houzel, Didier. 2000. "Working with Parents of Autistic Children." In *Work with Parents: Psychoanalytic Psychotherapy with Children and Adolescents,* edited by J. Tsiantis. London: Karnac Books.

Hraba, Joseph. 1994. *American Ethnicity,* 2nd ed. Itasca, IL: F. E. Peacock.

Hunter, Joyce, and Gerald P. Mallon. 2000 "Lesbian, Gay, and Bisexual Adolescent Development." In *Education Research and Practice in Lesbian, Gay, Bisexual, and Transgendered Psychology,* edited by B. Greene and G. Croom.

Hurrelmann, Klaus, and Stephen F. Hamilton. 1996. *Social Problems and Social Contexts in Adolescence: Perspective across Boundaries.* New York: Aldine de Gruyter.

Icard, L. 1986. "Black Gay Men and Conflicting Social Identities: Sexual Orientation versus Racial Identity." *Journal of Social Work and Human Sexuality* 4: 83–93.

Inhelder, Barbel, and Jean Piaget. 1972. *The Growth of Logical Thinking from Childhood to Adolescence.* London: Routledge and Kegan Paul.

Jackson, Sandy, and Hector Rodriguez-Tome. 1993. *Adolescence and Its Social Worlds*. Hove, UK: Lawrence Erlbaum.

Jones, Harold E., and Nancy Bayley. 1950. "Growth, Development, and Decline." *Annual Review of Psychology* 1: 1–8.

Jones, Mary C., and Paul H. Mussen. 1958. "Self-Conceptions, Motivations, and Interpersonal Attitudes of Early- and Late-Maturing Girls." *Child Development* 29(4): 491–501.

Josselson, Ruthellen. 1987. *Finding Herself: Pathways to Identity Development in Women*. San Francisco: Jossey-Bass.

Josselyn, Irene Milliken. 1952. *The Adolescent and His World*. New York: Family Service Association of America.

Kacerguis, Mary Ann, and Gerald R. Adams. 1980. "Erikson Stage Resolution: the Relationship between Identity and Intimacy." *Journal of Youth and Adolescence* 9: 117–26.

Kandel, D. B. 1985. "On Processes of Peer Influences in Adolescent Drug Use: A Developmental Perspective." *Advances in Alcohol and Substance Abuse* 4: 139–63.

Kandel, D. B. 1996. "The Parental and Peer Contexts of Adolescent Deviance: An Algebra of Interpersonal Influences." *Journal of Drug Issues* 26(2): 289.

Katchadourian, Herant A. 1977. *The Biology of Adolescence*. San Francisco: W. H. Freeman.

Keating, Daniel P. 1990. "Adolescent Thinking." In *At the Threshold: The Developing Adolescent*, edited by S. S. Feldman and G. R. Elliot. Cambridge, MA: Harvard University Press.

Keller, George, ed. 1997. *The Best of Planning for Higher Education*. Ann Arbor, MI: Society for Higher Education.

Keniston, Kenneth. 1965. *The Uncommitted: Alienated Youth in American Society*. New York: Dell.

Kimmel, Douglas C., and Irving B. Weiner. 1995. *Adolescence: A Developmental Transition*, 2nd ed. New York: Wiley.

Kitano, Harry H. L. and Roger Daniels. 1988. *Asian Americans: Emerging Minorities*. Englewood Cliffs, NJ: Prentice-Hall.

Kleijwegt, Marc. 1991. *Ancient Youth: The Ambiguity of Youth and the Absence of Adolescence in Greco-Roman Society*. Amsterdam: J. C. Gleben.

Kohlberg, Lawrence. 1969. "Stage and Sequence: The Cognitive-Developmental Approach to Socialization." In *Handbook of Socialization Theory and Research*, edited by D. A. Goslin. Chicago: Rand McNally.

Kohler, Wolfgang. 1947. *Gestalt Psychology*. London: Liveright.

Kolansky, Harold, and W. Thomas Moore. 1971. "Effects of Marijuana on Adolescents and Young Adults." *Journal of the American Medical Association* 3: 486–92.

Kroger, J. 2003. "Identity Development during Adolescence." In *Blackwell Handbook of Adolescence*, edited by G. R. Adams and M. D. Berezonsky. Malden, MA: Blackwell. 205–26.

Krouse, J., and P. Krouse. 1998. *Who's Who among American High School Students: 29th Annual Survey of High Achievers*. Lake Forest, IL: Educational Communications.

Kung, Shien-woo. 1962. *Chinese in American Life*. Seattle: University of Washington Press.

Ladd, Gary W. 2005. *Children's Peer Relations and Social Competence*. New Haven, CT: Yale University Press.

Laursen, Brett, Willard W. Hartup, and Ann L. Koplas. 1996. "Towards Understanding Peer Conflict." *Merrill-Palmer Quarterly* 42(1): 76.

Lerner, Richard M., and Christine M. Ohannessian, eds. 1999. *Adolescence: Development, Diversity, and Context; Risks and Problem Behaviors in Adolescence*. New York: Garland.

Lewin, K. 1939. "Field Theory and Experiment in Social Psychology." *American Journal of Sociology* 44: 873–84.

Lorenz, Konrad. 1965. *Evolution and Modification in Behavior*. Chicago: University of Chicago Press.

Lyman, Stanford M. 1986. *Chinatown and Little Tokyo: Power, Conflict, and Community among Chinese and Japanese Immigrants in America*. Millwood, NY: Associated Faculty Press.

Lynd, Robert S, and Helen Merrell Lynd. 1929. *Middletown: A Study in Contemporary American Culture*. New York: Harcourt, Brace.

Mahler, Margaret. 1968. *On Human Symbiosis and the Vicissitudes of Individuation: I. Infantile Psychosis*. New York: International Universities Press.

Marcia, J. 1980. "Identity in adolescence." In *Handbook of Adolescent Psychology*, edited by J. Adelson. New York: Wiley. 159–87.

Marshall, William A., and J. Tanner. 1974. "Puberty." In *Scientific Foundations of Pediatrics*, edited by J. A. Davis and J. Dobbing. Philadelphia: Saunders. 1224–41.

Masterson, J. F. 1968. "The Psychiatric Significance of Adolescent Turmoil." *American Journal of Psychiatry* 124: 240–68.

McCullers, Carson. 1946. *The Member of the Wedding*. Cambridge, MA: Riverside.

McGoldrick, Monica, Joe Giordano, and Nydia Garcia-Preto, eds. 2005. *Ethnicity and Family Therapy*, 3rd ed. New Cork: Guilford.

McKinney, John Paul, Lawrence B. Schiamberg, and Lawrence G. Shelton, eds. 1998. *Teaching about Adolescence: An Ecological Approach*. New York: Garland.

McLellan, Jeffrey A., and Mary Jo V. Pugh. 1999. *The Role of Peer Groups in Adolescent Social Identity: Exploring the Importance of Stability and Change*. San Francisco: Jossey-Bass.

Mead, Margaret. 1928. *Coming of Age in Samoa*. New York: Morrow.

Mead, Margaret. 1962. *The School in American Culture*. Cambridge, MA: Harvard University Press.

Mead, Margaret. 1963. "Why Is Education Obsolete?" In *The Teacher and the Taught*, edited by R. Gross. New York: Dell.

Miller, D. C., and J. P. Byrnes. 2001. "Adolescents' Decision-Making in Social Situations: A Self-Regulation Perspective." *Journal of Applied Developmental Psychology* 22: 237–56.

Mindel, Charles H., Robert W. Habenstein, and Roosevelt Wright. 1988. *Ethnic Families in America: Patterns and Variations*. New York: Elsevier.

Minuchin, Salvador. 1974. *Families and Family Therapy*. Cambridge, MA: Harvard University Press.

Minuchin, Salvador, and Charles Fishman. 1981. *Family Therapy Techniques*. Cambridge, MA: Harvard University Press.

Montgomery, L.M. 1983. *Anne of Green Gables*. New York: Grosset & Dunlap.

Morales, Edward S. 1989. "Ethnic Minority Families and Ethnic Minority Gays and Lesbians." *Marriage and Family Review* 14: 217–39.

Muuss, Rolf E. 1982. *Theories of Adolescence*, 4th ed. New York: Random House.

Muuss, Rolf E. 1986. *Theories of Adolescence*, 6th ed. New York: McGraw-Hill.

Mussen, Paul H., and Mary C. Jones. 1957. "Self Conceptions, Motivation and Interpersonal Attitudes of Late and Early Maturing Boys." *Child Development* 28: 243–56.

Myrdal, Gunnar. 1944. *An American Dilemma: The Negro Problem and Modern Democracy*. New York: Harper.

Newman, William M. 1973. *American Pluralism: A Study of Minority Groups and Social Theory*. New York: Harper & Row.

Offer, Daniel, and J. R. Offer. 1975. *From Teenage to Manhood*. New York: Basic Books.

Offer, Daniel, Eric Ostrov, Kenneth I. Howard, and Robert Atkinson. 1988. *The Teenage World: Adolescents' Self-Image in Ten Countries*. New York: Plenum.

Orenstein, Alan, and William Phillips. 1978. *Understanding Social Research: an Introduction*. Boston: Allyn and Bacon.

Oxford English Dictionary Online. 2008. Oxford: Oxford University Press. http://dictionary.oed.com/.

Parsons, Talcott, and Robert F. Bales. 1955. *Family: Socialization and Interaction Process*. Glencoe, IL: Free Press.

Piaget, Jean. 1932. *The Language and Thought of the Child*. New York: Harcourt, Brace.

Piaget, Jean. 1952. *The Origins of Intelligence in Children*. New York: International Universities Press.

Piaget, Jean. 1972. "Intellectual Evolution from Adolescence to Adulthood." *Human Development* 14: 1–12.

Piaget, Jean, and Barbel Inhelder. 1969. *The Psychology of the Child*. New York: Basic Books.

Prinstein, M. J., and A. M. LaGreca. 2002. "Peer Crowd Affiliation and Internalizing Distress in Childhood and Adolescence: A Longitudinal Follow-Back Study." *Journal of Research on Adolescence* 12(3): 325–52.

Purkey, William Watson. 1970. *Self Concept and School Achievement*. Englewood Cliffs, NJ: Prentice-Hall.

Radloff, R. 1966. "Social Comparison and Ability Evaluation." *Journal of Experimental Social Psychology*, Supp. 1: 6–26.

Rank, Otto. 1952. *The Trauma of Birth*. New York: Brunner. (Orig. pub. in English 1929.)

Redl, Fritz. 1966. *When We Deal with Children: Selected Writings*. New York: Free Press.

Redl, Fritz. 1974, October. "Something New Has Been Added on the Way to the Forum." Paper presented at the Second Annual Friends Hospital Clinical Conference, Philadelphia.

Rich, C. L., R. C. Fowler, D. Young, and M. Blenkush. 1986. "San Diego Suicide Study: Comparison of Gay to Straight Males." *Suicide and Life Threatening Behavior* 16: 448–57.

Robinson, Virginia P. 1930. *A Changing Psychology in Social Case Work*. Chapel Hill: University of North Carolina Press.

Rogers, Carl R. 1965. *Client-Centered Therapy*. Boston: Houghton-Mifflin.

Rokeach, Milton. 1973. *The Nature of Human Values*. New York: Free Press.

Rollin, Lucy. 1999. *Twentieth-Century Teen Culture by the Decades: A Reference Guide*. Westport, CT: Greenwood.

Rosario, Margaret, Heino F. L. Meyer-Bahlburg, Joyce Hunter, Theresa M. Exner, Marya Gwadz, and Anden M. Keller. 1996. "The Psychosexual Development of Urban Lesbian, Gay, and Bisexual Youths." *Journal of Sex Research* 33(2): 113–26.

Rose, Arnold Marshall, and Caroline Rose. 1948. *America Divided: Minority Group Relations in the United States*. New York: Knopf.

Rose, Arnold Marshall, and Caroline Rose. 1965. *Minority Problems: A Textbook of Readings in Intergroup Relations*. New York: Harper and Row.

Rosenblum, G. D., and M. Lewis. 2003. "Emotional Development in Adolescence." In *Blackwell Handbook of Adolescence*, edited by G. R. Adams and M. D. Berzonsky. Malden, MA: Blackwell.

Rotheram-Borus, Mary Jane, Margaret Rosario, and Cheryl Koopman. 1991. "Minority Youths at High Risk: Gay Males and Runaways." In *Adolescent Stress: Causes and Consequences*, edited by M. E. Colten and S. Gore. New York: Aldine de Gruyter.

Rubin, Kenneth H., William Bukowski, and Jeffrey G. Parker. 1998. "Peer Interactions, Relationships, and Groups." In *Handbook of Child Psychology: Social, Emotional and Personality Development, Vol. 3,* edited by W. Damon and N. Eisenberg. New York: Wiley.

Rubin, Kenneth H., and Robert J. Coplan. 1992. "Peer Relations in Childhood." In *Developmental Psychology: An Advanced Textbook,* edited by M. H. Bornstein and M. E. Lamb. Hillsdale, NJ: Lawrence Erlbaum.

Rubin, Kenneth H., Robert Coplan, Xinyin Chen, and Allison A. Buskirk. 2005. "Peer Relationships in Childhood." In *Developmental Science: An Advanced Textbook,* 5th ed., edited by M. H. Bornstein and M. E. Lamb. Mahwah, NJ: Lawrence Erlbaum. 469–512.

Rustin, Margaret. 2000. "Dialogues with Parents." In *Work with Parents: Psychoanalytic Psychotherapy with Children,* edited by J. Tsiantis. London: Karnac Books.

Ryan, Caitlin, and Donna Futterman. 1998. *Lesbian and Gay Youth: Care and Counseling.* New York: Columbia University Press.

Salinger, J. D. 1951. *The Catcher in the Rye.* Boston: Little, Brown.

Sánchez-Ayéndez, M. 1988. "The Puerto Rican American Family." In *Ethnic Families in America,* 3rd ed., edited by C. H. Mindel, R. Habenstein, and R. Wright, Jr. New York: Elsevier.

Sarafica, F. and D. Blyth. 1985. "Continuities and Changes in the Study of Friendship and Peer Groups during Early Adolescence." *Journal of Early Adolescence* 5: 267–83.

Sarason, S., and M. Klaber. 1985. "The School as a Social Situation." *Annual Review of Psychology* 49: 908–18.

Savin-Williams, Ritch C. 1990. *Gay and Lesbian Youth: Expressions of Identity.* New York: Hemisphere.

Savin-Williams, Ritch C. 1998. "*. . . And Then I Became Gay": Young Men's Stories.* New York: Routledge.

Schachter, Stanley. 1959. *The Psychology of Affiliation.* Stanford, CA: Stanford University Press.

Schlegel, Alice, and Herbert Barry III. 1991. *Adolescence: An Anthropological Inquiry.* New York: Free Press.

Schmid, Calvin F., and Charles E. Nobbe. 1965. "Socioeconomic Differentials among Nonwhite Races." *American Sociological Review* 30(6): 909–22.

Schoenberg, Robert. 2008, April 17. Director, Lesbian, Gay, Transvestite, Bisexual (LGTB) Center, University of Pennsylvania. Conversation with Vivian Seltzer.

Schoenberg, Robert, Richard S. Goldberg, and David A. Shore. 1984. *Homosexuality and Social Work.* New York: Haworth.

Sears, Robert A. 1957. *Patterns of Child Rearing.* Evanston, IL: Row, Peterson.

Sears, Robert R., Lucy Rau, and Richard Alpert. 1965. *Identification and Child Rearing*. Stanford, CA: Stanford University Press.

Sebald, Hans. 1984. *Adolescence: A Social Psychological Analysis,* 3rd ed. Englewood Cliffs, NJ: Prentice-Hall.

Sebald, Hans, and B. White. "Teenagers' Divided Reference Groups: Uneven Alignment with Parents and Peers." *Adolescence* 15: 979–84.

Selekman, Mathew D. 1993. *Pathways to Change*. New York: Guilford.

Seltzer, Vivian C. 1980. "Social Comparison Behaviors of Adolescents." In *Children in Cooperation and Competition*, edited by E. Pepitone. Lexington, MA: Lexington Books, D. C. Heath.

Seltzer, Vivian C. 1982. *Adolescent Social Development: Dynamic Functional Interaction*. Lexington, MA: Lexington Books, D. C. Heath.

Seltzer, Vivian C. 1989. *Psychosocial Worlds of the Adolescent: Public and Private*. New York: Wiley.

Seltzer, Vivian C. 1997. "Look Who's Coming to College." In *The Best of Planning for Higher Education,* edited by G. Keller. Ann Arbor, MI: Society for Higher Education.

Seltzer, Vivian C. 2002. "Themes from Adolescent Original Plays." Unpublished paper, University of Pennsylvania, Philadelphia.

Seltzer, Vivian C. 2008. "Cross-National Interest Levels of Junior and Senior High School Students in Peers' Future Plans." Unpublished paper, University of Pennsylvania, Philadelphia.

Seltzer, Vivian C., and Robert Cosner. 2006. "A Comparison of Findings from ARGI Studies of 1974, 1984, 2004." Unpublished paper, University of Pennsylvania, Philadelphia.

Seltzer, Vivian C., and Richard P. Waterman. 1996. "A Cross-National Study of Adolescent Peer Concordance on Issues of the Future." *Journal of Adolescent Research* 11(4): 461.

Seltzer, Vivian C., and Richard P. Waterman. 1998. "A Rausch Model Extension to Measure Relative Perceived Maturity: A Four Nation Study." Unpublished paper, University of Pennsylvania, Philadelphia.

Settersten, Richard A., Frank F. Furstenberg, Ruben G. Rumbaut, eds. 2005. *On the Frontier of Adulthood: Theory, Research, and Public Policy*. Chicago: University of Chicago Press.

Shaffer, David, P. Fisher, R. H. Hicks, M. Parides, and M. Gould. 1995. "Sexual Orientation in Adolescents who Commit Suicide." *Suicide and Life-Threatening Behavior* 25 (suppl.): 64–71.

Shakespeare, William. 1986. *Macbeth*. In *William Shakespeare: The Complete Works*, ed. Stanley W. Wells et al. Oxford, UK: Clarendon.

Shandler, Sara. 1999. *Ophelia Speaks: Adolescent Girls Write about Their Search for Self*. New York: Harper.

Singer, Mark I., Lynn T. Singer, and Trina M. Anglin. 1993. *Handbook for Screening Adolescents at Psychosocial Risk.* New York: Lexington Books.

Skinner, B. F. 1938. *The Behavior of Organisms.* New York: Appleton-Century-Crofts.

Skinner, B. F. 1950. "Are Theories of Learning Necessary?" *Psychological Review* 57: 193–216.

Skinner, B. F. 1970. *Walden Two.* New York: Macmillan.

Skinner, B. F. 1972. *Cumulative Record: A Selection of Papers,* 3rd ed. New York: Appleton-Century-Crofts.

Smetana, J. G., and E. Turiel. 2003. "Moral Development during Adolescence." In *Blackwell Handbook of Adolescence,* edited by G. R. Adams and M. D. Berezonsky. Malden, MA: Blackwell. 247–68.

Smith, Thomas E. 1985. "Group Work with Adolescent Drug Users." *Social Work with Groups* 8(1): 55–64.

Spindler, G. 1974. "The Transmission of Culture." In *Education and Cultural Process: Toward an Anthropology of Education,* edited by G. Spindler. New York: Holt, Rinehart & Winston.

Stapel, Diederik A., and Hart Blanton. 2007. *Social Comparison Theories: Key Readings.* New York: Psychology Press.

Strayer, F. F., and A. J. Santos. 1996. "Affiliative Structures in Preschool Peer Groups." *Social Development* 5: 117–30.

Steinberg, Laurence. 1996. *Adolescence.* New York: McGraw-Hill.

Steinberg, Laurence. 2001. "We Know Some Things: Parent-Adolescent Relationships in Retrospect and Prospect." *Journal of Research on Adolescence* 11(1): 1–22.

Stone, M. R., and B. B. Brown. 1999. "Descriptions of Self and Crowds in Secondary School: Identity Claims and Projections." In *The Role of Peer Groups in Adolescent Social Identity: Stability and Change,* edited by J. McClellan. San Francisco: Jossey-Bass.

Suarez-Orozco, Marcelo M. 1989. *Central American Refugees and U.S. High Schools: A Psychosocial Study of Motivation and Achievement.* Stanford, CA: Stanford University Press.

Sue, Derald Wing. 2006. *Multicultural Social Work Practice.* Hoboken, NJ: Wiley.

Sullivan, Harry Stack. 1953. *The Interpersonal Theory of Psychiatry.* New York: Norton.

Suls, Jerry M., and Richard L. Miller. 1977. *Social Comparison Processes: Theoretical and Empirical Perspectives.* Washington, DC: Hemisphere.

Sussman, Steve, Pallave Pokhrel, Richard D. Ashmore, and B. Bradford Brown. 2007. "Adolescent Peer Group Identification and Characteristics: A Review of the Literature." *Addictive Behaviors* 32: 1602–27.

Taft, Jessie. 1930. "The 'Catch' in Praise." *Child Study.*

Taft, Jessie. 1948. *Family Casework and Counseling: A Functional Approach*. Philadelphia: University of Pennsylvania Press.

Takaki, Ronald. 1989. *Strangers from a Different Shore: A History of Asian Americans*. Boston: Little, Brown.

Takaki, Ronald. 1993. *A Different Mirror: A History of Multicultural America*. Boston: Little, Brown.

Tanner, J. M. 1971. "Sequence, Tempo, and Individual Variation in the Growth and Development of Boys and Girls Aged Twelve to Sixteen." *Daedalus* 100: 907–30.

Thibaut, John W., and Harold H. Kelley. 1959. *The Social Psychology of Groups*. New York: Wiley.

Thomas, Alexander, Stella Chess, and Herbert George Birch. 1970. *The Origins of Personality*. San Francisco: W. H. Freeman.

Trebay, G. 2000, August 20. "Scrawn to Brawn." *New York Times*, ST1, ST4.

Tremble, Bob, Margaret Schneider, and Carol Appathurai. 1989. "Growing Up Gay or Lesbian in a Multicultural Context." *Journal of Homosexuality* 17: 253–67.

Turiel, E. 1974. "Conflict and Transition in Adolescent Moral Development." *Child Development* 45: 14–29.

Walvin, James. 1982. *A Child's World: A Social History of English Childhood 1800–1914*. Middlesex, UK: Penguin Books.

Waterman, A. 1982. "Identity Development from Adolescence to Adulthood: An Extension of Theory and a Review of Research." *Developmental Psychology* 18: 341–58.

Waters, Malcolm. 1994. *Modern Sociological Theory*. Thousand Oaks, CA: Sage.

Watson, John B. 1930. *Behaviorism*. New York: Norton.

Wertheimer, Max. 1944. *Gestalt Theory*. New York: s.n.

Wheeler, L. 1969. "Factors Determining the Choice of a Comparison Other." *Journal of Experimental Social Psychology* 5: 219–32.

White, Joseph L. 1989. *The Troubled Adolescent*. New York: Pergamon.

Windle, Michael, and Rebecca C. Windle. 2003. "Alcohol and Other Substance Use and Abuse." In *Blackwell Handbook of Adolescence*, edited by G. R. Adams and M. D. Berezonsky. Malden, MA: Blackwell. 450–69.

Wolman, Benjamin B. 1998. *Adolescence: Biological and Psychosocial Perspectives*. Westport, CT: Greenwood.

Wu, Frank H. 2002. *Yellow: Race in America beyond Black and White*. New York: Basic Books.

Yalom, Irvin D., and Molyn Leszcz. 2005. *The Theory and Practice of Group Psychotherapy*. New York: Basic Books.

Zink, Caroline. 2008. "Know Your Place: Neural Processing of Social Hierarchy in Humans." *Neuron* 58: 273–83.

Index

Regular index entries are followed by three sections affording access to pertinent concepts and protocols related to actual cases: Brief Case Examples, p. 330, Extensive Case Histories for Study, p. 331, and Tutorial for Peer Arena Lens (PAL) Group Therapy, p. 332.

BRIEF CASE EXAMPLES

TUTORIAL FOR PEER ARENA LENS (PAL) GROUP THERAPY

About the Author

VIVIAN CENTER SELTZER is Professor of Human Development and Behavior at the University of Pennsylvania. She also lectures and teaches internationally and collaborates with foreign colleagues on cross cultural research on adolescent psychological development and peer attachment. She is a licensed psychologist, a certified school psychologist, a certified marriage and family therapist, and a licensed and certified social worker. She is the author of *The Psychological Worlds of the Adolescent: Public and Private* and *Adolescent Social Development: Dynamic Functional Interaction*.